Trust Among Strangers

In the late eighteenth and early nineteenth centuries, the internal migration of a growing population transformed Britain into a "society of strangers." The coming and going of so many people wreaked havoc on the institutions through which Britons had previously addressed questions of collective responsibility. Poor relief, charity briefs, box clubs, and the like relied on personal knowledge of reputations for their effectiveness and struggled to accommodate the increasing number of unknown migrants. *Trust Among Strangers* recenters problems of trust in the making of modern Britain and examines the ways in which upper-class reformers and working-class laborers fashioned and refashioned the concept and practice of friendly society to make promises of collective responsibility effective – even among strangers. The result is a profoundly new account of how Britons navigated their way into the modern world.

PENELOPE ISMAY is Cooney Family Assistant Professor in History at Boston College.

Trust Among Strangers

Friendly Societies in Modern Britain

Penelope Ismay

Boston College

CAMBRIDGE
UNIVERSITY PRESS

University Printing House, Cambridge CB2 8BS, United Kingdom

One Liberty Plaza, 20th Floor, New York, NY 10006, USA

477 Williamstown Road, Port Melbourne, VIC 3207, Australia

314-321, 3rd Floor, Plot 3, Splendor Forum, Jasola District Centre, New Delhi - 110025, India

79 Anson Road, #06-04/06, Singapore 079906

Cambridge University Press is part of the University of Cambridge.

It furthers the University's mission by disseminating knowledge in the pursuit of education, learning and research at the highest international levels of excellence.

www.cambridge.org
Information on this title: www.cambridge.org/9781108459945
DOI: 10.1017/9781108560535

First published 2018
First paperback edition 2019

A catalogue record for this publication is available from the British Library

Library of Congress Cataloging in Publication data
Names: Ismay, Penelope, author.
Title: Trust among strangers : friendly societies in modern Britain / Penelope Ismay.
Description: 1 Edition. | New York : Cambridge University Press, 2018. | Includes bibliographical references and index.
Identifiers: LCCN 2018016880 | ISBN 9781108472524 (hardback) | ISBN 9781108459945 (paperback)
Subjects: LCSH: Societies–Great Britain–History–21st century. | BISAC: HISTORY / Europe / Great Britain.
Classification: LCC HS71.G74 I76 2018 | DDC 369.0941–dc23
LC record available at https://lccn.loc.gov/2018016880

ISBN 978-1-108-47252-4 Hardback
ISBN 978-1-108-45994-5 Paperback

Contents

Figures

Maps and Tables

Acknowledgments

I have many people to acknowledge in the making of this, my first book. I will begin where my intellectual life began, at the US Naval Academy (USNA). As a student dressed in uniform and marching through my days to the beat of someone else's drum, I was very attracted to the modern individual I learned about in my history classes, in all her unique and liberated glory. But when I returned to the Academy as an instructor and tried to teach her story, my students showed me with their questions that the modern individual was far more complicated than I thought. And so began my journey to understand how people really lived and cooperated in modern societies.

I thank my teachers in the History Department at USNA, who showed me what it means to be a historian and why it matters. Dan Masterson helped me to grasp the systems of reciprocity that characterized pre-Columbian Latin America, with patience, humor, and kindness. Nancy Ellenberger opened the world of gender history to me and proved a great support as I contemplated, and entered, graduate school. My special thanks to Bob Artigiani, who, among a million other things, taught me systems theory and how to think with it in history. He also made everything I have written – especially this book – better. With his considered criticism and energetic encouragement, he was teacher and friend in equal measure. Thank you for that gift, Bob, and to Susan and Erin for taking such good care of our family over the years.

Most of the research and thinking that made this book possible happened while I was a graduate student at Berkeley. I was extremely fortunate in my advising team of James Vernon, who encouraged me to keep thinking about big questions and challenged me to think more carefully about how they mattered, and Tom Laqueur, who agreed but also insisted that I connect those cosmic questions to particular historical problems. The facts of modernity and its theoretical discontents might describe their joint intellectual influence on me, but the other types of influence they had on me were equally important. Specifically, I learned that becoming a historian is an ongoing process that involves a whole family of scholars and a whole lot of emotions. My debt to them is enormous and growing. I know I cannot pay it back, but I promise to pay it forward. I also thank Carla Hesse, the late Susanna Barrows, Paul Rabinow, Yuri Slezkine, and Jonathan Sheehan for the always stimulating conversations and classes I had with them.

In the vast and wonderful intellectual family that they assembled beyond Berkeley, Tom and James introduced me to people who helped to broaden and deepen my thinking on just about everything. Gareth Stedman Jones met with me regularly when I was at Pembroke College; he helped me to refine some of my early arguments and also to think about new approaches. John Gillis read many of the first chapter drafts, always asking challenging questions and cheering me on when I figured something out. I am deeply thankful for John and Tina Gillis' generous friendship over the years. Deborah Valenze has read everything I have written even before this project began to materialize: she helped me to think about audience, to clarify and sharpen my argument, and to avoid historiographical sinkholes. Deborah is also my sea-momma, a mentor and friend who continues to help me navigate the challenges and opportunities of the profession; she does so with pinpoint accuracy and massive amounts of empathy.

Indeed, in a book where friendship figures so prominently, it will not be surprising how important these and all the friendships are that sustained me during its writing. The graduate students at Berkeley were (and are!) a motley crew of smart, funny, and thought-provoking friends and interlocutors. I want to thank India Mendelkern, Tehila Sasson, Alan Mikhail, David Anixter, Sarah Horowitz, Radhika Natarajan, Arpita Roy, and especially Alyse Han for the camaraderie and positive push-back. Caroline Shaw showed me the ropes of researching and proved a constant friend through the highs and lows of archival research. Daniel Usisshkin made it clear that serious thinking and serious humor can go hand in hand. Mary-Rose Cheadle gave me entry into stimulating seminars at Cambridge University and the pubs that surrounded it. Amy Connery kept me sane, run by run, and Sandy Friedland, hike by hike, on the trails of those marvelous Berkeley Hills. David Beecher and Grahame Foreman taught me as much about how to be a friend in the modern world as they did about modernity, although they taught me quite a bit in that department as well. I am eternally grateful for their company, commiseration, and "fantasticity."

Chris Motley and Neil O'Donnell deserve special mention in the category of friendship. They read much of the original dissertation, as well as most of the chapters of the book, with a critical eye and a generous heart. I drafted major parts of both at their home in San Francisco and their magical retreat in the hills above Monterey Bay. They celebrated every milestone along the way – no matter how small – punctuating the solitude of writing with fabulous dinners and toasts. They began as distant relations who became our dear friends during our years in Berkeley. They, in turn, introduced us to new friends who, in time, became family to us. Geri and Bill Weir and Julie and Kurt Sellerberg have given us a similar embrace on the east coast.

The way friendships develop in relation to the institutional frameworks in which they flourish is something I learned from studying friendly societies. I experienced it first hand as I left the sunny embrace of graduate school in Berkeley and cast off to the unknown world of professional academia. The sun may not shine quite as brilliantly in Boston, but you wouldn't know it by the warmth generated by my colleagues at Boston College. They are generous and congenial, on top of being wicked-smart scholars. Several of them have read chunks of this book at various stages, and many others offered to. Thanks to Prasannan Parthasarathi, Jim Cronin, Julian Bourg, and Kevin Kenny, in particular. Arianne Chernock, Alexis Peri, and Priya Lal deserve warm thanks for always knowing exactly what kind of advice to give – and when to give none at all – as I worked through the many iterations and emotional layers of editing. Pam and James Hansen and Jyoti and Martin Peters created the warm and loving village that makes it possible to be a human being while also being a scholar. My special thanks to Des Fitz-Gibbon: I would not have made it up this mountain without your always wise and often hilarious interventions, my friend. Thank you for sharing your canteen on those seemingly endless climbs and for your surprising irreverence and deep empathy throughout.

In my first year at Boston College, I was deeply honored to be named the Cooney Family Assistant Professor. I am so grateful to be part of an organization that values its junior faculty and for the clear and increasing commitment the college has made to the humanities at a time when other institutions of higher education are moving in the opposite direction. I would like to direct my special thanks to Bob and Loretta Cooney who, in addition to making the world a better place through their philanthropy, are smart, kind, and disarmingly down to earth. This project was well in the works before I got to Boston College, but the Cooney's generous funding has expanded both the time and space I had to work on it. Most importantly, their generosity made it possible for me to host a manuscript workshop at Boston College, which brought together many of my intellectual heroes into one room to discuss what I naively imagined was the penultimate draft. My special thanks to Margot Finn, Craig Muldrew, and Tim Alborn for their careful readings of that draft and for the astute feedback and the generous way in which they delivered it.

My students at USNA, University of California, Berkeley, and now Boston College have been some of my most provocative interlocutors. I particularly want to thank the students in my classes on "Revolution and Trust in Modern Europe," "The Credit Nexus," and "A Social History of Money." I was fortunate to have several students who helped with references and visualization, including Philip Verdirame, Pete Haskel, and the fabulous Christine Bertoglio, who made the maps and charts that appear in Chapters 4 and 5.

Parts of this book have been presented in various forms at conferences and workshops over the years. My years in graduate school coincided through some alignment of the stars with the Mellon Consortium on British History and Modernity that brought faculty and graduate students from Yale, Berkeley, and Chicago together over the course of five years. It is where I came of age intellectually, presenting my pre-research ideas about friendly societies at the first meeting, a very early chapter draft at the second, and a précis of the finished book as a new assistant professor at the final meeting. I want to thank all the participants – but particularly, Miles Ogborn, Chris Otter, William Deringer, Steve Pincus, and Brent Sirota for challenging me to think more sharply about the claims I was making. The Mellon Foundation also funded a conference on modernity that I organized at Berkeley, which helped me formulate the framework of this book. My thanks to the sparkly participants of the British History Writing Workshop at Berkeley, particularly Tehila Sasson and Michal Givoni. The article that resulted from that workshop became "Between Providence and Risk: Odd Fellows, Benevolence and the Social Limits of Actuarial Science, 1820s–1880s," *Past and Present*, (2015) 226(1):115–147. Parts of it have been reworked and appear in Chapters 4 and 5. I thank the participants of the much-missed British Studies Group at the Center for European Studies at Harvard, where I presented a brand-new version of my first chapter, and the Economic History Seminar at Yale, where I presented Chapter 3, with special thanks to Jose Espin-Sanchez, Rohit De, Naomi Lamoreaux, Tim Guinnane, Ariel Ron, and Simon Grote for their perceptive feedback.

The research for this book took me to archives all over Great Britain. There are many people who made an otherwise solitary experience more enjoyable. Bill Boyd granted me free access to the archives at the Odd Fellows Board of Directors in Manchester; Paul Eyre treated me to dinner with his family as he helped me to re-think the early history of the Order; Max Jones connected me with his neighbors and a lovely house in Heaton

Moor; Michael Rose took me on an illuminating tour of industrial Manchester and taught me a great deal about the poor laws. Special thanks to Jit and Patricia Uberoi for teaching me about alternative modernities and for their wonderful hospitality in Delhi. Thanks to the archivists and librarians at Cambridge University Rare Books Library, the British Library, John Rylands Library, Cardiff University Special Collections Library, the Local and County Record Offices in Derbyshire, Glamorgan, Preston, Lancashire, Knowsley, Bolton, Cornwall, Devon, Manchester Archives and Local Studies, and Manchester City Library. My thanks to the fantastic editors at Cambridge University Press, especially Liz Friend-Smith, Ian McIver, Divyabharathi Elavazhagan, the external reviewers, and the entire Editorial Services team. Their feedback was invaluable, greatly improving the shape of the book. And thanks to my wonderful style editor Srdjan Smajic, who helped me to refine my writing, in addition to producing the index.

Finally, because most importantly, I want to thank my family. My parents, Billy and Susan Donnelly, taught me how to think for myself, and my siblings, to stand up for myself. Mary and Arthur Ismay, my inlaws, were a source of constant support throughout the writing of this book. Most of all, I thank Dave, Julian, and Beatrice, who together make up Team Ismay. Every day, they fill my heart with their laughter, brilliance, and love. Julian was almost two when I filed my dissertation. The very next day he asked me if I had "turned my dissertation into a book yet." Undaunted when I told him I had not, he waited a whole twenty-four hours to ask me again. It became a morning ritual, one I enjoyed some days less than others. Thank you for asking, my love; I am happy to report a new answer. Beatrice, thank you for coming to us at just the right time and for the magnitude of your joy. It is to Dave, the partner of my life, who took it all in stride, even when I did not, who challenged and celebrated me in all the right moments, and who is the most genuinely good and easily the smartest person I know, that I dedicate this book.

Introduction
New Beginnings

[The friendly society] seems to be a Project that we are led to by Divine Rule and has such a Latitude in it, that, for ought I know, as I said, all the Disasters in the World might be prevented by it, and Mankind be secur'd from all the Miseries, Indigences and Distresses that happen in the world.[1]
Daniel Defoe, 1697

Provision is thereby made against the contingencies of fortunes, to which all are subject; and the nation, providing for such of its poor as are unable to provide for themselves, appears in the character of one great ... Friendly Society ... to which all may contribute according to their ability, and upon which all may come in misfortune.[2]
William Palmer, 1844

For, mutual assurance is economy in its most economical form; and merely presents another illustration of that power of co-operation which is working out such extraordinary results in all departments of society, and is in fact but another name for Civilization.[3] Samuel Smiles, 1875

So at last human society may become a friendly society – an Affiliated Order of branches, some large and many small, each with its own life in freedom, each linked to all the rest by common purpose, and by bonds that serve that purpose.[4]
William Beveridge, 1949

This book examines the ways in which the English, and later the British, grappled with questions of collective responsibility – of who owes what to whom and why – during the great transformation of British society from the late seventeenth century to the late nineteenth. They answered these questions in myriad ways over that vast expanse of time, but one answer that became increasingly important was the concept and practice of friendly society. As urbanization and commercialization transformed

---

[1] Daniel Defoe, *An Essay upon Projects* (London, 1697), 122.
[2] William Palmer, *Principles of the Legal Provision for the Relief of the Poor: Four Lectures Partly Read at Gresham College in Hilary Term, 1844* (London, 1844), 38.
[3] Samuel Smiles, *Thrift* (Chicago: Donohue, Henneberry & Co., 1875), 133.
[4] William H. Beveridge, *Voluntary Action: A Report on Methods of Social Advance* (London: Allen and Unwin, 1948), 324.

the social and economic landscape in this period, contemporaries adapted the concept to generate new relationships and to structure new organizations that could make promises of collective responsibility effective – even among strangers. At the same time, laborers and artisans refashioned their own practices of mutuality by designing new kinds of mutual aid societies capable of linking local clubs to those in distant places, ultimately connecting millions of working people into international networks of reciprocity.

While this second story about friendly societies, where laborers joined together for mutual aid, is familiar to us, the first is not. That is to say, we do not usually think of friendly society as a concept. The term friendly society has become synonymous with the working-class mutual aid society that proliferated throughout the nineteenth century. In some ways, it is not surprising that we associate the term friendly society exclusively with the eponymous working-class organization. Nineteenth-century friendly societies comprised the largest social movement of the age and provided significant financial security for millions of working-class households. These societies provided some form of what we would now call social welfare – material relief during periods of unemployment due to accident or illness, a lump sum for a proper burial, and pub-based sociability. The majority of these organizations were exclusively for men, but women formed friendly societies that also provided financial assistance during sickness and burial, as well as for sex specific needs like lying-in.[5] While friendly societies were mostly concentrated in the

---

[5] Building on Anna Clark's work on female friendly societies, scholars have taken up the question of the material impact that male-only clubs had on the lives of women and the household economy, as well as the extent to which female-only friendly societies were a result of their exclusion from male societies or a function of differing needs. Because this book focuses on the institutional problem of trust among strangers from the local to the national, I do not specifically address female friendly societies, which with few exceptions remained local through the period I study. Although they represented a bigger proportion of the whole in the late eighteenth century, by the early 1870s, female friendly societies represented only 1 percent of the friendly societies in existence. (Simon Cordery, *British Friendly Societies, 1750–1914* (New York: Palgrave Macmillan, 2003), 24.) For more on female friendly societies, see Anna Clark, *The Struggle for the Breeches: Gender and the Making of the British Working Class*, Studies on the History of Society and Culture, No. 23 (Berkeley: University of California Press, 1995); Daniel Weinbren, "The Fraternity of Female Friendly Societies," In *Gender and Fraternal Orders in Europe, 1300–2000*. (London: Palgrave Macmillan, 2010), 200–222; Evelyn Lord, "'Weighed in the Balance and Found Wanting': Female Friendly Societies, Self Help and Economic Virtue in the East Midlands in the Eighteenth and Nineteenth Centuries," *Midland History* 22, no. 1 (June 1997): 100–112; Dot Jones, "Self-Help in Nineteenth Century Wales: The Rise and Fall of the Female Friendly Society," *Llafur*, 4, no. 1 (1984): 14; Andrea A. Rusnock and Vivien E. Dietz, "Defining Women's Sickness and Work: Female Friendly Societies in England, 1780–1830," *Journal of Women's History* 24, no. 1 (2012): 60–85.

industrial cities of the northwest, they were a regular feature of the social landscape throughout Britain and much of its vast and growing empire. They hosted a great number of social events where they opened their doors to the community, including their annual feasts, dances, lectures, and charity dinners of all kinds. Particularly in towns in the American south and west as well as in towns all over the West Indies and Australia, friendly societies became the center of social life. By the middle of the nineteenth century, their membership numbers were bigger than those of trade unions, cooperatives, and Methodist societies combined.[6] By 1913, 6.6 million Britons were members of registered friendly societies, with an estimated 2.4 million more in unregistered friendly societies. This means that friendly societies provided welfare benefits to something like 75 percent of the British workforce.[7] Along with other "approved societies," they became the basis for national welfare distribution in 1911 under the National Insurance Act, and William Beveridge proposed to continue using them in the later National Insurance Acts, which formed the basis of the welfare state.[8]

Given their obvious importance as a working-class organization, Eric Hobsbawm admonished historians in 1957 for leaving friendly societies "surprisingly, and quite unnecessarily neglected."[9] Since then, social and labor historians have worked to remedy that neglect. We now know a great deal about the institutional life of friendly societies, particularly their numbers, growth, and geographic distribution, as well as their socio-economic and occupational composition.[10] Because the biggest concentrations of friendly societies were found in industrial, northwestern, urban centers and seemed to comprise a largely working-class membership, historians first interpreted them as evidence of an "independent working-class

---

[6] P. H. J. H. Gosden, *The Friendly Societies in England, 1815–1875* (Manchester: Manchester University Press, 1961), 7.

[7] David G. Green, *Reinventing Civil Society: The Rediscovery of Welfare without Politics*, Choice in Welfare, No. 17 (London: IEA Health and Welfare Unit, 1993), 26, 34. The estimate that friendly societies insured 75 percent of the workforce comes from David Green, "The Evolution of Friendly Societies in Britain" (caledonia.org, 1993), www .caledonia.org.uk/friendlies.htm.

[8] Beveridge, *Voluntary Action: A Report on Methods of Social Advance*, see chapter 2.

[9] Eric Hobsbawm, "Friendly Societies," *Amateur Historian* 3, no. 3 (1957): 98.

[10] David Neave, *Mutual Aid in the Victorian Countryside: Friendly Societies in the Rural East Riding, 1830–1914* (Hull: Hull University Press, 1991); Geoffrey Crossick, *An Artisan Elite in Victorian Society: Kentish London, 1840–1880* (London: C. Helm, 1978); Dot Jones, "Did Friendly Societies Matter? A Study of Friendly Society Membership in Glamorgan, 1794–1910," *Welsh History Review* 3, no. 2 (1985): 324–349; Martin Gorsky, "The Growth and Distribution of English Friendly Societies in the Early Nineteenth Century," *Economic History Review* 51, no. 3 (1998): 489–511; Gosden, *The Friendly Societies in England, 1815–1875.*

culture," as E. P. Thompson put it. Consequently, these organizations figured prominently in the debates over working-class political action, the "labour aristocracy," and standards of living among the working classes.[11]

Friendly societies emerged from these debates with their working-class credentials somewhat tarnished, however. In particular, it seemed that they never took full advantage of the fact that the Friendly Society Act (1793) made them the only type of association in which it was legal for laborers to meet freely, an opportunity otherwise denied to the working classes by the repressive legislation of the late eighteenth and early nineteenth century.[12] To be sure, there were cases where friendly societies supported trade unions out of their funds or organized and participated in strikes.[13] And, there were trade unions that hid their activities under the guise of a friendly society.[14] On the whole, however, friendly

---

[11] E. P. Thompson, *The Making of the English Working Class* (New York: Vintage, 1966), 460–461; E. J. Hobsbawm, *Labouring Men; Studies in the History of Labour.* (New York: Basic Books, 1965), 273–274; Crossick, *An Artisan Elite in Victorian Society: Kentish London, 1840–1880*; Robert Gray, *The Labour Aristocracy in Victorian Edinburgh* (Oxford: Clarendon, 1976).

[12] The British government's stance on friendly societies differed markedly from its continental neighbors. In France, the relationship between the state and the *sociétés des secours mutuel* vacillated between repression and direct control during the various regime changes of the nineteenth century. In Prussia, whose welfare programs became the model for Bismarck's late nineteenth-century reforms, membership in trade-based or municipal-welfare organizations was generally compulsory. In Britain, by contrast, friendly societies remained voluntary throughout the century. Indeed, even as the state became increasingly interested in their potential as a national system of social welfare through the nineteenth century, registration remained voluntary. For more on welfare and insurance reform in Europe, see Michael David Sibalis, "The Mutual Aid Societies of Paris, 1789–1848," *French History* 3, no. 1 (March 1, 1989): 1–30; Paul V. Dutton, *Origins of the French Welfare State: The Struggle for Social Reform in France, 1914–1947* (Cambridge: Cambridge University Press, 2002), chapter 2; Jean-Louis Robert, Antoine Prost, and Chris Wrigley, eds., *The Emergence of European Trade Unionism* (Aldershot: Ashgate Pub Ltd, 2004), 218; George Steinmetz, *Regulating the Social: The Welfare State and Local Politics in Imperial Germany: The Welfare State and Local Politics in Imperial Germany* (Princeton, N.J.: Princeton University Press, 1993), 125–126; Timothy Guinnane, Tobias Jopp, and Jochen Streb, "The Costs and Benefits of Size in a Mutual Insurance System: The German Miners' Knappschaften, 1854–1923," In *Welfare and Old Age in Europe and North America: The Development of Social Insurance*, Perspectives in Economic and Social History, No. 21 (London: Pickering & Chatto, 2012).

[13] Francis Place, *The Affairs of Others: The Diaries of Francis Place, 1825–1836*, ed. James Alan Jaffe, Camden Fifth Series, v. 30. (New York: Cambridge University Press for the Royal Historical Society, 2007); W. H. Oliver, "Tolpuddle Martyrs and Trade Union Oaths," *Labour History*, no. 10 (1966): 5–12; Herbert Vere Evatt, *The Tolpuddle Martyrs: Injustice within the Law* (Sydney: Sydney University Press, 2009).

[14] "Union at Derby," *Preston Chronicle*, December 14, 1833. Some of the confusion on this point is due to the fact that many trade unions offered the same benefits that friendly societies did. For more on this point, see Malcolm Chase, *Early Trade Unionism: Fraternity, Skill and the Politics of Labour* (Aldershot and Brookfield, VT: Ashgate, 2000), 2, 107; Cordery, *British Friendly Societies, 1750–1914*, 45, 54–55, 135.

societies were some of the most visible supporters of the Victorian moral and social order and openly courted elite patronage.[15] Because of this, friendly societies eventually became an important part of the explanation for why the working classes failed to live up to the radical potential implicit in their organizational structures. And thus, the largest working-class organization of the nineteenth century consequently drifted to the margins of British history.[16]

Focusing on the failure of friendly societies in this respect, however, leaves us with some rather puzzling questions. Why did late eighteenth-century British parliamentarians, who also noted the radical potential of friendly societies, nevertheless offer them special legal protections? The year 1793 was an inauspicious time to grant an organization that involved regular, alcohol-fueled gatherings of workers the right to meet freely and to roam the country without regard to settlement restrictions. With the alarming rise of political radicalism and poverty at home and the French Revolution raging on the continent, why should friendly societies warrant such gentle, even generous, treatment at the very moment when all other working-class associations in the country were outlawed? And, why did the upper classes continuously offer them patronage when friendly societies steadfastly refused to allow these outsiders any influence on the operations of their societies?

Beyond their radical credentials, questions about the role friendly societies played in providing social welfare have also proved vexing for historians. Rather than use their precarious funds exclusively for the purpose of providing financial assistance to members, friendly societies also spent their money on expensive practices of ritualized sociability, including regular club-night drinking. Data collected internally by the leading Affiliated Orders constitutes most of what we know about the health of the working classes in the nineteenth century. The data that they collected on sickness and death rates in the 1850s led to significant advances in actuarial science, especially with respect to morbidity

---

[15] Of course, this was a two-way relationship. Aspiring local elites patronized friendly societies to help establish their authority both in the agricultural south of the eighteenth century and the industrializing north of the nineteenth. For examples, see Paul Langford, *Public Life and the Propertied Englishman, 1689–1798* (Oxford: Clarendon Press, 1991); Theodore Koditschek, *Class Formation and Urban-Industrial Society: Bradford, 1750–1850* (Cambridge: Cambridge University Press, 1990); Dan Weinbren, "'Imagined Families': Research on Friendly Societies," *Moving the Social [Online]* 27 (September 2014), 130.

[16] In *British Friendly Societies, 1750–1914*, Simon Cordery makes a convincing case that friendly societies may not have been radical, but they were far more politically active than earlier labor historians had understood.

predictions. In spite of this, most friendly societies did not reform in accordance with actuarial principles until the very end of the nineteenth century. And even those societies that did make some financial reforms nevertheless refused to give up their ritualized practices of sociability. Historians are generally sympathetic toward friendly society finances in the first part of the century before accurate actuarial tables existed, but they have deemed the continued refusal to reform after 1850 and the insistence on maintaining practices of sociability "unconscionable."[17] Indeed, while some scholars of the welfare state in Britain attribute the demise of voluntary friendly societies in the early twentieth century to the competition posed by state administered programs,[18] the consensus view is that friendly societies destroyed themselves from within due to this so-called inherent conflict between the demands of fraternalism and insurance.[19]

The fixation on what friendly societies did not do once again leaves us with unanswered questions, however. Why, it seems worth asking, were friendly societies so insistent on maintaining their practices of sociability in the face of dwindling resources and contemporary critics who railed against what they called the "utter incongruity in combining notions of beer and insurance?"[20] Why did the societies continue to engage in these practices even after they began actuarial reforms in the second half of the century? More to the point, if fraternalism and insurance were inherently at odds, how was it that the societies with the most elaborate and expensive social lives became the most popular *and the most successful*

---

[17] The idea that there was a necessary contradiction between the demands of fraternalism and those of insurance is generally assumed among historians, but it originated in the work of Gosden and Bentley. (Gosden, *The Friendly Societies in England, 1815–1875*, 11, 220; Bentley B. Gilbert, *The Evolution of National Insurance in Great Britain: The Origins of the Welfare State.* (London: Joseph, 1966), 170–171.)

[18] Stephen Yeo, "Working-Class Association, Private Capital, Welfare and the State in the Late Nineteenth and Twentieth Centuries," In *Social Work, Welfare, and the State*, Noel Parry, Michael Rustin, and Carole Satyamurti, eds., (Beverly Hills, CA: Sage Publications, 1980); David Green and Lawrence G. Cromwell, *Mutual Aid or Welfare State: Australia's Friendly Societies.* (Sydney: G. Allen & Unwin, 1984); David T. Beito, *From Mutual Aid to the Welfare State: Fraternal Societies and Social Services, 1890–1967* (Chapel Hill: University of North Carolina Press, 2000); E. P. Hennock, *The Origin of the Welfare State in England And Germany, 1850–1914: Social Policies Compared* (Cambridge: Cambridge University Press, 2007).

[19] Two important exceptions are John Macnicol, *The Politics of Retirement In Britain, 1878–1948* (Cambridge: Cambridge University Press, 1998); Nicholas Broten, "From Sickness to Death: Revisiting the Financial Viability of the English Friendly Societies, 1875–1908," In *Welfare and Old Age in Europe and North America: the Development of Social Insurance*, Perspectives in Economic and Social History, No. 21 (London: Pickering & Chatto, 2012).

[20] "Mr. Tidd Pratt's Office Can Be No Sinecure," *The Times*, November 6, 1863.

providers of social welfare in the second half of the nineteenth century? The neglect of friendly societies by British historians has been remedied, then, but the results are muddled, and some important questions remain unanswered.

What has escaped the notice of historians – and can help answer these questions – is that friendly society had ethical as well as institutional dimensions. The working-class friendly society that appeared in the nineteenth century was just one iteration of a larger conceptual and practical mode of organizing reciprocity. Since at least the sixteenth century, the term *friendly society* was used to describe the various kinds of mutualities and obligations among different groups of people. In particular, the term was often associated with the virtues of brotherly love, harmony, and "mutual charity," which clergymen and secular humanists alike deemed critical for the proper functioning of the community. Writing in 1593, English ecclesiastical reformer Myles Coverdale, best known for producing the first complete translation of the Bible into English, relies on this usage when he remarked that "among all living creatures, there is none created to a more loving and friendly society and fellowship than man. Hereunto serve all sciences and handy crafts, that men after a friendly manner agreeing among themselves, may relieve one another's necessities and want, and help bear one another's burthen[s]."[21] Note that Coverdale was not talking about friendly society as an organization but rather as a mode of mutuality. He was saying that humans require the help of others to live, and so they design by agreement mutually conducive relations of reciprocity.

One type of agreement about mutuality could constitute a particular friendly society. But the term friendly society itself could refer to any understood relations of reciprocity. The basis for and conditions of reciprocity in friendly society could vary widely – so too could the purpose to which those reciprocal relations were put. From Daniel Defoe's perspective, writing in the late seventeenth century, the concept of friendly society had "such a Latitude in it, that ... all the Disasters in the World might be prevented by it."[22] Friendly society retained its conceptual richness all the way through to the twentieth century. Defoe was interested in solving particular social problems with his various conceptions of friendly society, as we will see in Chapter 1. But as the epigraphs at the beginning of this chapter from William

---

[21] Myles Coverdale, *Fruitfull Lessons, upon the Passion, Buriall, Resurrection, Ascension, and of the Sending of the Holy Ghost* ... (London, 1593).
[22] Defoe, *An Essay upon Projects*, 122.

Palmer, Samuel Smiles, and William Beveridge make clear, nineteenth-
and twentieth-century Britons believed that friendly society also had the
potential to refigure the basis of human society itself.

By paying attention to the more capacious sense of the term as well as
to the particular institutional iterations of it in this book, I demonstrate
that friendly societies were so much more than muddled might-have-
beens on the margins of British history. The concept and practice of
friendly society was, in fact, a robust and nimble cultural resource for
thinking about and working through some of the most pressing questions
facing British society in a period marked by rapid social and economic
change. Questions about what people in a society owe to each other are
foundational – the answers structure and legitimate social order. The
reciprocity that one comes to expect from others, and the conditions
under which those expectations are met, produce the diffuse bonds of
social trust that hold societies together.[23] The transformation of British
society from a collection of trading towns and agricultural communities
to a highly mobile, industrial, and urban society in this period put
pressure on the mechanisms through which Britons had long met those
expectations. In particular, the institutions that made it possible to
facilitate collective responsibility in the past, such as the charity brief
and the poor laws, depended on knowing the reputations of the people
involved. The same was true for the local mutual aid clubs that laborers
started forming in the eighteenth century. As internal migration and
urbanization made local knowledge difficult to access, much less stabil-
ize, Britons were forced to grapple with the problem of how to make
social obligations effective among people who did not know each other.
Trust Among Strangers tells a story about how Britons used friendly
societies to think and work their way through various iterations of this
problem. In doing so, the book restores both the concept of friendly
society and the organizations called friendly societies to their rightful
place at the heart of modern British history.

This study also has implications for our understanding of trust in
modern societies. Social scientists tell us that trust among strangers is
critical to the functioning of modern societies and that it is substantively
different from the kind of personal trust among familiars that held pre
modern societies together. In the modern world, nearly every aspect of
our lives involves trusting people we do not know. We get on planes
piloted and buses driven by strangers; we regularly give our birth date,

---

[23] I borrow my definition from John C. Scott who treats social trust as "a kind of all-
purpose social *glue*." (John C. Scott, *Geographies of Trust; Geographies of Hierarchy,
Democracy and Trust* (New York: Cambridge University Press, 1999), 275.)

social security number, and our mother's maiden name to unknown entities online. We have created systems of interdependence where it is in the interest of everyone involved to ensure that planes do not randomly fall out of the sky. When they do, we expect explanations that conform to our belief that, if everything had been working properly, a catastrophe could have been avoided. It is not so much the pilot that we put our trust in when we board a plane, in other words, but in the vast systems of regulations, training, markets, and science that keeps her focused on flying safely. Sociologists call the trust we place in these systems *social trust* and describe it as a coping mechanism – a "protective cocoon," as Anthony Giddens puts it, or a means of "reducing uncertainty," in Niklas Luhmann's words.[24] We trust because if we did not, we would be paralyzed by the infinite number of variables we would have to take into account in order to make a decision about the most mundane aspects of everyday life.

But this is how social trust works if a modern society is working properly. There are other, less savory ways of reducing uncertainty. People and their intentions can be made transparent through stricter security measures and more information, on the one end, or force, on the other. And if that fails, enemies can be named and separated from society. Endless and anxiety-producing shades of grey can be made to conform to clear distinctions of black and white. Under such conditions, strangers, usually of specific types, do not fare so well. This is where the current research on social trust falls short. While there is broad consensus among social scientists about the critical importance of social trust for the functioning of modern societies, there is little agreement on how to rebuild trust when it breaks down and devolves into distrust. In other words, we know what function social trust serves, but we do not fully understand the processes through which it comes into being or how it can be rebuilt when existing foundations are undermined.

A historical perspective can help. A historical perspective can also move us beyond false dichotomies between a personal, "premodern" world and an anonymous, modern one. We have historical evidence that can help us trace the actual transformation in Britain from a society where reciprocity was administered and structured through the local relationships of the parish community, to one that Adam Smith

---

[24] Anthony Giddens, *Modernity and Self-Identity: Self and Society in the Late Modern Age* (Stanford, CA: Stanford University Press, 1991), 3; Niklas Luhmann, *Trust and Power* (New York: John Wiley, 1980), 4. There is a voluminous social scientific literature on social trust and the role it plays in modern societies. A good place to start is Barbara Misztal, *Trust in Modern Societies: The Search for the Bases of Social Order* (Cambridge, UK: Polity Press, 1996).

described as a society of strangers.[25] Yet, while personal trust may have been based on face-to-face relationships in the early modern period, with the exception of family and close intimates, the relationships comprising local communities were not, as Keith Wrightson puts it, "in the final analysis, personal."[26] Instead, early modern Britons "personalized" social relationships, which were themselves guided by convention. Just as the term *local community* should not be reduced to an idealized image of a small, tight-knit group of people who mutually cared for one another, so *society of strangers* should not necessarily signal an atomized world of anonymous individuals. Strangers are not, as Georg Simmel pointed out, simply those who are unknown in a society, but rather those who have "not belonged to it from the beginning."[27] The question *Trust Among Strangers* addresses is how did Britons, over the course of roughly two centuries, create conditions of belonging that could incorporate people who were unknown to each other – and who could remain strangers?

What constituted "belonging" and "the beginning" in the case of England and later Britain will be considered more fully throughout this book. I will tackle it in a preliminary fashion here, however, in order to introduce how specific historical problems of trust forced Britons to develop new conditions of belonging and how friendly societies played a critical role in creating them.

For centuries in England and Wales, the parish and the various cor- porate bodies that structured civic life had been the specific places where governance happened, justice was served, and deprivation was amelior- ated.[28] All the customary rights associated with the parish – the right to the commons, charity, poor relief, and employment, for example – belonged to those who lived within the parish bounds. When the old

---

[25] Adam Smith, *The Wealth of Nations*, 5th ed. (New York: The Modern Library, 1789), 85–86, 456; For more on Smith's characterization of Britain as a society of strangers, see Richard Teichgraeber III, "Rethinking Das Adam Smith Problem," *The Journal of British Studies* 20, no. 2 (Spring 1981): 106–123; And for more on the social conditions that produced a society of strangers, see James Vernon, *Distant Strangers: How Britain Became Modern* (Berkeley: University of California Press, 2014), especially the introduction.

[26] Keith Wrightson, *English Society: 1580–1680* (New Brunswick, NJ: Rutgers University Press, 2003), 72.

[27] Georg Simmel, *The Sociology of Georg Simmel*, trans. Kurt H. Wolff (New York: The Free Press, 1950), 402.

[28] For more on the importance of local structures of governance and belonging throughout the early modern and modern periods, see David Eastwood, *Government and Community in the English Provinces, 1700–1870* (New York: St. Martin's Press, 1997); Brodie Waddell, *God, Duty and Community in English Economic Life, 1660–1720* (Woodbridge: Boydell Press, 2012); K. D. M. Snell, *Parish and Belonging: Community, Identity and Welfare in England and Wales, 1700–1950* (Cambridge: Cambridge University Press, 2006).

poor laws were first created in the late sixteenth century, they enhanced, rather than diminished, the importance of the parish and its boundaries in this respect.[29] Belonging was more than a matter of mere residence, however.[30] If the rich were to help the poor of their own parishes, they needed to know that the poor had fulfilled their part of the reciprocal agreement. It was this information that proved so difficult to establish. For it was a moral knowledge about a laborer's willingness to work, and that knowledge was produced and accrued over a lifetime. In times of plenty and social peace, there was little reason to take note of such information. Questions about a laborer's moral character only arose when he or she was out of employment and was seeking poor relief. If a laborer had been in such a situation before, a record of past work history might be stored in centralized, parish records. Such information, however, was more commonly dispersed in the memories of the people comprising the community.[31] Parish officers did not always personally know the person who asked for relief, particularly in large parishes. So even within the parish community, parishioners had to demonstrate their right to belong.

Migrating strangers, however, posed a threat to both the material and moral bases of local relationships of reciprocity. Even if the strangers came from close by, as they crossed parish boundaries in search of work, they triggered questions about their intent, moral probity, and who was going to be responsible for paying for relief should they fail to find work. Strange laborers in the early modern period were generally seen as potential charges on parish resources or as vagrants, that is to say, potential criminals.[32] They could only prove themselves through their

---

[29] Paul Slack, *The English Poor Law, 1531–1782*, Studies in Economic and Social History, No. 9 (Basingstoke: Macmillan, 1990), 20–21, 26–29; Joanna Innes, "The 'Mixed Economy of Welfare' in Early Modern England: Assessments of the Options from Hale to Malthus (c.1683–1803)," In *Charity, Self-Interest and Welfare*, Martin Daunton, ed., (New York: St. Martin's Press, 1996).

[30] The Act of Settlement (1662 and later acts) stipulated the particular and changing conditions of belonging. Settlement might be a function of birth, long-term residence, or occupation. Women and children had access to settlement through these means, but their settlement was more commonly derived from their father's. For more on the complexity of women's settlement, see Pamela Sharpe, "Parish Women: Maternity and the Limitations of Maiden Settlement in England, 1662–1834," In *Obligation, Entitlement and Dispute under the English Poor Laws*, Peter Jones and Steven King, eds., (Newcastle upon Tyne, UK: Cambridge Scholars Publishing, 2015).

[31] It was not until 1819 that vestries were legally required to keep records of their meetings. (Eastwood, *Government and Community in the English Provinces, 1700–1870*, 42.)

[32] Parish officers kept a sharp eye out for visibly pregnant women, whom they actively excluded, and Snell noted examples where the laborers of one parish threw stones at any strange laborers venturing too close to the parish boundaries. (Snell, *Parish and Belonging*, 51.)

deference and their "willingness to work."[33] But while deference could be observed in a person's social conduct, measuring his or her willingness to perform labor was a different matter. Like known parishioners, migrating laborers could not simply say that they were willing to work; proof was necessary. Such proof could come in the form of letters from parish priests, passes or certificates verified by the appropriate authority, or a demonstration of the readiness to work by actually performing labor. Legislators had been chasing this problem for more than two centuries because "not belonging from the beginning" had been the norm in England for a long time. Laborers were no longer traveling the great distances they had in the sixteenth century, but most laborers moved out of their parish of birth at some point in their lives. The laws of settlement, which delineated the legal conditions of belonging to a parish, vacillated between protecting the parish and its limited resources from "hordes of vagrants," on the one hand, and enabling laborers "to take their labor to the best market," on the other. What brought this system to a crisis point in the late eighteenth century was the rapidly growing proportion of single, able-bodied men who were out of work and asking for relief. Were these laborers still willing to work, some observers wondered, or had the guarantee of relief pauperized them? In any case, how could one know for sure?

To be sure, late eighteenth-century property owners worried about paying for the ever-escalating poor rates – but the source of their more potent fear was what those rising rates indicated. With political and social radicalism on the rise, they worried that the system that did so much to maintain social order, reinforce trust between the classes, and relieve poverty was no longer capable of doing that work. From the 1780s to the mid-1830s, the best minds in Britain, and a great many others besides, discussed new ways of thinking about collective responsibility that could deal with the emergent social problems of a commercializing and urbanizing society. The solutions they proposed were quite diverse, involving garden and cow allotments, soup kitchens, forced emigration, workhouses, public works projects, and national insurance schemes.[34]

---

[33] Steve Hindle notes other attributes that parish officers looked for, including a fear of God, deference, thrift, and sobriety, but he argues that the Elizabethan poor laws were first and foremost designed to instill work discipline in the laboring poor. (Steve Hindle, *On the Parish?: The Micro-Politics of Poor Relief in Rural England c. 1550–1750* (Oxford: Oxford University Press, 2004), 379–398, for his argument about the importance of work, see chapter 3.)

[34] For a close examination of some rather sophisticated proposals for systematic, actuarial based, national insurance, see Gareth Stedman Jones, *An End to Poverty? A Historical Debate* (London: Profile Books, 2004); Arthur Young, *An Inquiry into the Propriety of Applying Wastes to the Better Maintenance and Support of the Poor. With Instances of the*

Additionally, co-operative mills and utopian socialist experiments like Robert Owen's New Lanark mill sought to avert these problems by transforming the conditions of capitalism itself.[35] The idea that helped contemporaries conceptualize a path from a system based on local knowledge to one that could accommodate great numbers of strangers spread over vast distances, however, was the myriad possibilities for organizing reciprocity contained in the concept of friendly society. Indeed, because the basis of mutuality in a friendly society could vary quite widely, these organizations appealed to reformers across the political spectrum. Some saw them as a way to reestablish traditional, patriarchal hierarchies within the parish community. Others saw in them a way to imagine a new, risk-based social order, one that did not rely on personal knowledge for its effectiveness nor on the existence of poverty for its legitimacy.

While upper-class reformers borrowed many of their insights from early modern theologians, mathematicians, and social observers, it was the surprising proliferation of the laborer's "box club" that convinced them they had the right solution. The fact that laborers had established societies for their mutual relief all over the country during some of the worst years of grain scarcity stood as powerful proof that the English laborer had not been pauperized. By the end of the eighteenth century, there were an estimated 7,200 societies, comprising 648,000 members and providing mutual aid to nearly a quarter of the population of England and Wales.[36] Reformers began to regard membership in one of these "box clubs" or "sick clubs" as proof of the laborer's trustworthiness. After all, the cost of membership required hard work, joining signaled forethought, and continuing to pay one's dues demonstrated independence. When laborers traveled through foreign parishes, their membership served as a passport, rendering this moral knowledge readily apparent for all to see. It was because of these virtues that Parliament granted these clubs legal protection in 1793. As I show in Chapter 1,

Great Effects (Bury, UK, 1801); *An Account of the Proceedings of the Acting Governors of the House of Industry* (Dublin, 1799).

[35] Peter Gurney, *Co-Operative Culture and the Politics of Consumption in England, 1870–1930* (New York: St. Martin's Press, 1996), 11–14; Robert Owen, *New View of Society. Mr. Owen's Report to the Committee of the Association for the Relief of the Manufacturing and Labouring Poor, Laid before the Committee of the House of Commons, on the Poor's Laws, in the Session of 1817* (London, 1817).

[36] Frederick Eden made this estimate based on the number of societies registered under the 1793 Friendly Society Act and the average number of members in those societies. He then raised that number by a third, based on responses he received from queries to town clerks about the number of unregistered friendly societies. (Frederick Eden, *Observations on Friendly Societies for the Maintenance of the Industrious Classes during Sickness, Infirmity, Old Age and Other Exigencies* (London, 1801), 6–8.)

poor law reformers re-christened these box and sick clubs as friendly societies in order to build on what laborers were doing. But they also expanded on the laborer's efforts so that this model of reciprocity encompassed all of British society.

While focusing on trust opens new ways of seeing the shifting relationships between the classes in this period, "a history of trust is of necessity a history of distrust."[37] This is true because new outsiders were created as new conditions of belonging were delineated, which will become clear in Chapter 2. But it is also true because social trust is based on expectations about the general fairness and security of the entire social system, and it is difficult to establish such expectations while the system itself is changing so rapidly.[38] The two years following the Napoleonic Wars, when tens of thousands of troops were demobilized into a glutted labor market and poor rates climbed to unprecedented levels on a radicalized political stage, relations between the classes were permeated by a distrust that bordered on paranoia.[39] As we will see in Chapter 3, the initiative that the working classes had shown in forming mutual aid societies all on their own, so attractive only a few years earlier, suddenly looked suspicious. In such dangerous times, even the most outspoken advocates of friendly societies abruptly withdrew their support and began patronizing savings banks instead. Savings banks were upper-class inventions and required nothing from the laborer but to deposit her savings. It did not take long for the inadequacy of individual savings to become clear and for friendly societies to return to center stage. But, as I will show, this economic solution to a social problem raised its own problems of trust. In this case, laborers struggled to read the intentions of patrons who seemed to want to get control over their money. This episode is remarkable for the ways in which both laborers and reformers directly addressed emergent problems of distrust. The final outcome of these negotiations was a new model of friendly society, called the New Friendly Society, which combined the social power of mutual insurance with the economic incentives of individual savings.

---

[37] Geoffrey Hosking, "Trust and Distrust: A Suitable Theme for Historians?" *Transactions of the Royal Historical Society* 16 (2006): 114.

[38] For an especially good example of this in the aftermath of the French Revolution, see Sarah Horowitz, *Friendship and Politics in Post-Revolutionary France* (University Park, PA: The Pennsylvania State University Press, 2013).

[39] Anthony Page, *Britain and the Seventy Years War, 1744–1815: Enlightenment, Revolution and Empire*(New York: Palgrave Macmillan, 2014), 137. While absolute rates would rise above the 1818 level in the late 1820s, when calculated as a proportion of population poor rates peaked in 1818 at roughly £8 million. (J. R. Poynter, *Society and Pauperism: English Ideas on Poor Relief, 1795–1834* (London: Routledge & Kegan Paul, 1969), 295.)

Laborers were not, of course, waiting around for reformers to figure out a new system of reciprocity for them. They were grappling with problems of trust in their own mutual aid clubs. As we will see in Chapter 4, in the 1810s and 1820s, when urbanization rates reached their highest level in the nineteenth century, local clubs were also forced to deal with the problem of migrating strangers. In the local club, relief was a by-product of the relationships forged through regular meetings and, with the exception of a small number of trade-based friendly societies, these benefits were not transferable to other clubs. While poor law reformers worried about the problem of transferable benefits as they experimented with their own versions of friendly societies, it was laborers who actually solved it – albeit not in a way that middle-class reformers (or modern historians, for that matter) found satisfactory. In their own models, upper-class patrons did away with the alcohol, the rituals, and the meetings, as well as the use of funds for anything not stipulated in the society rules. These practices made no sense to reformers who wanted to put every last penny of the laborers' hard-earned money toward their future welfare. Laborers, by contrast, saw pub-based sociability as critical to their practice of mutual aid. Rather than undermining club finances, the solidarity produced through friendly society had a multiplying effect on what people of limited means could do. The Affiliated Orders used a scaled-up version of ritualized sociability to create bonds of reciprocity between distant branch lodges. It was these bonds that enabled the Odd Fellows, the most popular of the Orders, to accommodate trust at a distance, transforming separate lodges into an international system of mutual aid.

This success, however, created a new set of problems. By mid-century, a number of forces, including a spectacular case of fraud involving a prominent Odd Fellow, combined in a way that suggested sociability, and the mutual benevolence it fostered, was no longer enough to secure the financial future of the Affiliated Orders. Instead of limiting gifts to what was available in the box or through ad hoc collections, it had become standard practice among friendly societies to specify the sickness and burial benefits members could expect. In other words, pre-determined out-payments were promised without being associated with a designated income. Since the Affiliated Orders were critical for working-class welfare at this point, their financial stability was of vital importance to the state. From the perspective of the actuaries that the government consulted, more members meant more liabilities. From the perspective of the members, however, increasing numbers meant an increased number of brothers on whom they could count in time of need. Furthermore, for members, financial reform was more than a matter of calculating liabilities. It also required trusting that a stranger and his strange assortment of numbers provided a better guide to the future than their own commitment to mutuality. The leadership of the Affiliated Orders worked hard to get members to trust in actuaries and their science – and they eventually succeeded. But they continued to make fraternalism central to their organization because, as I will show in Chapter 5, the commitment to brotherhood secured members against contingencies that even actuarial science was incapable of predicting. Indeed, it was this peculiar mix of "science and altruism" that William Beveridge wanted to draw on when he proposed using friendly societies as the basis for the twentieth-century welfare state, so that "at last," as he put it, "human society may become a friendly society."[40]

The fact that people like Beveridge wanted the bonds of trust without the messy and seemingly irrational means through which the working-class members of friendly societies maintained them, however, highlights obvious class dimensions of social trust, as well as less obvious gender dynamics. In particular, the very different methods for producing trust that upper class reformers and working class Odd Fellows employed had a significant impact on the kinds of people who could be accommodated within a friendly society. Poor law reformers, for example, had little trouble encompassing women alongside men in their schemes because the key flow of reciprocity was between the classes. They always graduated membership costs according to one's ability to pay – whether it was due to the customarily low wages of women, for example, or to special life-cycle considerations like childbirth or age. Any shortfalls could be subsidized out of paternal obligation or actuarial calculation, as we will see in Chapter 2. As long as the working-class members paid some contribution, they signaled their willingness to belong and made their trustworthiness legible to upper-class patrons. In this way, patronized friendly societies (as well as savings banks) were used to reinforce a cross-class patriarchy, even if they were capable of facilitating mixed-sex belonging within classes.

For the largely working-class Odd Fellows, by contrast, trust between equals was forged through a masculine form of sociability, which precluded women. As we will see in Chapter 4, the exclusion of women was at first due to cultural norms that dominated associational life in early modern Britain as well as the new gendered division of labor that

---

[40] Abb Landis, *Friendly Societies and Fraternal Orders; a History of the Legislation, Supervision, Mortality Experience, Management, Reforms, Rates of Assessment and Present and Past Financial Condition of the English Friendly Societies* (Winchester, TN, 1900), 49; Beveridge, *Voluntary Action: A Report on Methods of Social Advance*, 324.

emerged with industrialization.[41] Women and men of the laboring classes often drank together informally in pubs, but rarely in the more formal setting of a club – especially those clubs that involved heavy drinking, like the Odd Fellows.[42] Yet, the increased emphasis on conviviality that helped the Odd Fellows to overcome the challenges associated with extra-local trust coincided with a separation of alcohol from the clubs and societies of "respectable," middle-class Britons in the first decades of the nineteenth century.[43] The Odd Fellows responded by adopting emergent middle-class forms of masculinity to deflect negative attention away from their increasingly outmoded drinking culture. Showing that they cared for their own dependents, they argued, proved that friendly society members were characterized by a "manly independence" even if they also engaged in less respectable practices like ritualized drinking. The exclusion of women, which began as a kind of cultural default, was thus institutionalized in the 1830s. Such justifications were no longer tenable in the late nineteenth century, however, when actuarial science made it possible to think of sex and occupational differences as merely posing different liabilities whose costs could be calculated. By the end of the century, the Affiliated Orders finally admitted women. Focusing on problems of trust, then, can help explain specific shifts in the rhetoric of gender and class.

Early modern and modern historians of economic life were the first to discover the critical role that trust played in the way British society developed in this period.[44] By paying attention to the pervasiveness of personal credit and debt relations that underpinned the British domestic and imperial economy from the sixteenth century on, they have

---

[41] On the former point, see Mark Hailwood, *Alehouses and Good Fellowship in Early Modern England* (Woodbridge: Boydell Press, 2014), 194–203; Clark, *The Struggle for the Breeches*, 30–31; on the latter, see Cordery, *British Friendly Societies, 1750–1914*, 24–25.

[42] Peter Clark argues that the exclusion of women was common to the vast majority of clubs in the eighteenth-century. Peter Clark, *British Clubs and Societies 1580–1800: The Origins of an Associational World* (New York: Oxford University Press, 2000), 198–204. The Methodists created a rival friendly society Order called the Rechabites in 1835, in order to get men out of the pub. The fact that the Rechabites and other temperance societies admitted both men and women supports the idea that mixed-sex clubbing was not supposed to involve drinking.

[43] M. J. D. Roberts, *Making English Morals: Voluntary Association and Moral Reform in England, 1787–1886* (Cambridge: Cambridge University Press, 2004), 116–17; Simon Gunn, *The Public Culture of the Victorian Middle Class: Ritual and Authority in the English Industrial City 1840–1914* (Manchester: University of Manchester Press, 2000), chapter 2.

[44] Craig Muldrew's work on what he calls the "economy of obligation" is particularly important in this respect. He demonstrates that the early modern economy was composed not of a cash-nexus but of vast networks of personal credit held together by bonds of trust. (Craig Muldrew, *The Economy of Obligation: The Culture of Credit and Social Relations in Early Modern England* (Basingstoke: Palgrave Macmillan, 1998).)

demonstrated that the entire economy was held together by relationships of trust.[45] Thus, notwithstanding the conventional economist's story, their work demonstrates that our understanding of "the economy" cannot be abstracted from the social relationships and cultural systems that made it work.[46] Eighteenth-century creditors would have loved it if Adam Smith had been describing reality when he claimed that butchers, brewers, and everyone else simply took their goods to market and "exchange[d] them for money."[47] Instead of anonymous cash transactions that ended at the point of sale, the vast majority of exchanges from the sixteenth through the late nineteenth century were conducted on the basis of credit, which means that the relationship between buyer and seller continued into the future.[48] In the absence of complete knowledge about financial wealth, creditors had "to read debtors' personal worth and character" from an assortment of barely legible social and moral cues as they worked to distinguish the trustworthy from the

[45] Nuala Zahedieh, *The Capital and the Colonies: London and the Atlantic Economy 1660–1700* (Cambridge: Cambridge University Press, 2010); David Hancock, *Citizens of the World: London Merchants and the Integration of the British Atlantic Community, 1735–1785* (Cambridge: Cambridge University Press, 1997); Miles Ogborn, *Global Lives: Britain and the World, 1550–1800* (New York: Cambridge University Press, 2008); John J. McCusker and Kenneth Morgan, *The Early Modern Atlantic Economy* (Cambridge: Cambridge University Press, 2000); Jacob M. Price, *Overseas Trade and Traders: Essays on Some Commercial, Financial, and Political Challenges Facing British Atlantic Merchants, 1600–1775* (Brookfield, VT: Variorum, 1996).

[46] As Britain developed the institutional means to reinforce the credit economy in the modern period, including new kinds of courts and new legal sanctions, trust continued to be of paramount importance to economic exchange. Margot Finn shows how courts continued to gauge the trustworthiness of the claimants who appeared before them in cases involving retail credit while creditors and debtors drew on cultural beliefs about character to shape their own claims to creditworthiness well into the nineteenth century. (Margot C. Finn, *The Character of Credit: Personal Debt in English Culture, 1740–1914* (Cambridge: Cambridge University Press, 2003); For late nineteenth-century working-class credit networks, see Paul Johnson, *Saving and Spending: The Working-Class Economy in Britain* (Oxford: Oxford University Press, 1985).) And James Taylor's work on mid-nineteenth-century joint stock companies shows that even laws that look like the embodiment of *laissez-faire* were actually efforts to make the trust so critical to corporate capitalism more visible to shareholders so that they could better hold directors accountable. (James Taylor, "Company Fraud in Victorian Britain: The Royal British Bank Scandal of 1856," *English Historical Review* 122, no. 497 (June 2007): 700–724; James Taylor, *Boardroom Scandal: The Criminalization of Company Fraud in Nineteenth-Century Britain* (Oxford: Oxford University Press, 2013).) Historians have learned a great deal from and contributed to the way literary scholars have approached the culture of the economy and the economy of culture. See, for example, Deidre Lynch, *The Economy of Character: Novels, Market Culture, and the Business of Inner Meaning* (Chicago: University of Chicago Press, 1998).

[47] Smith, *The Wealth of Nations*, 36.

[48] Even cash was not without a social life and was subject to questions of trust, as Deborah Valenze shows in her brilliant study of money. (Deborah Valenze, *The Social Life of Money in the English Past* (Cambridge: Cambridge University Press, 2006).)

untrustworthy.[49] The social and moral embeddedness of economic action give lie to the idea that Britain became a "market society" in this period, where the laws of the market became the laws of society.[50]

Yet, if both the reality of "market society" and the "death of the moral economy have been greatly exaggerated," as James Taylor pithily notes, we need to expand our focus beyond economic exchange in order to understand the many ways in which the relations of economic life were re-moralized again and again throughout the modern period.[51] In particular, the social relationships and cultural systems that creditors used to make assessments of trustworthiness were not created for the purpose of facilitating the credit economy – rather, they formed the *social* fabric through which *economic* life was woven. *Trust Among Strangers* works to recenter questions of collective responsibility and the way that the concept and practice of friendly society helped contemporaries to grapple with them. In doing so, this book fleshes out this larger social world. If self-reliance was one answer to such questions, it neither dominated nor exhausted the other ways of thinking about how to make social obligations effective among strangers. Indeed, if the perfectly rational and transparent economic man was a figment of Adam Smith's imagination, the self-helping and independent man who needed nothing from society was just as much a fictional creation – one that reformers were forced to revise as their ideas clashed with the new social realities of urbanization and industrialization. Focusing on problems of trust, in short, keeps us from treating ideological fantasies as history, and will enable us to rethink the processes through which Britons navigated the great transformation of their society.

As such, the new story I tell in *Trust Among Strangers* has implications for how we understand modernity more broadly. We have rightly moved away from accounts of modernity that emphasized a radical break with the past – the rise of the individual and the decline of community; the rise of the market economy and the decline of moral economy; the rise of science and the expert and the decline of religion and faith; and the rise of bureaucratic institutions and the decline of personal relationships, to name a few. Such binary conceptions of modernity could not explain the persistence of traditional forms and practices anywhere in the world, including Europe. Part of what these models got wrong was a fixation on

---

[49] Finn, *The Character of Credit*, 21.
[50] Karl Polanyi, *The Great Transformation: The Political and Economic Origins of Our Time* (Boston: Beacon Press, 1957), 3, 57.
[51] Taylor, "Company Fraud in Victorian Britain," 700.

what was new.[52] Historians who employed such models used the new as the goal toward which their stories were headed. But in doing so, they rendered incomprehensible so much of what made the new possible. The history of friendly societies has been told, for example, as if they were trying to become modern forms of working-class consciousness and modern forms of insurance. The actual methods that friendly societies employed to secure their vulnerabilities (the drinking, rituals, regalia, etc.) make no sense in that story. In *Trust Among Strangers*, I try to take friendly societies on their own terms and, as A. O. Hirschman did in another context, I offer "evidence that the new arose out of the old to a greater extent than has generally been appreciated."[53]

When the problems of trust that were so critical to the making of modern Britain are recentered in our historical accounts of those processes, the history of friendly societies can finally break free from its hitherto residual status. As a robust set of ethics and institutional possibilities, friendly society helped Britons grapple with some of the most pressing issues of their day. Yet, what was so significant about friendly societies was neither their ethical basis nor their institutional form, but the way Britons shaped them to fit the problems at hand for more than 200 years. Friendly societies are still with us. Stories of their purported demise, due to internal negligence or competition with the welfare state, are evidence of the limitations of treating them exclusively as working-class mutual aid institutions. As we will see in the epilogue, friendly societies continue to do important social work in Britain. Indeed, thinking about the malleability of the practice and concept of friendly society in the twenty-first century may offer us a new set of historical resources to mine as we continue to grapple with how to trust strangers in our modern world.

---

[52] James Vernon has recently addressed the inadequacies of these radical-break models of modernity in his *Distant Strangers*. Conceptualizing modernity as a dialectical process, he argues that modernity is a social condition produced by the problems of living with, governing, and exchanging with strangers. Instead of fixating on the new forms of governance like statistics or centralized bureaucracies that emerged in response, however, Vernon argues that what made them effective solutions was the way in which they were re-embedded in older institutions, relationships, and traditions. I am indebted to James for helping me to think about modernity in new ways, and for so much else. (Vernon, *Distant Strangers*.)

[53] Albert O. Hirschman, *The Passions and the Interests: Political Arguments for Capitalism before Its Triumph* (Princeton, NJ: Princeton University Press, 1977), 4.

1   Friendly Society before Friendly Societies

> Among all living creatures, there is none created to a more loving and friendly society and fellowship than man. Hereunto serve all sciences and handy crafts, that men after a friendly manner agreeing among themselves, may relieve one another's necessities and want, and help bear one another's burthen[s].[1]   Myles Coverdale, 1593

The origin of friendly societies has long and confidently been associated with the demise of the medieval trade and craft guilds in England in the sixteenth and seventeenth centuries.[2] The family resemblance the eighteenth and nineteenth-century laborer's mutual aid society shared with these earlier corporate forms is remarkable, both in terms of the benefits they provided and the ritualized social life that occurred within them. Mutual aid and, more specifically, sickness and burial relief were common features of many types of late medieval and early modern associational life.[3] And many of the ceremonies, feasts, regalia, and symbols found in nineteenth-century friendly societies were very clearly borrowed from these earlier corporate forms. But while the functional relationship is strong, there is something about the term friendly society that this lineage does not adequately capture. Indeed, it is strange that the mutual aid societies that laborers founded in the eighteenth century

---

[1] Coverdale, *Fruitfull Lessons*.

[2] Cornelius Walford, *Gilds: Their Origin, Constitution, Objects, and Later History* (London: George Redway, 1888); Gosden, *The Friendly Societies in England, 1815–1875*; Victoria Solt Dennis, *Discovering Friendly and Fraternal Societies: Their Badges and Regalia* (Malta: Osprey Publishing, 2005); Anthony Black, *Guild and State: European Political Thought from the Twelfth Century to the Present* (New Brunswick, NJ: Transaction Publishers, 2003). For an important exception, see Dan Weinbren and Bob James, "Getting a Grip: The Roles of Friendly Societies in Australia and Britain Reappraised," *Labour History*, no. 88 (2005): 87–103. See also James' essay "Problems with UK and US Odd Fellow Literature" (www.takver.com/history/benefit/ofshis.htm).

[3] For a discussion of important similarities and differences between laborers' benefit societies and craft guilds, see Ilana Krausman Ben-Amos, *The Culture of Giving: Informal Support and Gift-Exchange in Early Modern England* (Cambridge: Cambridge University Press, 2008), 106–111.

should have been called friendly societies at all since actual members rarely used the term. More commonly, they referred to their societies as "box clubs," "sick clubs," or "benefit clubs." For instance, in 1745, James Robinson, who kept a public house in Drury Lane, gave testimony on behalf of his friend Benjamin Stevens who was on trial, accused of murdering his own wife. Speaking in defense of his friend, Robinson explained, "I belong to a Benefit Club with Stevens, where they allow some Money for burying of Wives ... ."[4] This case may have been extraordinary, but his use of the term benefit club was not.

Box clubs became friendly societies in the 1780s, when poor law reformers first discovered them in villages, towns, and cities all over Britain. When these reformers wrote about these clubs in the context of the debate over the poor laws, they acknowledged the terminology in common usage among laborers but then rechristened the clubs friendly societies. For example, when Revd. John Acland published one of the first widely read pamphlets on the subject in 1786, he titled it, "A plan for rendering the poor independent [of] public contribution; founded on the basis of the friendly societies, commonly called clubs."[5] So they were commonly called clubs, but Acland called them friendly societies. Other writers, too, rebranded box clubs as friendly societies. Frederick Eden, whose massive investigation of poverty in England did the most to popularize friendly societies in the context of the poor law debates, referred to them in dual terms as "the Benefit Clubs, or Friendly Societies."[6] The shift from using multiple terms to the single phrase *friendly society* happened in 1793, with the first major legislation protecting these clubs. The Friendly Society Act attached legal meaning to the term that continues to be in force today.[7] Only thirty-six years earlier, by contrast, when Parliament required that London coalheavers contribute to a fund for their mutual relief, they did not call this a friendly society. The law passed to protect them simply referred to what they were doing as a "relief fund."[8]

---

[4] "The Tryal &c. of Benjamin Stevens; (a Shoemaker) for the Murder of His Wife, Who with the Other Malefactors, Was Executed on Tuesday at Tyburn," *Penny London Post*, July 10, 1745.

[5] John Acland, *A Plan for Rendering the Poor Independent on Public Contribution; Founded on the Basis of the Friendly Societies, Commonly Called Clubs* (Exeter, 1786).

[6] Frederick Eden, *The State of the Poor: Or, an History of the Labouring Classes in England, from the Conquest to the Present Period*, 3 vols., vol. 1 (London, 1797), xxiii.

[7] 33 Geo.III. c. 54.

[8] "An Act for Relief of the Coalheavers working upon the River Thames; and for enabling them to make a Provision for such of themselves as shall be Sick, Lame or past their Labour, and for their Widows and Orphans." (31 Geo.II. c. 76.)

Why did poor law reformers, social thinkers, and legislators in the late eighteenth century suddenly start calling benefit clubs friendly societies? What, in other words, was in a name? Quite a lot, it turns out. Myles Coverdale's sixteenth-century usage of the term *friendly society* makes it clear that what he had in mind was a certain kind of reciprocity and the social ethics of community, more broadly. As we will see, the basis for reciprocity in a friendly society, and the practices used to police its boundaries, could vary quite widely. It was this nimbleness that raised friendly society in importance compared to other conceptions of cooperation that were so important to the social, religious, and economic life of parish communities in the seventeenth century. Ethical practices like neighborliness, for example, which had been so effective in the local context of the parish throughout the sixteenth and in the first half of the seventeenth century, began to lose traction toward the end of the seventeenth and into the eighteenth century. In this context, contemporaries drew on and adapted the concept of friendly society to pick up some of that ethical work. In addition to making it possible to connect people in networks of trust that extended beyond local boundaries, the concept of friendly society also became an important cultural resource for working out how to deal with questions of collective responsibility in a society of strangers.

Indeed, when nineteenth century reformers began grappling with new versions of these same problems, they redubbed the laborer's mutual aid association a friendly society. That story is the subject of Chapters 2 and 3. By examining the early modern history of the term in this chapter, it should become clear what poor law reformers hoped to invoke when they changed the name "box club" to "friendly society."

★★★

In the sixteenth and seventeenth centuries, friendly society was a much more capacious concept than it became in the nineteenth century. Early modern English men and women used the term "friendly" to emphasize the pleasures and responsibilities that members of a self-defined "society" could expect from, or ought to give to, each other.[9] It could simply mean being "in company" or in the "society of friends," the latter of which was used less frequently but interchangeably with "friendly society." Sometimes pleasure or conviviality was the main purpose of friendly

---

[9] Phil Withington has recently shown that in the early modern period "society" was defined as "purposeful and deliberate association." (Phil Withington, *Society in Early Modern England: The Vernacular Origins of Some Powerful Ideas* (Cambridge: Polity, 2010), 109.)

society, as in a dining club where the cost for the feast passed from member to member.[10] Similar in purpose, although less formally structured, "being in friendly society" could connote the pleasure of being in the company of a close friend or friends and the mutual help implied in those friendships.[11]

If the term *friendly* signaled the ethical relationship between the members of a society, it also indicated how those ethics could be fulfilled. Building on the work of ancient philosophers and medieval thinkers, early modern theologians believed that friendliness begot society and that togetherness fostered mutual care, harmony, and solidarity. A passage from the Anglican clergyman Simon Patrick's popular devotional book *Mensa Mystica* (1660) is worth considering because it clearly illustrates the mutually constitutive relationship between friendly society and solidarity. Clarifying the social role of communion, Patrick explained that breaking bread with fellow Christians was as much about "entering into a strict League of Friendship" with all the members of the church as it was about affirming one's relationship with God. The act of feasting together was not merely a symbolic act of unity, in other words; it also served a specific social function. "It is well known," he continued, "that eating and drinking together was anciently such a sign of unity, conjunction of minds, and Friendly Society, that the word *Companis*, and *Companio*, in old Latine, is the same with *Socius*." To be and, especially, to feast together in company created a bond that fostered mutuality. "And hence it is that all our *Companies* and *Fraternities* in Cities have their *Guild Halls* where they meet," Patrick went on, "and their Feasts likewise at

---

[10] The English translation of Giovanni Boccaccio's *Decameron* (1620) illustrates this usage of the term. "[I]n diverse places of *Florence,* men of the best houses in every quarter, had a sociable and neighborly assembly together, creating their company to consist of a certain number, such as were able to supply their expenses; as this day one, and tomorrow another: and thus in a kind of friendly course, each daily furnished the Table, for the rest of the company." (Giovanni Boccaccio, *The Decameron*, trans. John Florio (London, 1620), 14.) Friendly society was also used synonymously with college, as in College of Physicians, which Gideon Harvey explained to detractors was simply a *"voluntary friendly Club, Society, or Association of Doctors of Physick, mutually consented, and agreed unto, under certain just and equal Conditions, Rules, Laws . . . "* (Gideon Harvey, *The Art of Curing Diseases by Expectation with Remarks on a Supposed Great Case of Apoplectick Fits* (London, 1689), 206.)

[11] Richard Sibbes, *Bowels Opened* (London, 1639), 46; Michel de Montaigne, *Essays*, trans. John Florio (London, 1613), 520; Marcus Tullius Cicero, *A Panoplie of Epistles, or, a Looking Glasse for the Unlearned*, trans. Abraham Fleming (London, 1576), 405; Giovanni Francesco Biondi Sir, *Eromena, or, Love and Revenge*, trans. James Hayward (London, 1632), 35.

certain times for the maintaining of love and amicable correspond-ence."[12] Like many other political and religious thinkers in this period, Patrick put great stock in the importance of friendly society as both a cooperative ethic that promoted mutuality and the institutional means of achieving that ethic.

Friendly society thus stood in a constellation of related early modern terms – the most important of which was neighborliness, the Christian duty to be in charity with fellow Christians – that emphasized cooper-ation and mutual aid in the parish and the Christian nation more broadly. After the Reformation in England, maintaining friendly society, or being "in charity with one's neighbor," was no longer central to "the efficacy of the sacraments and of intercession."[13] Yet, such friendliness, charitable-ness, and neighborliness continued to be an important ideal for one's individual spiritual life as well as for the social harmony of the parish. In the mid-seventeenth century, friendliness and neighborliness were used interchangeably in the context of the local community. In an exposition on the book of Job published in 1643, for example, Joseph Caryl explained, "Much of the comfort of our lives is brought in by the society of friends. Woe be to him that is alone (saith Solomon) two are better than one, and especially in times of trouble. As our comforts are multi-plied upon them that are neere us, so our sorrowes are allayed and eased by them." To be without friends, Caryl reckoned, was "(if not a hell yet) one of the greatest afflictions on the earth."[14] In a well-known work published in 1660, the Cambridge Platonist Nathaniel Ingelo also put special emphasis on how friendly society was critical in a world marked by mutual dependence.

[S]ince you are made to live in the Company of others like your selves in Nature, the pleasure of your life depends very much upon friendly Society, and therefore you must endeavour to preserve an entire Charity with all your Neighbours, and as you hope to be lov'd by others, you must love them so truly, as never to do that to them which you would not have them doe to you.[15]

---

[12] Simon Patrick, *Mensa Mystica: Or, a Discourse Concerning the Sacrament of the Lord's Supper*, 7th ed. corr. (London, 1660), 99.

[13] Keith Wrightson, "The 'Decline of Neighbourliness' Revisited," In *Local Identities in Late Medieval and Early Modern England*, Norman Leslie Jones and Daniel R. Woolf, eds., (New York: Palgrave Macmillan, 2007), 39.

[14] Joseph Caryl, *An Exposition with Practical Observations upon the Three First Chapters of the Book of Job* (London, 1643), 364.

[15] Nathaniel Ingelo, *Bentivolio and Urania* (London, 1660), 378. In the same vein, the Anglican clergyman and Bishop Isaac Barrow explained how that love must be developed: "We are ... obliged heartily to love, that is to bear good-will to, to wish well to, to rejoice in the welfare, and commiserate the adversities of all men ... Love is the only sure cement, that knits and combines men in friendly society ... " According to

If maintaining friendly society and being in charity with one's neighbors was supposed to promote the harmony of the parish, selfishness, fighting, haggling, and dishonesty were understood as destructive of it. The Puritan clergyman and writer Richard Bernard made this clear in a 1627 book featuring a mock trial of several prisoners accused of "disturbing both the Church and common-wealth." During the trial, the character "Master Neighborhood" offers some rather damning testimony. "My lord," he said,

> this unhappy man hath altogether disunited men's affections, so as in our Towne there is very little love: hardly will one do another a good turn freely, but either it must be one for another, like for like, or in certain future hope for gain. This wretch hath almost banished all friendly society; every man is so now for himself, as he neglecteth his neighbor almost wholly.[16]

Like neighborliness, the ethic of friendly society, then, worked to mollify the socially corrosive effects of self-interest as well as the inequalities of a highly stratified society. Being friendly to those around you meant practicing the golden rule, which in turn brought not only mutual help, but pleasure too. Maintaining friendly society, like neighborliness, formed an important boundary of the "moral community" of the parish.[17] Being unfriendly or unneighborly, by contrast, put one outside these bounds.

In addition to being spiritual and social ideals, these modes of achieving cooperation were critical in the context of local credit networks, which by the end of the sixteenth century formed some of the key sinews of parish communities. The perennial shortage of coin in England meant that parishioners, rich and poor, were all mutually indebted to each other.[18] What Craig Muldrew calls an "economy of obligation" entailed

---

Barrow, if this love were mere passive emotion, it would have "appeared rather a suspicious strangeness"; instead he preached, "when for our preservation, or comfortable accommodation of life, [other men] need our help or our advice, we are readily to afford them; when they are in want or distress, we are to minister to them what comfort and relief we can." (Isaac Barrow, *Of the love of God and our neighbour, in several sermons* (London, 1680), 234–235.)

[16] Richard Bernard, *The Isle of Man* (London, 1627), 202–203.

[17] Wrightson, *English Society*, 61–63.

[18] On the ubiquity of credit relationships in medieval and early modern England and the interdependence that they created in local communities, see Craig Muldrew, "Interpreting the Market: The Ethics of Credit and Community Relations in Early Modern England," *Social History* 18, no. 2 (May 1, 1993): 163–183; Muldrew, *The Economy of Obligation*; Alannah Tomkins, *The Experience of Urban Poverty, 1723–82: Parish, Charity and Credit* (Manchester: Manchester University Press, 2006); Chris Briggs, *Credit and Village Society in Fourteenth-Century England* (Oxford: Oxford University Press, 2009); Phillipp R. Schofield and N. J. Mayhew, eds., *Credit and Debt in Medieval England, c.1180–c.1350* (Oxford: Oxbow Books, 2002); Peter Spufford, *Money and Its Use in Medieval Europe* (Cambridge: Cambridge University Press, 1989).

vast webs of interconnected personal credit networks based on little more than the word of the borrower and the trust of the lender. From the informal, often unrecorded loans between individuals in local communities, to the strictly kept accounts of the merchants who were creditors to the government, nearly every economic transaction in the sixteenth and seventeenth centuries was based on the personal familiarity and mutual trust of the parties involved.[19]

Credit networks in local parishes were maintained through acts of neighborliness, which both signaled a parishioner's reputation for trustworthiness and helped keep credit flowing when the serial repayment of debts got interrupted.[20] Much of the social and religious life of the parish was oriented around the creation or maintenance of a trustworthy reputation. "[T]he trustworthiness of neighbors came to be stressed as the paramount communal virtue, just as trust in God was stressed as the central religious duty."[21] Relationships of credit were dependent on the ethics of Christianity, and there was a great deal of crossover between the two. Christian ethics like the practice of stewardship, for example, helped to reinforce credit relationships by connecting one's actions in the worldly "Commonwealth" with their meaning in the "godly commonwealth." As Deborah Valenze explains, "Gaining money and giving it away represented opposite sides of a balance sheet of spiritual accounting ... " The wealth that Christians accumulated was "part of the common stock, devolving upon the individual in much the same way as a long-term loan, with strings attached ... "[22]

If the pressure to be a good Christian neighbor in order to gain a reputation for trustworthiness produced a mutually reinforcing relationship between spiritual and material life in the parish, the punishment for being a bad neighbor had significant implications on both registers as well. People who hoarded money rather than immediately paying their debts, for example, were seen in an especially negative light because their greed kept other people in the network from being able to pay their debts

---

[19] Using analysis conducted by Richard Grassby and Peter Earle, Craig Muldrew estimates that even the merchants who held large reserves of coin were fifteen times more likely to use credit instruments rather than cash. (Craig Muldrew, "'Hard Food for Midas': Cash and Its Social Value in Early Modern England," *Past & Present*, no. 170 (February 1, 2001): 93; Richard Grassby, *The Business Community of Seventeenth-Century England* (Cambridge: Cambridge University Press, 2002), 246–249; Peter Earle, *The Making of the English Middle Class: Business, Society, and Family Life in London, 1660–1730* (Berkeley: University of California Press, 1989), 121.)

[20] "The very extension of credit required trust, and such trust was both acquired and maintained through neighbourly relations." (Muldrew, "Interpreting the Market," 177.)

[21] Muldrew, *The Economy of Obligation*, 194–195.

[22] Valenze, *The Social Life of Money in the English Past*, 103, 109–112.

in turn, thereby inhibiting the fulfillment of obligations that kept social ties amicable and the whole community running smoothly.[23] In the same vein, allowing more time for repayment of a debt, and even forgiving a debt altogether, was considered an expression of good faith because it recognized the community-wide consequences of an individual's actions. It was in each person's interest to keep credit flowing because any breakdown could have a cascading effect on the entire credit network. In fact, people who gained a reputation for insisting on prompt repayment regardless of the social consequences might find themselves excluded from credit altogether. This was a very serious consequence, for when a man's credit, "the life blood of his trade," is gone, Daniel Defoe explained in *The Complete English Tradesman* (1726), it is "the death of [him]."[24]

Because so much depended on one's ability to ascertain the trustworthiness of others, the means through which reputations were circulated gained renewed emphasis in the seventeenth century. Muldrew argues that "there was a reordering of notions of community relations towards a highly mobile and circulating language of judgment...about the creditworthiness of households."[25] People circulated their "currency of reputation" through various forms of sociability. Through their conversations (including gossip and rumors), letters, gifts, acts of hospitality, and so on, parishioners cultivated and circulated their own reputations and those of others.[26] Bad reputations also circulated in this way.[27] Yet even among people who knew each other well, determining the value of such a volatile currency was difficult. Hosting a dinner party could serve to communicate a family's trustworthiness and to advertise its financial solvency to its neighbors. But deciphering such signals required a keen eye. Guests, who were almost always also creditors, took to scrutinizing everything – from the plate service and the number of servants to the quality (and quantity) of the meat served – in an effort to determine

---

[23] Ibid., 112.

[24] Defoe from *The Complete English Tradesman* (London, 1726) quoted in Julian Hoppit, *Risk and Failure in English Business, 1700–1800* (Cambridge: Cambridge University Press, 1987), 26. Having suffered the consequences of being a double bankrupt himself, Defoe knew well that in England bankruptcy was seen as "a Crime so Capital, that [the bankrupt] ought to be cast out of Human Society and expos'd to Extremities worse than Death." (Defoe, *An Essay upon Projects*, 97.)

[25] Muldrew, *The Economy of Obligation*, 3.

[26] David Steven Pennington, "Women in the Market Place: Gender, Commerce, and Social Relations in Early Modern English Towns" (PhD Dissertation, Washington University in St. Louis, 2007), chapters 6 & 8; Muldrew, *The Economy of Obligation*, 93–94; chapter 6.

[27] Laura Gowing, *Domestic Dangers: Women, Words, and Sex in Early Modern London*, Oxford Studies in Social History (Oxford: Clarendon Press, 1998), 125–133.

whether or not the host family was capable of paying its debts.[28] Maintaining credit locally required almost constant social vigilance.

Changes to the character of the parish in the seventeenth century strained neighborliness as an ethic and sociability as a conduit through which credit circulated. Even as preachers continued to exhort their flocks to be good neighbors, the parish community to which neighborliness referred changed dramatically. The reasons were complex and manifold, involving religious, economic, and social structural changes, but the effect was to undermine the effectiveness of neighborliness both as a practice and an ideal. The increasing number of dissenting religious communities, for example, which were often regional or national in geographic scope, made it difficult to talk about the Anglican parish as co-extensive with one's "community." Seventeenth-century enclosures also led to major reconfigurations of local social and economic relationships, sometimes replacing a neighborly relationship with a more contractual one between landlords and tenants.[29]

But the change that had the biggest impact on local communities, whether urban or rural, and on the ethic of neighborliness that was supposed to govern relations within them, was population growth and migration within Britain. The sharp rise in population in the mid-sixteenth century – that continued for another hundred years – put a great deal of pressure on local economies, which, in turn, led to a "great tide of internal migrants" who traveled the country in search of work.[30] Migration vastly increased the population of London in particular, despite a concomitant rise in mortality rates.[31] The considerable loss of life during the Great Plague in 1665, and the massive dislocation of large swaths of the city's inhabitants a year later in the Great Fire merely intensified the city's potential for anonymity. As Laura Gowing explains, people were "living in communities where they had a relatively short personal history and no family past... [T]o their neighbors, they were, to some extent, an unknown quantity."[32] Indeed, of the 575,000 people

---

[28] Felicity Heal, *Hospitality in Early Modern England* (Oxford: Oxford University Press, 1990). Signaling creditworthiness through hospitality was so critical, in fact, that some people even bankrupted themselves in the process of displaying it. (Muldrew, *The Economy of Obligation*, 158, 298–300.)

[29] Wrightson, "The 'Decline of Neighbourliness' Revisited," 35.

[30] E. A. Wrigley, "British Population during the 'Long' Eighteenth Century, 1680–1840," In *The Cambridge Economic History of Modern Britain*, Roderick Floud and Paul Johnson, eds., (Cambridge: Cambridge University Press, 2004), 57–95.

[31] For more on the population of London in the seventeenth century, see Peter Spufford, "Population Movement in Seventeenth Century England," *Local Populations Studies*, 1970, 41–50.

[32] Gowing, *Domestic Dangers*, 20.

living in the city in 1700, most "were born outside the capital."[33] All roads may have led to London, but these migrants changed the face of the local communities they traveled through and the ones they left behind, as well. The preamble to the Settlement and Removal Act (1662), where laborers were legally associated with a particular parish through birth or forty days residence as a condition of relief, demonstrates the kind of mobility that continued to characterize English laborers in the second half of the seventeenth century. Poor people, it reads,

> are not restrained from going from one parish to another, and, therefore, do endeavor to settle themselves in those parishes where there is the best stock, the largest commons or wastes to build cottages, and the most woods for them to burn and destroy; and when they have consumed it, then to another parish, and at last become rogues and vagabonds, to the great discouragement of parishes to provide stocks, where it is liable to be devoured by strangers.[34]

Because neighborliness was an ethic most immediately applicable to the parish neighborhood and to the kinds of relations that ought to obtain between neighbors who resided there, it began to lose traction as the character of the parish changed. Indeed, the way in which the meaning of the term "neighbor" itself changed maps this transformation. In the early eighteenth century "to know someone 'as a neighbor'" merely implied living in proximity, and that, most likely, "one did not know that person very well at all."[35] Being a neighbor, then, no longer evoked the set of ethical relationships it once did. Yet, while the ethic of neighborliness was in decline, the behaviors inspired by it continued to be critical to the functioning of that community.[36]

It was in response to this problem that contemporaries began to draw on and expand upon conceptions of friendly society. Neighborliness had been a capacious concept, encompassing a broad range of behaviors with spiritual, social, and economic dimensions, as we have seen. New conceptions of friendly societies were used to pick up two kinds of work that neighborliness had done in local communities, enhancing one's reputation for creditworthiness and encouraging mutual aid among parishioners. The concept and practice of friendly society became important for creating bonds of trust between creditors in different parts of the country as credit networks outgrew the local practices of sociability that had kept

---

[33] Jeremy Boulton, "London, 1540–1700," In *The Cambridge Urban History of Britain*, Peter Clark, David M. Palliser, and Martin Daunton, eds., (Cambridge: Cambridge University Press, 2000), 318.

[34] 13 & 14 Car. II, c.12.

[35] Wrightson, "The 'Decline of Neighbourliness' Revisited," 34.

[36] Muldrew, "Interpreting the Market."

them secure. Just as important, friendly society became important for securing the promises of mutually obligated strangers to help each other during particular kinds of crises.

Even though credit continued to be highly personal in nature, the end of the seventeenth century saw an enormous expansion of the credit economy rather than the reverse. As credit networks grew more complex – because of the number of parties involved, the distances between them, and the types of financial instruments used – local reputations became a proportionally weaker basis for making determinations of creditworthiness.[37] This problem was two-fold. On the one hand, without familiarity, it was difficult for trustworthy people to signal their honesty and good faith where loans were concerned. And it was easy for untrustworthy people to take advantage of the almost infinite opportunities for concealment that major urban centers like London offered, on the other. Social and legal sanctions were only effective if they resulted in ostracizing bad debtors from credit networks. Yet one could always move out of range of his or her own bad reputation, as Defoe's fictitious character Moll Flanders repeatedly did.[38] The problem of determining trustworthiness under these conditions is recorded in the growing number of debt cases brought to the new small-claims courts and the increase in the number of cases involving forged private credit instruments.[39] So if population mobility undermined the ethic of neighborliness and the "serial sociability" of the credit economy, how did an economy based on familiarity and trust not only function but also expand enormously in this period?[40]

There were several ways in which friendly society helped to answer this question, some more important than others. Late seventeenth century clergymen continued to encourage their flocks to maintain friendly society with neighbors and creditors, but they began to put new emphasis on the material incentives for doing so. In 1681, for example, the prominent Anglican theologian John Scott admonished Britons to practice friendly society on earth, which he explained in terms of the golden rule, in preparation for what he called the "friendly society of heaven." Yet, to

---

[37] Muldrew, *The Economy of Obligation*, chapter 4.

[38] Daniel Defoe, *Moll Flanders* (New York: Knopf: Distributed by Random House, 1991).

[39] For more on debt litigation, see Craig Muldrew, "The Culture of Reconciliation: Community and the Settlement of Economic Disputes in Early Modern England," *The Historical Journal* 39, no. 4 (December 1, 1996): 915–942; Muldrew, *The Economy of Obligation*, ch. 7 & 8; And for more on credit fraud, see Randall McGowen, "From Pillory to Gallows: The Punishment of Forgery in the Age of the Financial Revolution," *Past & Present*, no. 165 (November 1, 1999): 107–140.

[40] Wrightson, "The 'Decline of Neighbourliness' Revisited," 20; Muldrew, *The Economy of Obligation*, 151.

a degree his critics found alarming, he also emphasized the earthly advantages of doing unto others in this way.[41] "[A] *good Name* [is] the Ground of Trust and Credit," he explained, "and Credit [is] the main Sinew of Society ... "[42] Heavenly rewards were part of maintaining friendly society with others, as he put it, but "[t]here are a World of Necessaries and Conveniences *without* which we cannot be happy, and *with* which we cannot be supplied without each other's aid and assistance."[43]

It was only when the general concept of friendly society was tied to specific friendships, however, that term began to gain greater cultural traction in this context. Historians have long emphasized the critical importance of family, religion, and ethnic ties in shoring up the credit economy throughout the eighteenth century.[44] Not surprisingly, kinship formed the first and most important of such relationships.[45] Yet, Naomi Tadmor has recently shown that friendship became increasingly important for expanding the bonds of kinship to include non-kin and for cementing extra-local ties. As she put it, "it was along the lines of 'friendship' that [Britons] mobilized many of their social and economic interests, thus forming regional networks well beyond their immediate neighborhoods."[46] Beginning in the early eighteenth century, friendship

---

[41] One critic noted that the treatise was "Practical, but generally wanting in evangelical views ... " (Edward Bickersteth, *The Christian Student: Designed to Assist Christians in General in Acquiring Religious Knowledge* (New York: R. B. Seeley & W. Burnside, 1829), 515.)

[42] John Scott, *The Christian Life from Its Beginning to Its Consummation in Glory* (London, 1681), 91, 184.

[43] Ibid., 176.

[44] Laurence Fontaine, *The Moral Economy: Poverty, Credit, and Trust in Early Modern Europe* (Cambridge: Cambridge University Press, 2014); Muldrew, *The Economy of Obligation*; T. S. Ashton, *An Eighteenth Century Industrialist - Peter Stubbs of Warrington 1756 – 1806* (Manchester: Manchester University Press, 1961); Margaret R. Hunt, *The Middling Sort: Commerce, Gender, and the Family in England, 1680–1780* (Berkeley: University of California Press, 1996); Richard Grassby, *Kinship and Capitalism: Marriage, Family, and Business in the English-Speaking World, 1580-1740* (Cambridge: Cambridge University Press, 2001); Earle, *The Making of the English Middle Class*; Reliance on family and co-religionists was especially important in far-flung merchant networks. See Price, *Overseas Trade and Traders*; Zahedieh, *The Capital and the Colonies*; Leanore Davidoff and Catherine Hall, *Family Fortunes* (New York: Routledge, 2002); Hancock, *Citizens of the World*; the same is true in the Merchant networks in other parts of the world. See, for example, Susan Migden Socolow, *Merchants of Buenos Aires 1778–1810: Family and Commerce* (Cambridge: Cambridge University Press, 2009); Xabier Lamikiz, *Trade and Trust in the Eighteenth-Century Atlantic World: Spanish Merchants and Their Overseas Networks* (Rochester: Boydell Press, 2013).

[45] Ben-Amos, *The Culture of Giving*, chapter 1.

[46] Naomi Tadmor, *Family and Friends in Eighteenth-Century England* (Cambridge: Cambridge University Press, 2001), 214.

came to include relationships both between kin and non-kin, between equals and non-equals, between men and women, and between neighbors and people who lived far away. Friendship could expand the purview and increase the nimbleness of the relationships between co-religionists, families, and ethnic groups. Indeed, friendship was often overlaid onto and between religious, ethnic, and neighborhood affiliations, and "kinship shaded into friendship" in important ways.[47]

Yet, friendship was not as restricted as other social relationships. Whereas religious and ethnic networks were limited, the act of naming a friend could forge bonds between virtually anyone. Literature, letters, and diaries from this period show that friendship was not undertaken lightly, however. It might begin in shared affection, but the responsibilities of friendship went beyond simply enjoying one another's company. As Tadmor puts it, "Friends worked together and for each other, lent and borrowed money and goods, bought and sold to and from each other, recommended themselves to other 'friends,' and exchanged many other 'favours' and 'services.'"[48] Because of the social and economic obligations incurred in friendships, they were also careful to choose friends who were "honest, godfearing, literate, and ... sober people."[49] Being capable of friendship and actually having friends, then, became an explicit sign of trustworthiness. It meant that other people trusted and relied on you – and if worse came to worst, they could stand surety for or even help pay a debt that you could not. Not only was friendship a powerful relationship that traveled well, it also had a multiplying effect. New friends brought their own society of friends into the relationship, thus increasing the potential number of people one could call on in time of need.[50]

Friendship became such a powerful conduit for transmitting trust and trustworthiness because, at the same time that it became an increasingly expansive relationship, the bond itself was quite specific. It was a voluntary relationship, and its boundaries were governed by the intensity of the emotions that bound the friends, the oath made between them, and the social sanctions that punished people who did not take the obligations of friendship seriously enough. The image of helplessness and destitution evoked when one was 'left entirely "friendless," gives some indication of

---

[47] Wrightson, *English Society*, 58.
[48] Tadmor, *Family and Friends in Eighteenth-Century England*, 212.   [49] Ibid., 214.
[50] For more on the ways in which friendship and membership in mutual aid societies expanded the networks to which one had access, see Ben-Amos, *The Culture of Giving*, chapter 3, esp. 109.

the importance of friendship in this period.[51] The descriptor "poor and friendless" went together for good reason, and it was often used in pleas for charity to help people in debtor's prisons, workhouses, and the highways and byways of the country.[52]

Adding shared faith to friendship made it more powerful still and, in fact, bound co-religionists all over the world in the eighteenth century. Few religious communities did this better than the Quakers. Friend, of course, had special theological significance for them, as in "friend of God" or "friend of Christ." Early adherents took on the name Friend in the same way that they used the pronouns "thou" and "thee," to emphasize that there was "no respect of persons," that God had made all humans equally capable of receiving the light of truth.[53] In their early years, however, what it meant to be a "friend of God" was so open to individual interpretation, it left little room for friendships to form laterally between other "friends of God." It was actually the unfriendliness of civil authorities that first grouped Friends together under the common and, originally, pejorative term *Quaker* and, in that grouping, shaped the early boundaries of their community. Quakers began to develop their own earthly friendships with other "Friends" as a result of official persecution under the Act of Uniformity (1662). Because Friends were imprisoned, fired from jobs, and excluded (or excluded themselves) from parish relief, they began to develop their own practices of friendly society, which included visiting their sick, relieving their poor, lending money, and bringing food and other necessities to those who had been imprisoned.

Friends policed the boundaries of their friendly society through the auspices of the Local Monthly Meetings, which emerged as a means of helping members to keep their everyday, "outer life" from interfering with their pursuit of the "inner Light." To this end, Friends kept alert to the economic lives of each member, nipping in the bud the first sign of poor business judgment, prodigality, or idleness.[54] Friends who

---

[51] Tadmor, *Family and Friends in Eighteenth-Century England*, 256.

[52] See, for example, Thomas Whincop, *A Sermon Preached before the Right Honourable the Lord-Mayor, the Aldermen, and Governours of the Several Hospitals of the City of London* (London, 1701), 11; Defoe, *An Essay upon Projects*, 188; Finn, *The Character of Credit*, 148.

[53] William C. Braithwaite, *The Beginnings of Quakerism* (London: Macmillan and Co., 1912), 494.

[54] The financially savvy among them "dissuade[d] those who had no property from undertakings which seemed likely to endanger their economic status." (Auguste Jorns, *The Quakers as Pioneers in Social Work*, trans. Thomas Kite Brown (Montclair, NJ: Kessinger Publishing, LLC, 1969), 69.) If a member did run into financial trouble, Friends had standard procedures for addressing it. If a Friend contracted debts he could not pay, for example, he had to appear before his Monthly Meeting with an account of his debts and assets and the Friends would decide how to get him out of debt, sometimes

nevertheless fell short, who became bankrupts or contracted bad debts, were expelled.[55] In the late seventeenth century, London Friends extended this system so that it applied to and connected Friends nationally. In 1693, Quakers in London had become alarmed by the increasing problem of provincial members who moved to the metropolis without sufficient means to sustain themselves. The solution London Friends came up with was for migrating Friends to get a certificate from their Monthly Meeting attesting to their financial ability to make the move. These preventive measures extended the effect of local vigilance into a far-reaching network that could both facilitate credit and mutual aid as well as detect fraud before it happened.[56] Spiritually fit and financially solvent, Quakers thus created the first nationwide friendly society. When they officially began calling themselves *The Society of Friends* in the late eighteenth century, they had created some of the most trustworthy credit and mutual aid networks in the world and had become – not coincidentally – some of the richest non-noble families in Britain.[57]

At the same time that Quakers were adapting the concept and practice of friendly society to meet the needs of their persecuted community, others

paying the debt themselves. If that member stayed out of debt, he would be forgiven. (Arnold Lloyd, *Quaker Social History, 1669–1738* (London: Longmans, Green and Co., 1950), 37.) For more on how Quakers maintained creditworthy friendly society in the eighteenth century, see Ann Prior and Maurice Kirby, "The Society of Friends and Business Culture, 1700–1830," In *Religion, Business and Wealth in Modern Britain*, David Jeremy, ed., (New York: Routledge, 2006).

[55] When the methods used to contain bad business decisions and debt failed, Friends could be quite ruthless to the financially failed among them. Unheeded warnings about paying off debts could lead to expulsion. For aggravated cases like bankruptcy, the punishment was immediate expulsion. (Lloyd, *Quaker Social History*, 73). See also, Ann Prior and Maurice Kirby, "The Society of Friends and the Family Firm, 1700–1830," In *Family Capitalism*, Geoffrey Jones and Mary Rose, eds., (Brookfield, VT: Frank Cass, 1993), 78; John Coakley Lettsom, ed., *Memoirs of John Fothergill, M.D. &c.* (London, 1786), 100.

[56] For more on the Society of Friends' business practices in the eighteenth and nineteenth centuries, see Prior and Kirby, "The Society of Friends and Business Culture, 1700–1830."

[57] As the Quaker merchant William Stout said of the Quaker tradesman Henry Coward, he was "very much respected and trusted, not only by the people of his own religious profession, but with all others of all professions and circumstances." (Muldrew, "Interpreting the Market," 178.) For the Friends' success in business in this period, see Jacob M. Price, "The Great Quaker Business Families of Eighteenth-Century London," In *The World of William Penn*, Richard S. Dunn and Mary Maples Dunn, eds., (Philadelphia: University of Pennsylvania Press, 1986); Jordan Landes, *London Quakers in the Trans-Atlantic World: The Creation of an Early Modern Community* (Basingstoke: Palgrave Macmillan, 2015). As was well known at the time, their effectiveness relied a great deal on their ability to expel untrustworthy members. So while it might have been true, as one of their admirers claimed, that the Quakers were "the only people on earth free from poverty," it was equally true that "there may be, and no doubt are, many [poor persons] ... who *have been* Quakers." (Eden, *The State of the Poor*, 1: 589; Lloyd, *Quaker Social History*, 43.)

worked to make the ethics of friendly society effective in contexts without such clearly defined boundaries. If neighbors were supposed to help each other in times of need in local communities, individuals or communities were supposed to be able to solicit mutual aid from the Christian nation at large through what was called a "charity brief." Briefs were basically a license granted by the crown to solicit charity for a loss too big for a local entity to deal with on its own. In 1633, for example, James Savell submitted a brief requesting funds for his town which had been "devastated by a fire in the gunpowder house." Making his case, Savell wrote that, "105 buildings in what had been a thriving clothing town, which had maintained a great multitude of poor people" were burnt to the ground. Additionally, his brief stated that the fire made one hundred people lame and killed thirty-seven men, women, and children, "with four other women, lying in childbed, who with their young infants newly borne were all burnt to ashes."[58] This brief was signed by the local curate who swore to the brief's veracity. From there, the brief was sent to the crown for approval. Once it received the royal seal, it would then be circulated to the parishes, about 15,000 in all, and read from the pulpits. When the service ended, a collection would be taken and then forwarded on to the victim or victims, in this case, the town.

The charity brief was, on the one hand, a way of redistributing social risks and, as such, acted like a kind of social insurance. Briefs were regularly issued throughout the sixteenth and seventeenth centuries, for instance, for Christians taken captive by "Turks" or Barbary pirates.[59] Travel by sea was critical both to the wealth and the defense of the nation, and most people either knew someone who had been taken captive or had read about someone's captivity.[60] On the other hand, these briefs and the causes to which they could be put reflected and reinforced the moral order of English society. Supporting Protestant refugees and paying for the release of Christians at the hands of their Muslim captors was part of the religious cosmos that Britons inhabited. Closer to home, giving toward Savell's brief where a whole town lost its livelihood to fire, something that could happen to anyone at a time when most structures were still built primarily with wood, makes it clear that the charity brief was basically a call to "neighborliness" to the Christian nation at large.

---

[58] Cornelius Walford, *Kings' Briefs, Their Purposes and History* (London: Royal Historical Society Transactions, 1882), 19–20.

[59] Ibid., 14, 26.

[60] From 1660 – 1710, there were five nationwide campaigns to raise ransom money for people taken captive by Barbary. For more on the use of charity briefs to solicit funds to pay ransoms for English captives, see Linda Colley, *Captives: Britain, Empire and the World, 1600–1850* (New York: Anchor Books, 2004), 76, 77–79.

The charity brief had long been plagued by the difficulty of relying on Britons' sense of duty to help distant strangers. But in this period, it also suffered from the lack of consensus on what the Christian nation entailed and, more importantly in the English context, on what kind of Christians constituted that community. The sectarianism and internal migration that undermined the parish community also poked holes in the idea that the nation was simply the parish writ large. The fact that Quakers and other dissenting sects refused to contribute to briefs illustrates this point.[61] Increasing instances of fraud also made the briefs themselves suspicious, and the new modes of protecting against those frauds made people feel less obligated to give.

The frauds riddling the history of the charity brief were similar to those perpetrated in credit networks. As printing grew more sophisticated and printers proliferated toward the end of the century, there was a significant increase in outright forgery. Briefs would be printed up and passed with a forged royal seal. False claims were made about churches that did not exist or fires that never happened.[62] In fact, John Savell's brief, the one described above, was a fraud. The fire never happened; it was a total fabrication. The most egregious aspect of Savell's fraud was that he played on key contemporary cultural concerns – property destruction by fire, the deaths of innocent children, even newborns in their mother's arms, the loss of livelihood through injury, and the poverty all of this senseless destruction caused. Like the problems plaguing extra-local credit networks, the difficulty of verifying the word of strangers made it difficult to know whom to trust.

As the local institutions and practices that had made the charity brief trustworthy lost their effectiveness, the state attempted to prevent fraud by instituting new uniform procedures for charity briefs. In the 1630s, for example, the signatures of local notables who could attest to the validity of the claim were required. But the new procedures only introduced new ways of defrauding the system. The less scrupulous of those local notables began charging a fee for their signature. Another new require-ment that invited new kinds of abuses was the monopoly granted to royal printers for the exclusive right to print charity briefs. Intended to limit the printing of charity briefs to trustworthy printers, the monopoly royal printers enjoyed allowed them to charge exorbitant fees. These protec-tions and others like them made the process of soliciting charity in this manner so complex that the object of charity was seldom in a position to undertake it alone and was forced to pay a fee to an "undertaker" to do

---

[61] Walford, *Kings' Briefs, Their Purposes and History*, 51.
[62] For some examples, see ibid., 19–20.

so. Often, at the end of the process, more money would have been expended in fees than was ever collected in donations.[63]

But the cost of securing charity briefs against fraud, however, was only the beginning of the new abuses committed against them. The practice that especially irked contemporaries was the "farming of briefs." Because briefs had become so difficult to process, and because any given brief represented a potential monetary value, a market emerged for discounting briefs. People began purchasing briefs from the would-be recipient for less than the presumed value. The victim would then be ensured at least some money and the buyer, if his gamble paid off, could turn a profit. Samuel Pepys noted this for-profit alms collection in his diary with disgust.[64] "To church, *where we observe the trade of briefs is come now up to so constant a course every Sunday that we resolve to give no more to them.*"[65] Thus, the mechanism used to distribute large-scale social risks while at the same time reinforcing moral order had earned a poor reputation. Pepys and his contemporaries had no way to evaluate the credibility of the cause described in a brief. And they had no way to determine how much of their contributions would actually reach the victim or get siphoned off instead to feed the veritable industry of interested parties that had grown up around briefs.[66] The breakdown of the charity brief left victims of catastrophes without recourse to the aid that their neighbors and countrymen were socially and spiritually obligated to give.

The emergence of friendly societies as they came to be understood in the late eighteenth century has never been connected to the demise of the charity brief. Indeed, we only know about the charity brief at all because of the role it conventionally plays as a kind of prehistory for modern insurance, fire insurance in particular.[67] Historians use the charity brief

---

[63] Wyndham Anstis Bewes, *Church Briefs, or, Royal Warrants for Collections for Charitable Objects* (London: Adam and Charles Black, 1896), 34–37. Also see Richard Burn, *Ecclesiastical Law: With Notes and References by Simon Fraser*, 7th ed., vol. 1 (London, 1809), 253.

[64] Pepys was not alone in registering his disgust. See the section on fraud in Bewes, *Church Briefs, or, Royal Warrants for Collections for Charitable Objects*, 26–46.

[65] Samuel Pepys, June 30, 1661, quoted in Walford, *Kings' Briefs, Their Purposes and History*, 3.

[66] These abuses (and others) finally led to the abolishment of charity briefs in 1828. (9 Geo. IV. c. 42.)

[67] Insurance historians generally rely on Cornelius Walford's *The Insurance Cyclopaedia*, vol. 3 (London: Charles and Edwin Layton, 1871), 439 for the early history of insurance. And his work on charity briefs, or "king's briefs" as they were also called, was for a long time one of the few works to cover the brief. (Walford, *Kings' Briefs, Their Purposes and History*; M. Harris, "'Inky Blots and Rotten Parchment Bonds': London Charity Briefs and the Guildhall Library," *Historical Research* 66 (1993): 98–110; Bewes, *Church Briefs, or, Royal Warrants for Collections for Charitable Objects*.) In a recent article, R. A. Houston places the charity brief back into the "economy of makeshifts" of charity and welfare.

to distinguish premodern strategies for dealing with risk from "modern" insurance.[68] "Modern" modes of insurance replaced the charity brief from this perspective because they solved the "high moral hazard" problem inherent in the charity brief. By waiting to collect funds after a loss had occurred, historians argue, the charity brief invited fraud and gave no incentive for people to adopt measures to prevent fires.[69] This all changed in the wake of the Great Fire of London, which destroyed some 13,200 houses, eighty-seven parish churches, fifty-two Company Halls, St. Paul's Cathedral, the Royal Exchange, the Guildhall, and several other civic buildings. Between sixty-five and eighty thousand people were left homeless and financially ruined. In 1681, Nicholas Barbon, a man famous in economic history for being one of the first advocates of what we now think of as a "free market," started the "Fire Office," a company that historians consider to be the first to offer modern fire insurance. Barbon was well placed to invent a market in fire insurance because he had led the way in speculating in the massive building boom that followed the Great Fire. He also lost much of his newly acquired fortune by overextending himself. In the early 1670s, he turned to underwriting the very houses he had helped to build, at first on his own and then, in the early 1680s, with partners in the newly established Fire Office. By 1682, the company was underwriting 4,000 houses in London.

But even in the late seventeenth century, fire insurance was more controversial than this story suggests. Fire insurance was not merely an economic problem in need of an economic solution. Insurances of various kinds, especially in maritime applications, had been around for a while at this point, yet they were seen at best as a kind of credit and at worst as a form of gambling, rather than a way to manage risk as we understand it today.[70] Beyond the associations insurance had with gambling, however, property destruction by fire had long been in a special category. Fires had periodically devastated London, and yet, all those wooden houses continued to go uninsured because of the association that fire had with special acts of providence. This is why the charity brief was so important. When God wrote his messages in fire, the charity brief offered a chance for the entire community to engage in an act of communal sacrifice and atonement. Charles II's proclamation for an

---

(R. A. Houston, "Church Briefs in England and Wales from Elizabethan Times to 1828," *Huntington Library Quarterly* 78, no. 3 (2015): 493–520.)

[68] For example, see Robin Pearson, *Insuring the Industrial Revolution: Fire Insurance in Great Britain, 1700–1850* (Aldershot, UK: Ashgate, 2004), 4.

[69] Ibid., 4.

[70] Geoffrey Wilson Clark, *Betting on Lives: The Culture of Life Insurance in England, 1695–1775* (Manchester: Manchester University Press, 1999), chapter 5.

annual day of atonement after the Great Fire makes this clear. September 2nd became a day of "humiliation and fasting," so that Britons "may ... reflect seriously upon their manifold iniquities," the proclamation read, "which are the unhappy causes of such judgments."[71] The need for some kind of fire insurance was well recognized long before the Great Fire, but efforts to start companies in the past had always been thwarted by the belief that "Providence might be tempted" by such interference.[72] The Fire Office may have been the first "modern" fire insurance company, then, but by collecting funds in advance Barbon introduced a moral hazard that many of his contemporaries were unwilling to embrace.

In fact, when Barbon and his partners petitioned James II "to grant them the Office of making and registering all Assurances, Policies, and contracts of houses from Fire, within the Bills of Mortality for thirty-one years," the King balked.[73] Instead, he initially granted the patent to a rival company called The Friendly Society. Even though the patent was eventually granted to both companies, the reasoning James gave for first refusing to give it to the Fire Office is telling. As he put it, the "way of Ensuring Houses by the Friendly Society is of more benefit and satisfaction to the publick than by the Fire Office."[74] This was because the Friendly Society was a charity brief writ small. Rather than calculate premiums in advance, they collected the people in advance. Those people paid a small amount of money up front to indicate their commitment to contribute toward the rebuilding of any member's house should the need arise. Unlike the charity brief which also collected money after the fact, however, The Friendly Society did not rely on the hope that fellow Christians would fulfill their social obligations to their neighbors. The originators, Henry Spelman and William Hale, capitalized on the concept of friendly society that had been around for a long time at this point and secured the commitment to pay up with mutually reinforcing social and moral protections. In addition to asking the contributors to signal their willingness to help each other in advance, he also asked them to sign a contract binding themselves to do so.

[71] Francis Boyer Relton, *An Account of the Fire Insurance Companies ... in Great Britain and Ireland During the 17th and 18th Centuries Including the Sun Fire Office* (London: Swan Sonnenschein & Co., 1893), 16. For a later example of how actual Britons reacted to such proclamations, see Thomas Turner's favorable description of the day of fasting and humiliation designated on March 12, 1762. (Thomas Turner and David Vaisey, *The Diary of Thomas Turner, 1754–1765* (Oxford: Oxford University Press, 1984), 246.)

[72] Walford, *The Insurance Cyclopáedia*, 439.

[73] Relton, *An Account of the Fire Insurance Companies ... in Great Britain and Ireland During the 17. and 18. Centuries Including the Sun Fire Office*, 40.

[74] Minutes of the Privy Council quoted in ibid., 42.

Since a contract, like credit, was only as good as the people involved, Spelman further reinforced the contractual obligation with creditworthy people. In his initial advertisement, he was very specific in listing the names of the distinguished men with whom members would be contractually bound in this friendly society: "the Right Honorable the Lord Mayor, and others, Sir *Francis Pemberton*, Sir *William Dolben*, and Mr. *Trinde*," besides, he added, "a great Number of Eminent Lawyers and Persons of Honour and Quality have already made themselves Members of the said Society," the prospectus announced.[75] Once The Friendly Society was well established some years later, losses were secured by the estates of several trustees, including Sir Christopher Wren, Sir James Smith, Sir Cyril Wich, and Sir William Pritchard.[76] Land, of course, was the gold standard in terms of security in this period. Just as important, the reputations of these men were well known in London and, unlike ordinary people, it was more difficult for them to hide from the consequences if they reneged on the contract. By 1706, The Friendly Society was thought to have insured 18,000 houses. Their success encouraged the proliferation of many rival copycat companies that insured by mutual contribution. Indeed Nicholas Barbon, never one to miss out on a lucrative opportunity, began to offer insurances out of the Fire Office "by mutual contribution" in addition to premium type insurance in 1693.[77]

There is no doubt that, beginning in the late seventeenth century, premium-based fire insurance companies were an important means through which Londoners managed their collective risks. But if these companies replaced the charity brief, they did so only in a very limited sense. The Friendly Society was far more important in this respect because it had implications both for reinforcing the moral order and distributing collective risks of all kinds. In particular, it suggested a model for creating contingency-specific "neighbors" who were contractually bound to fulfill a particular "duty" to a stipulated "neighborhood." In his 1697 *Essay Upon Projects*, Daniel Defoe recognized the potential for non-profit versions of The Friendly Society. In his mind, the applications to which these friendly societies could be put were boundless, "[a]ll the

---

[75] Henry Spelman, *The Friendly Society, or a Proposal of a New Way of Method for Securing Houses from Considerable Loss by Fire, by Way of Subscription and Mutual Contribution* (London, 1684), 2, 4.

[76] Walford, *The Insurance Cyclopáedia*, 465.

[77] Relton, *An Account of the Fire Insurance Companies ... in Great Britain and Ireland During the 17. and 18. Centuries Including the Sun Fire Office*, 44. Of the first nine fire insurance companies started, three were proprietary like the Fire Office, and the rest were mutual. It was only after 1715 that proprietary companies became the norm. (Walford, *The Insurance Cyclopáedia*, 529–530.)

contingencies of life might be fenced against by this method (as fire is already)," he exclaimed, "as thieves, floods by land, storms by sea, losses of all sorts, and death itself, in a manner, by making it up to the survivor."[78] Defoe imagined transforming the social obligations that had once been covered by acts of neighborliness as well as the charity brief into disaggregated risks that were each covered by different friendly societies composed of people who shared those same risks. "[O]ne thing is particularly required in this way of assurances," Defoe explained, "none can be admitted but such whose circumstances are (at least, in some degree) alike, and so mankind must be sorted into classes; and as their contingencies differ, every different sort may be a society upon even terms." Organizing people by the risks they shared would coordinate their interests so that their mutual interdependence became visible in the same way that spiritual and material interests were aligned in the Society of Friends.[79] By aligning people's interest in this way, Defoe made it thinkable for even strangers to obligate themselves to each other. And he figured out a way to make obligations among strangers effective.

In the friendly society for seamen that Defoe proposed, for example, merchant sailors, who were regularly reduced to poverty because of the dangers inherent in their profession, could join together with other sailors to assure what Defoe called their "estate," that is to say, their body parts. Sailors were critical to the defense and wealth of this island nation's growing empire. But their occupation was so dangerous, Defoe and others called them, "*les enfants perdus*, the forlorn hope of the world."[80] Being a sailor was not merely dangerous. It was often deadly. The survival rates were grim: 70 percent of working sailors and seamen were between the ages of fifteen and twenty-nine; 90 percent were under forty.[81] The state already recognized the precariousness of their lives by granting navy sailors who served during wartime a pension upon death and a set value for the loss of particular body parts – namely, eyes, arms, hands, and legs. Merchant sailors, however, had no such protection.

Defoe reasoned that private sea captains would find their own sailors more willing to fight off pirates if they knew that any injuries incurred would be compensated. If 4,000 sailors joined together in such a friendly society, the individual cost when a claim was made would be minimal. But what would induce payment from these notoriously rough characters, whose dangerous livelihood, in Defoe's own words, "so hardened them that we find them the worst of men?" Each sailor would pay his

---

[78] Defoe, *An Essay upon Projects*, 83.   [79] Ibid., 80.   [80] Ibid., 124.
[81] Keith Wrightson, *Earthly Necessities: Economic Lives in Early Modern Britain* (New Haven: Yale University Press, 2000), 310.

share, Defoe made clear, just "as they expect to be relieved if the same or the like casualty should befall them."[82] What Defoe did, in other words, was to create a contractually bound version of the golden rule with an incentive that was prescribed and specific rather than vague and general. A sailor would pay his share because he wanted the other sailors to feel the obligation to pay theirs when the time came – which, as every sailor well knew, it would.

Defoe's method of aligning interests in a friendly society in order to give force to duties had implications for general poverty. "The same thought might be improved into methods that should prevent the general misery and poverty of mankind," Defoe wrote, "and at once secure us against beggars, parish poor, alms-houses, and hospitals; by which not a creature so miserable or so poor but *should claim subsistence as their due* and not ask it of charity."[83] Because everyone faced the risk of either being poor or paying for poverty through the poor rates, the shared risk brought all Britons within the purview of this friendly society. In Defoe's plan, laborers would no longer have to rely on poor relief or the charity of the rich when they were "past their labor." They could anticipate this condition in advance and join together with other laborers, using present health and youth to underwrite future sickness and age.[84] Because some members of this friendly society would not get sick as often and some would be able to work well into old age, the good fortune of the few would translate into surplus funds for the less fortunate. Everyone, even the rich, had strong incentive to pay their share because the accumulated funds that were not used to relieve claims on it would be improved either by lending it to the government or investing it in the burgeoning money market in London. Defoe concluded his proposal by declaring,

I desire any man to consider the present state of this kingdom, and tell me, if all the people of England, old and young, rich and poor, were to pay into one common bank 4s. per annum a head, and that 4s. duly and honestly managed, whether the overplus paid by those who die off, and by those who never come to want, would not in all probability maintain all that should be poor, and for ever banish beggary and poverty out of the kingdom.[85]

---

[82] Defoe, *An Essay upon Projects*, 87.   [83] Ibid., 142.

[84] For example, a subscription of 4s. per year could be collected from the 100,000 laborers Defoe estimated to live in the combined parishes of Stepney and Whitechappel. Members could not collect any benefits for sickness or old age until a year had passed and enough interest had accrued on their combined funds. The lucky lost their share but retained their health; the unlucky got more than their share but paid the price of ill health – and together they would keep society free from poverty.

[85] Defoe, *An Essay upon Projects*, 107.

For Defoe, friendly society was a way of re-inscribing the circle of any obligation, of naming the concerned parties in advance, and of paying one's share because, as he put it,

> ... for as 'tis kind that my Neighbor shou'd Relieve me if I fall into Distress or Decay; so 'tis but Equal he shou'd do so if I agreed to have done the same for him; and if God Almighty has Commanded us to Relieve and Help one another in Distress, sure it must be commendable to bind our selves by Agreement to Obey that Command ...[86]

In Defoe's hands, friendly society recreated the conditions under which the ethic of neighborliness could once again be effective. Like Spelman's Friendly Society, Defoe's friendly society was a charity brief writ small. But it was also a neighborhood parish writ large. It gave Britons a means of fulfilling any social obligation by joining together with others, even strangers, who shared the same risk. Their common interests, rather than their familiarity with each other or their shared spiritual fate, would encourage each member to contribute when the time came. And it had as many applications in Defoe's mind as there were "Miseries, Indigences and Distresses" in the world, as he put it. He did not need to conjure traditional justifications for loving one's neighbor. Instead, he demonstrated that everyone in society would be affected by certain social risks like poverty, old age, widowhood, etc. Joining together to insure against them just made good sense.

His design for friendly societies spawned an entire family of similarly structured organizations that flourished throughout the eighteenth century. In fact, Defoe's intervention gave added meaning to the term friendly society; it became understood as a method for securing against a particular social risk. The founders of the "Friendly Society for Widows," for example, stated in their 1697 advertisement that assurances were conducted *"by way of Friendly Society."*[87] In addition to friendly societies that provided assurances to widows, others were established to secure members against a wide variety of contingencies like sickness, death, "female afflictions," lying-in, children, charity schools, marriage, as well as those associated with specific trades.[88] They were

---

[86] Ibid., 83.

[87] *The Friendly Society for Widows: Being a Proposal for Supplying the Defect of Joyntures, and Securing Women from Falling into Poverty and Distress at the Death of Their Husbands* (London, 1696).

[88] While laborers' clubs would be restricted to men only, these patronized friendly societies from the seventeenth and throughout the eighteenth and nineteenth centuries generally advocated for societies comprising both sexes. For some examples, see Henry Grimstone, *A List, or Short Account of the Various Charitable Institutions in Great Britain...* (York, 1794), 47–52.

also founded for the benefit of "People of Color in the Metropolis" and for enslaved (and formerly enslaved) people in the West Indies.[89] Clergymen continued to encourage Britons to maintain friendly society throughout the eighteenth century and indeed took the practice of mutual aid in the Defoe-inspired friendly societies as a sign that brotherly love was still possible in the commercial society of strangers Britain was rapidly becoming.[90]

These early modern usages of the term do not simply comprise the "pre-history" of friendly society. The dual, and importantly dynamic, understanding of friendly society as an ethical relationship and the institutional means of achieving that ethic persisted well into the nineteenth century. But the concept of friendly society went beyond the working class mutual aid associations that we most commonly associate with it. The concept also figured prominently in the great eighteenth century debates among moral philosophers about the basis of solidarity in commercial societies. The Scottish Enlightenment thinker Francis Hutcheson's use of the term suggested that there was widespread agreement about the importance of friendly society in this respect. As he put it, "Now since a friendly society with others, and a mutual intercourse of offices, and the joint aids of many, are absolutely necessary not only to the pleasure and convenience of human life, but even to the preservation of it; which is so obvious that we need not reason upon it."[91] The pleasures and obligations of friendliness, for Hutcheson, constituted a fundamental social virtue; it emanated out from the individual to include his family, friends, neighbors, countrymen, and, ultimately, humanity in friendly societies of ever increasing scope.[92]

What was in the name friendly society, then, had grown quite large by the end of the eighteenth century. When late eighteenth-century poor law reformers *saw* benefit clubs and *said* friendly societies, then, they did so with intention. Benefit clubs might provide relief for their members. Friendly societies, by contrast, opened up the possibility of transforming

[89] Ibid., 47; James A. Thome and J. Horace Kimball, *Emancipation in the West Indies a Six Months' Tour in Antigua, Barbadoes, and Jamaica, in the Year 1837* (New York: American Anti-Slavery Society, 1838).

[90] There are hundreds of such sermons. For a representative example, see *Sermon Preached to the Friendly Society, at Aldborough, At Their Annual Feast, on Whit-Monday, May Sixteenth, 1796, by the Rev. P. Johnson* (Norwich, 1796).

[91] Arguing against his colleagues who placed the origin of human society in the problems that self-interested individuals experienced in a state of nature, Hutcheson held that man was born into society and the pleasure of and need for friendship fostered cooperative behavior. (Francis Hutcheson, *A Short Introduction to Moral Philosophy: In Three Books; Containing the Elements of Ethicks and the Law of Nature* (Glasgow, 1747), 120–121.)

[92] Ibid., chapter 5.

the basis of the entire social order. Rather than poverty and its relief, relationships between the rich and the poor could be based on a recognition of their interdependence and a realignment of their common interests. As we will see in Chapters 2 and 3, it was the possibility of creating a new moral economy appropriate to a commercial society that made friendly societies so important to late eighteenth-century social thinkers. In particular, Defoe's version of friendly society helped poor law reformers imagine a new system of welfare that could give a commercially sound and socially meaningful basis for the relationships between the higher and lower classes. The early modern origins of the concept and practice of friendly society gave early nineteenth-century Britons a new model of belonging and a new way of thinking about community.

2 Friendly Societies and the Meaning of the New Poor Law

> It is manifest that our laws consider all the inhabitants of a parish as forming one large family, the higher and richer part of which is bound to provide employment and relief for the lower and labouring part.[1]
>
> David Davies, 1795

> The legislature is called on to stay this evil from motives higher and more dignified than any which self-interest can dictate. Every feeling of humanity and love of man for man, implanted in the hearts of all, bids us restore happiness and respectability to two millions and a half of fellow-Englishmen.[2]
>
> John Curwen, 1817

In the late eighteenth century, Defoe's broad conception of friendly society, through which "Mankind [could] be secur'd from all the Miseries, Indigences and Distresses that happen in the world" attracted a lot of interest in the debates over poverty. The Elizabethan poor laws had been criticized for a wide variety of reasons ever since they were introduced in the late sixteenth century.[3] In the late eighteenth century, however, calls for reform gained critical impetus. The most immediate reason for this was the sharp increase in poor rates, the tax on property that funded the relief of the poor. In 1785, the amount raised for the relief of the poor reached a record high of £2,167,760, having increased by 26 percent in only eight years. By 1803, the rates more than doubled, reaching £5,348,205.[4] But while the debates grew more heated with each new

---

[1] David Davies, *The Case of Labourers in Husbandry Stated and Considered, in Three Parts ... A View of Their Distressed Conditions ... The Principal Causes Of ...* (Bath, 1795), 28.

[2] Mr. Curwen's Motion for a Committee on the Poor Laws (HC Deb February 21, 1817, Vol 35 cc506–531).

[3] Richard Burn, *The History of the Poor Laws* (Clifton: Augustus M. Kelley, 1764/1973); J. D. Marshall, *The Old Poor Law, 1795–1834*, 2nd ed. (London: Macmillan, 1985); Slack, *The English Poor Law, 1531–1782*, L. A. Clarkson, ed., *Studies in Economic and Social History* (London: Macmillan, 1990).

[4] Frederick Purdy, "The Statistics of the English Poor Rate before and since the Passing of the Poor Law Amendment Act," *Journal of the Statistical Society of London* 23, no. 3 (1860): 289.

report on the rates, reform proved difficult. The poor laws were so deeply enmeshed in the social, cultural, and economic relationships within parishes and between them that reforming one aspect of them could have a cascading effect on a great many others. Frederick Eden, the author of the most extensive investigation into the causes of poverty in the eighteenth century, described this dilemma well. The various provisions of the poor laws were, he said,

so peculiarly interwoven with many excellent, and (perhaps) with many defective institutions that it becomes extremely difficult to determine, whether it is their joint, or separate influence, that affects the community: still more difficult is it...to say that a radical alteration will correct the evil complained of. The system has insinuated itself into every crack and aperture of the edifice, and, like the spreading ivy, has at length overshadowed the building that supported it: cropping it's luxuriant shoots may check it's encroachments; but cutting it's roots might perhaps endanger the fabric, which the feeble plant first undermined, and now holds together.[5]

The concept and practice of friendly society helped poor law reformers find their way out of this quagmire. Of the 517 major treatises, pamphlets and journal articles written on the poor laws between 1780 and 1834 found in the Goldsmiths's-Kress Library of Economic Literature, for example, 193 of them advocated friendly societies either as a replacement for or supplement to the poor laws.[6] Given how divisive these discussions were, that level of consensus is significant. Perhaps more impressive than the numbers, the variety of people and diversity of political views represented is significant. Local magistrates, ministers, manufacturers, the Board of Agriculture, the Society for Bettering the Condition and Increasing the Comforts of the Poor, Members of Parliament, and even the Prime Minister, all used friendly societies in their proposals for poor law reform. While the poor laws that were so hotly debated applied exclusively to England and Wales, and the problem was concentrated even more specifically in rural regions of those countries, the solutions found in friendly societies and the people thinking with them ranged all over Britain and its Empire.[7] Not only were they talked about a lot by a

[5] Eden, *The State of the Poor*, 1:6.
[6] Using Poynter's *Society and Pauperism* as an initial guide to the debates and the Goldsmiths'-Kress Library of Economic Literature as a data pool, I included "provident societies," "benefit societies," and "box clubs" in the tabulation of friendly society usage. These numbers are only meant to give an approximate sense of proportion. Goldsmiths'-Kress increases its holdings on a regular basis.
[7] In addition to the Scottish and Irish commentators who proposed friendly society models and implemented them locally, which will be discussed later in this chapter, Anglican, Methodist, and Moravian ministers also founded friendly societies for enslaved Africans and free laborers of color in the West Indies. The first was the St. John's Friendly Society,

wide variety of people, friendly societies also featured in every major, even if abortive, legislative effort to reform the poor laws in those years.[8] Each contained a contributory scheme based explicitly on the principle of friendly societies.[9]

Yet, the importance of friendly societies to social policy in this period is little known. The New Poor Law of 1834 represented such a radical departure from the past that the fifty years of debates leading up to it are given little causal weight in the making of the new policy.[10] Even J. R. Poynter, the only historian to study the debates as a whole, accords them little sway, concluding that "the principles of 1834 did not emerge as the culmination of a debate producing an essential consensus; rather the battle-axe of the Royal Commission cut the Gordian knot of intellectual confusion."[11] Although scholars disagree about what caused such a radical shift, there is little disagreement on what the "principles of 1834" were.[12] As E. P. Thompson put it, the New Poor Law was "the most sustained attempt to impose an ideological dogma, in defiance of the evidence of human need, in English history."[13] According to the consensus view, the principles of 1834 were modern market principles. The system would be made efficient by removing it from the hands of local parish officers and standardizing relief through a centralized bureaucracy. And the new system would be cost effective since relief for the able-bodied would be dis-incentivized by requiring them to enter a workhouse to receive it and would be less generous than what a laborer

started by Revd. R. Holberton in 1829 in Antigua (Flannigan and Lanaghan, *Antigua and the Antiguans a Full Account of the Colony and Its Inhabitants from the Time of the Caribs to the Present Day, Interspersed with Anecdotes and Legends: Also, an Impartial View of Slavery and the Free Labour Systems: The Statistics of the Island, and Biographical Notices of the Principal Families* ... (London: Saunders and Otley, 1844), 260.)

[8] Thomas Gilbert's (1786), Baron de Maseres's (1789), William Young's (1788), William Pitt's (1796), and Samuel Whitbread's (1807), each of the bills they produced contained a friendly society scheme in conjunction with poor law reform.

[9] Other contributory schemes that were talked about in political circles but never made it into the form of a bill include those by Thomas Paine (1795), Jeremy Bentham (1811), and Robert Owen (1812).

[10] Gareth Stedman Jones has pointed out the ideological reasons for ignoring this period. "Neo-conservative historiography belittles the importance of this episode in the history of social thought as little more than an eccentric tinkering with Poor Law reform. Old left historiography minimizes its significance because it is still fixated upon the 'bourgeois' limitations of such programmes." (Gareth Stedman Jones, *An End to Poverty?: A Historical Debate* (London: Profile Books, 2004), 10.)

[11] Poynter, *Society and Pauperism*, 309–310.

[12] The question for poor law historians has long been whose interests did the new law serve. For a concise account, see Peter Mandler, "The Making of the New Poor Law Redivivus," *Past & Present* 1, no. 117 (1987): 131–132.

[13] E. P. Thompson, *The Making of the English Working Class* (New York: Vintage, 1966), 295.

could earn in the market. Labor discipline would be instilled by exposing the poor to the unmediated forces of the market.

The tendency to ignore the content of the poor law debates between 1780–1834 is so common and the consensus on the market ethos informing the New Poor Law is so complete, in fact, that the work of a single figure, Joseph Townsend, is often used as historical shorthand for the whole period. In one account, for example, a quote from Townsend's work is used to represent five decades worth of thinking leading up to the New Poor Law: "Hunger will…teach decency and civility, obedience and subjection, to the most brutish, the most obstinate, and the most perverse."[14] The author then concludes that for both Townsend, whose work was published in 1786, and for the Royal Commission into the Operation of the Poor Laws, which produced its landmark report in 1834, "poverty was a goal, encouraging virtue, hard work, and a sense of social hierarchy."[15] Another poor law historian casts Townsend not as the strict paternalist, but rather as a representative of a "new breed of economic writer." This historian argues that "the only solution" for Townsend was "the abolition of mandatory assessment and relief. Only then could the wholesome discipline of the market take effect, bringing the poor face to face with harsh economic realities and the necessity of developing the qualities of character to survive."[16]

Townsend is not a bad choice in some ways. He was one of the first to attack the poor laws themselves as the cause of poverty and his *Dissertation on the Poor Laws* gave Malthus the key to his theory of population. But this interpretation oversimplifies Townsend's ideas about abolition. It also, and more importantly, misses an entire complex of ideas undergirding the alternative social configurations that Townsend and his contemporaries thought possible – and in which they invested a great deal of money and time promoting. A broader consideration of Townsend's *Dissertation on the Poor Laws* (1786) will make it clear why friendly societies were one of the most important of those alternatives.

To be sure, Townsend wanted to abolish relief for the able-bodied – but only gradually and in conjunction with friendly societies and private charity. Townsend saw in friendly societies a way to restore to the poor the resources they needed to rise above destitution – even if he also believed they would never be entirely free from poverty. His solution, so far from leaving the poor to starve, was to legislate mandatory and

---

[14] Joseph Townsend quoted in Lynn Hollen Lees, *The Solidarities of Strangers: The English Poor Laws and the People, 1700–1948* (Cambridge: Cambridge University Press, 1998), 14.
[15] Ibid., 14.
[16] Anthony Brundage, *The English Poor Laws, 1700–1930* (New York: Palgrave, 2002), 30–31.

universal friendly societies to which every laborer, while single, would contribute a quarter of his wages and, when married, "not more than one thirtieth of his income."[17] In order "to drive them into these societies," Townsend suggested that "no man should be entitled to relief from the parochial fund who did not belong to one of these."[18] He envisioned that the poor laws would gradually be superseded by a combination of subsidized friendly societies and private benevolence. This principle of abolishing poor relief for the able-bodied on the one hand and encouraging friendly societies on the other would supply both the fear – and the hope – Townsend thought necessary to inspire industry and frugality in the laboring poor. Equally important, the benevolent contributions that the rich would make to subsidize their frugality would restore the proper relations between the classes, which for him was a strict patriarchy marked by "due subordination."[19]

Townsend's model of society where charity and deference formed the basis of reciprocity was backward looking and his view of the poor was ungenerous in the extreme. But the push-pull mechanism he articulated – where a harsh poor law would act as the stick to the carrot of friendly society membership – is the key to understanding the poor law debates. Very few people agreed with Townsend's characterization of the poor, but most agreed with him about the importance of work as a form of social discipline for laborers and about the potential for relief to undermine that discipline.

The volume of discussion about poverty and how to deal with it in the late eighteenth and early nineteenth century was unprecedented and has only been matched very recently.[20] By returning friendly societies to their rightful place in this discussion, I have no intention of diminishing the importance of the New Poor Law of 1834 as a major turning point, or of ignoring the new kinds of thinking that influenced it. Instead, I argue that the New Poor Law and the market ethos that can be gleaned from its strictures do not provide a complete guide to what that turning point means. However harsh and impersonal the new law seemed in comparison with the old, its goal was to deter the able-bodied poor from asking for relief. Yet, as it pushed them away from the old system, the critical question for contemporaries was: toward what? The answer had to deal with not only poverty, but also with social order and "mutually reinforcing expectations about reciprocity" – that is to say, with social

---

[17] Joseph Townsend, *A Dissertation on the Poor Laws. By a Well-Wisher to Mankind* (London, 1786), 89.
[18] Ibid., 90.   [19] Ibid., 19, 87, 90.
[20] Martin Ravallion, *The Economics of Poverty: History, Measurement, and Policy* (New York: Oxford University Press, 2015).

trust.[21] The poor laws had never done so perfectly, but they had long been recognized as the basis for reciprocity between the propertied ratepayers and the poor of their parish.[22] The poor felt they had a "right to relief" and those with property were supposed to provide relief on the condition that the laborer exhibited a willingness to work. The fact that the poor survived through an "economy of makeshifts" where poor relief was only one and not always the most important source of relief does not diminish the symbolic importance of the poor laws as a potent symbol of reciprocity.[23] Unlike charity, gleaning, help from kin, mutual aid, and the many other means through which the poor survived, which varied widely depending on the region of the country, the collection of poor rates was universal in England and Wales by the late eighteenth century.[24] So, when the poor rates kept rising even after periods of obvious crisis had ended, observers worried that this relationship had come undone.[25] And they were terrified by what they thought the world would look like if it did.

***

The rise in poverty in the late eighteenth century was a complex phenomenon the details of which are still being debated. Rising population, enclosures, stagnant or declining wages in some regions amidst rising prices, the decline of cottage industry in the south, as well as the tactic that some farmers employed to use poor relief as a form of labor insurance, these and other factors all contributed to different degrees.[26] The structural aspects of poverty were exacerbated by the war with France and a series of harvest crises (most notably, 1795–1796 and 1800–1801). Contemporaries recognized many of these economic issues as contributing factors but because the poor laws were so intertwined with social life more generally, the rates represented much more than the cost of

---

[21] Scott, *Geographies of Trust; Geographies of Hierarchy*, 275.

[22] Thomas Mackay, *A History of the English Poor Law Vol. 3: 1834–1898.* (London: P.S. King, 1904), 103–104. Also, on this point, see K. D. M. Snell, *Annals of the Labouring Poor: Social Change and Agrarian England, 1660–1900* (Cambridge: Cambridge University Press, 1985), chapter 3. For how the poor laws legitimated the paternalist social order, see Marco H. D. van Leeuwen, "Logic of Charity: Poor Relief in Preindustrial Europe," *The Journal of Interdisciplinary History* 24, no. 4 (1994): 589–613.

[23] Steven King and Alannah Tomkins, *The Poor in England, 1700-1850: An Economy of Makeshifts* (Manchester: Manchester University Press, 2003). The term was first used in the French context. See Olwen H. Hufton, *The Poor of Eighteenth-Century France 1750–1789* (Oxford: Clarendon Press, 1974).

[24] Slack, *The English Poor Law, 1531–1782*, 18.   [25] Poynter, *Society and Pauperism*, 17.

[26] For an assessment of these different factors, see George R. Boyer, *An Economic History of the English Poor Law, 1750–1850* (New York: Cambridge University Press, 1990).

poor relief. Instead, they acted like a canary in the coalmine, signaling a problem with the entire social system. Rates were "widely regarded as a real indicator of malaise in the system or society at large. It was usually assumed that the rates ought not to rise, and that something was wrong since they did rise."[27]

In order to appreciate the broader cultural meaning given to rising rates, it is worth considering the way that poverty and its relief served to structure and legitimate the social order in England and Wales. "The poor ye will have with ye always" was a commonplace belief in the early modern period, not simply because of theories about the utility of poverty.[28] Contemporaries recognized that there would always be people who could not take care of themselves; that is to say, the so-called impotent, or helpless poor, which included the elderly, the chronically ill, orphans, pregnant women, and, with growing importance in the later eighteenth century, households with young, growing families. They also recognized that poverty threatened anyone who had to rely on her labor for work. The "necessity to labor" had been the definition of poverty for a long time.[29] Without resources other than labor to sustain a person during periods when he could not work, being a laborer meant being part of the "laboring poor."[30] Able-bodied laborers would not be able to work at some point in their lives due to illness, accident, age, pregnancy, not to mention harvest crises, war, natural disaster, and the seasonal nature of many occupations.[31] The only question was

---

[27] Poynter, *Society and Pauperism*, 17.

[28] Boyd Hilton, *Age of Atonement: The Influence of Evangelicalism on Social and Economic Thought, 1785–1865* (Oxford: Clarendon Press, 1986), 100.

[29] The insecurity of labor would continue to be defined as poverty into the nineteenth century. Patrick Colquhoun, for example, followed Bentham in defining poverty as "the necessity of working for a living," when he distinguished it from indigence, which he defined as the "inability to make a living by working . . . " (Quoted in Poynter, *Society and Pauperism*, 202.)

[30] The term "labouring poor" was apparently coined by Daniel Defoe in 1701, but Paul Slack has shown that the concept existed as far back as the sixteenth century. (Slack, *The English Poor Law, 1531–1782*, 12.) Edmund Burke famously found the term controversial because he wanted there to be a clear distinction between what he understood as the helpless poor and the able-bodied – those who could not work and those who could. This distinction will be discussed further later in this chapter. (Edmund Burke, *Maxims, Opinions and Characters, Moral, Political and Economical, from the Works of the Right Hon. Edmund Burke*, 2nd ed., vol. 2 (London, 1811), 64–66.)

[31] Eastwood, *Government and Community in the English Provinces, 1700–1870*, 125. Somewhere between 5–15 percent of the population was in receipt of some form of parish relief at any given time. But this snapshot hides the short-term relief that a great many more laborers received. Expanding the window to include an entire year, historians estimate that 25–30 percent of the population received relief due to either life-cycle contingencies or economic fluctuations over the course of the year. (Peter M. Solar, "Poor Relief and English Economic Development before the Industrial Revolution," *The Economic History Review* 48, no. 1 (1995): 1–22.)

when. The poor laws acknowledged the insecurity of labor and stood as a testament of the propertied classes' commitment to take care of the helpless and laboring poor in times of need.[32]

The question was not whether the poor should be relieved, but rather how. Throughout the early modern period, contemporaries worried about the form that relief took and under what conditions it was given. The Elizabethan poor laws made two distinctions in this respect. The chronically ill and the elderly, for example, could be relieved with cash or in-kind payments without that relief being detrimental to their morals. In order to protect the able-bodied from the twin dangers of idleness or dependence, however, the poor laws mandated that the poor be "set on work." In England, the upper classes did not hesitate to acknowledge the importance of labor to national wealth. And by the late seventeenth century, political economists were beginning to calculate the extent of the laborer's contribution with increasing refinement.[33] But as we saw with Townsend, the moral discipline of work every bit as much as the economic value was thought to be the best prevention of and antidote to a multitude of sins. Work, doing it when it was available, or being willing to do it even when it was not, formed an important boundary condition of the moral community.

These boundaries were constantly disturbed in practice throughout the early modern period, but they continued to inform how people thought about social and moral order. Most parishes tended to give both the able-bodied and impotent poor "outdoor relief" due to the prohibitive cost and inconvenience of relieving them with "indoor relief," i.e., in workhouses, or creating what we would call make-work schemes.[34] It is clear, however, that outdoor relief was acceptable only because it was considered short-term, temporary relief. If relief to the able-bodied became long term, however, contemporaries would panic about demoralizing the laborer. As we have seen, it was widely believed that long-term relief to the able-bodied – without requiring them to work – would ultimately render them *unable* to work.[35] During episodes where relief

---

[32] For more on the way that poor relief had become a "customary expectation," see Tim Hitchcock, Peter King, and Pamela Sharpe, *Chronicling Poverty: The Voices and Strategies of the English Poor, 1640–1840* (New York: St. Martin's Press, 1997), 10–13.

[33] For an early elaboration of a labor theory of value, see William Petty, *A Treatise of Taxes and Contributions* (London, 1685).

[34] Geoffrey Oxley, *Poor Relief in England and Wales 1601–1834* (London: David & Charles, 1974), 62–63, 90; Slack, *The English Poor Law, 1531–1782*, 27.

[35] As the Scottish Enlightenment thinker Lord Kaimes explained, when a laborer got used to a "certain provision against want, he relaxes gradually till he sinks into idleness: idleness leads to profligacy: profligacy begets disease: and the wretch becomes an object of public charity before he has run half his course." (Lord Kaimes quoted in

to the able-bodied extended for a longer period, there would be a spate of proposals for workhouses and labor schemes.[36] But then the pressure of the crisis would abate, and most parishes would resume the practice of relieving all paupers in the same manner – with outdoor relief – regardless of their helpless or able-bodied status.

If contemporaries worried about the impact the manner of relief might have on the poor, the problem of determining who among the able-bodied "deserved" relief became more exigent with increases in internal migration. In small parishes, officials were familiar enough with their own parishioners to make such determinations.[37] Strangers posed a different kind of problem because their character and work histories were unknown. The Laws of Settlement and the Vagrancy laws helped local authorities make some distinctions. After 1697, for example, laborers might carry a "settlement certificate" attesting to a good character and making clear that their home parish would care for them if they came into need.[38] There were other documents that helped parish officers determine the intent of a stranger. The various "licenses to beg," charity briefs, testimonials carried by servants attesting to the termination of their employment, passports carried by artisans, warrants given to demobilized sailors, and so on told parish officers that these people could be

A Letter to Thom. Gilbert, Esq., M.P. On His Plan for the Better Relief and Employment of the Poor (London, 1782), 5.)

[36] See, for example, William Hay, *Remarks on the Laws Relating to the Poor. With Proposals for Their Better Relief and Employment. By a Member of Parliament* (London, 1735). For a sense of how common they were, see Defoe's critique of them in Daniel Defoe, *Giving Alms, No Charity, 1704; A Proposal for Relief and Punishment of Vagrants, Particularly Such as Frequent the Streets and Publick Places of Resort, within This Kingdom* (London, 1748).

[37] Most poor law officials had authority over only a few hundred families. (Mark Blaug, "The Myth of the Old Poor Law and the Making of the New," *Journal of Economic History* 23 (1963): 130. Also see Boyer, *An Economic History of the English Poor Law, 1750–1850*, 20.)

[38] In 1697, Justices of the Peace were empowered to issue a resident who was leaving in search of work a "settlement certificate," which stated his or her parish of legal residence and guaranteed that should the traveler become chargeable in a foreign parish, the parish of legal settlement would pay all maintenance expenses; in 1731, the parish of residence was further required to pay "removal" expenses as well. For more on the laws of settlement, see James Taylor, *Poverty, Migration, and Settlement in the Industrial Revolution: Sojourners' Narratives* (Palo Alto, CA: Society for the Promotion of Science & Scholarship, 1989); James Taylor, "The Impact of Pauper Settlement 1691–1834," *Past and Present* 73 (1976); Keith Snell, "Settlement, Poor Law and the Rural Historian," *Rural History* 3 (1992): 145–172; Norma Landau, "The Regulation of Immigration, Economic Structures and Definitions of the Poor in Eighteenth-Century England," *The Historical Journal* 33, no. 3 (1990): 541–571; Steve Hindle, *On the Parish? The Micro-Politics of Poor Relief in Rural England, c. 1550–1750*.

trusted not to disturb the social order.[39] For a while, even without such documentation, clear social characteristics aided parish officers in differentiating the migrant, who tended to travel with families, from the vagrant, who was "marked out ... by an absence of complete families and a predominance of single men among them."[40] If the case was unclear and the stranger could give "no reckoning how he or she might get his or her living ... ," the vagrancy laws gave wide berth for local authorities to punish them and send them back to their parish of origin.[41]

The late eighteenth century rise in able-bodied poverty caused alarm, just as previous increases had in the past. But because single, able-bodied men came to represent the largest class of internal migrants and also a growing proportion of relief recipients in the rural parishes of the southeast in this period, there was renewed emphasis on how these unemployed men were relieved.[42] As these parishes dealt with the increased need, they developed various means of marrying relief with employment. Some gave allowances-in-aid of wages, the most famous of which was the Speenhamland system, which included elaborate bread scales. Others gave wage subsidies, family allowances, or short-term payments during seasonal downtimes. Some used the "roundsmen system," where laborers were hired out to local farmers who paid reduced wages, which were brought up to subsistence level by the parish rates.[43] In each case, laborers continued to earn what they could through work, and the parish made up the rest out of the rates. Leaving aside the hysteria with which the Poor Law Commissioners talked of these methods in 1834, what is clear is that parish officers were trying to relieve the able-bodied laborers in their communities in a way that, from their perspective, preserved both their morals and their lives, and thus social order.

---

[39] Edward Higgs, *Identifying the English: A History of Personal Identification 1500 to the Present* (London: Continuum, 2011), 80–91; Steve Hindle, "Technologies of Identification under the Old Poor Law," *Local Historian* 36, no. 4 (2006).

[40] Paul A. Slack, "Vagrants and Vagrancy in England, 1598–1664," *The Economic History Review* 27, no. 3 (1974): 365–68. About 50 percent of vagrants were single men, 25 percent single women, and the rest were married or claimed to be married. (A. L. Beier, "Vagrants and the Social Order in Elizabethan England," *Past & Present*, no. 64 (1974): 8–9.)

[41] Taylor, *Poverty, Migration, and Settlement in the Industrial Revolution*, chapter 1.

[42] Paul Fideler, *Social Welfare in Pre-Industrial England: The Old Poor Law Tradition*, Jeremy Black, ed., *Social History in Perspective* (New York: Palgrave Macmillan, 2006).

[43] Some parishes asked laborers to enter workhouses, but until 1834, such institutions were generally only used to house the helpless poor. (James Taylor, "The Unreformed Workhouse 1776–1834," In *Comparative Development in Social Welfare*, Ernest Walter Martin, ed., (London: Allen & Unwin, 1972), 65.)

As poor rates continued their rapid climb in the first two decades of the nineteenth century, however, a creeping panic spread over the country. Added to the ever-rising rates were other signs of social disorder – property destruction in particular – not only in the agricultural districts most affected by poverty, but in the growing cities of the northwest, as well. Contemporaries interpreted the urban reports that detailed rising crime, alcohol consumption, violence, and vagrancy as further indications that the social order was unraveling. It was in this context that the restriction of relief "became an almost universal aim. The problem was where and how to draw it, and on what principle."[44]

The poor law debates lasted for many decades because while most contemporaries recognized that the system of poor relief as it stood could no longer grapple with the shifting geography and structure of the economy, it was unclear how to fix it without "endanger[ing] the fabric, which the feeble plant first undermined, and now holds together," as Eden put it. The system was fundamentally local with a local vision of what social order should look like. Even though the settlement laws were designed to facilitate the movement of laborers to areas with greater employment opportunities, they could also be used defensively to protect parish resources against newcomers, which then acted like a break on labor mobility.[45] The questions that reformers asked in these years took them in circles for a long time because they could not figure out how to relieve poverty without demoralizing labor, on the one hand, or to trust laborers to travel freely in search of work without threatening social order, on the other. If the system remained local, how could relief be designed so that it met material needs without undermining the social discipline of labor? What was the most equitable way to fund local relief when regional and national growth was so unevenly distributed? And finally, who should contribute to relief and on what principle?

★★★

Friendly societies helped reformers work their way through this previously intractable set of problems. But the most generative thinking on these organizations happened at first outside of the poor law debates. As we saw in the last chapter, the concept and practice of friendly society had been around for a long time by the late eighteenth century. New ways of conceiving of society more broadly through moral philosophy,

---

[44] Poynter, *Society and Pauperism*, 43.
[45] For the increasing instance and cost of litigation between parishes and the way in which the local administration of relief incentivized a defensive posture against newcomers, see Snell, *Parish and Belonging*, 66–70.

political economy, and statistics made it possible to use a friendly society mode of reciprocity to do new things. The work in which Daniel Defoe was engaged in the early eighteenth century, where he figured out how to address the problem of distributing collective risks while also dealing with the problem of trusting strangers to pay for them, was taken up by a new generation of more statistically-minded thinkers in the 1770s. These men, radical dissenters like the Arian minister Richard Price, had strong political and ideological reasons for using numbers to make claims to political authority.[46] When such methods were applied to friendly societies, the implications were equally radical. These numbers had the potential to blow up the entire conception of poverty as necessary to social order and work as the only means of disciplining labor. The impact of their thinking on the enlarged role that friendly societies could have in a new system of welfare was profound.

Richard Price, "Britain's foremost authority on actuarial mathematics" at the time, was not at first interested in friendly societies, or box clubs as they were still called when he was writing in the early 1770s.[47] And he was not actively engaged in the debates over poverty. He wrote his *Observations on Reversionary Payments* in large part to fix the middle-class insurance schemes that proliferated throughout the eighteenth century.[48] According to Price, they were nothing but bubbles whose bursting was simply a matter of time.[49] In the process of detailing actuarially sound bases for these annuity societies and pension schemes, Price added a footnote noting that the box clubs of the lower orders were marred by the same problems.[50] In it, he suggested a method for creating an actuarial relationship between contributions and benefits in these clubs and even designed a statistical model for calculating average rates of sickness by age, which was the first of its kind.[51] Price's model turned out to be

---

[46] I thank Timothy Alborn for alerting me to this reference and for his intellectual generosity more generally. Peter Buck, "People Who Counted: Political Arithmetic in the Eighteenth Century," *Isis* 73, no. 1 (1982): 28–45.

[47] Geoffrey Wilson Clark, *Betting on Lives: The Culture of Life Insurance in England, 1695–1775* (Manchester: Manchester University Press, 1999), 123.

[48] Price's work was first published in 1771, with several updated editions running into the 1810s.

[49] Richard Price, *Observations on Reversionary Payments on Schemes for Providing Annuities for Widows, and for Persons in Old Age; the Method of Calculating the Values of Assurance on Lives; and on the National Debt* (London, 1772), 117.

[50] Ibid., 120, note (a).

[51] According to Walford, "This was probably the first attempt which was made to fix the rate of contributions by the members of friendly societies with some regard to the benefits to be received." (Walford, *The Insurance Cyclopáedia*, 385.) Price suggested two payment plans he considered sufficient to secure their funds. The first, presuming a constant membership of 100 with an average age of 36, if each member paid 4 pence

flawed, especially for the elderly.[52] And the values he assigned for contributions and sick pay were far higher than most laborers could have afforded.[53] But this short footnote was important. Like most box club payments, poor rates were collected after poverty had become a reality. Price's formulation introduced the critical element of time to keep the able-bodied laborer from ever being exposed to poor relief. The possibility of transforming able-bodied poverty into a simple liability that could be quantified, calculated, and therefore prepared for in advance was a radical departure from the way in which poverty had been conceived of at the time.

This scheme had a powerful effect on how people started talking and thinking about the problem of able-bodied poverty. Most immediately, Baron Francis de Maseres, a fellow mathematician and social reformer, elaborated on Price's distinction between the relief of the able-bodied laborer and the impotent poor and proposed a detailed way to make that separation self-sustaining. He also brought this pre-emptive method of removing able-bodied laborers from the purview of the poor laws to the attention of Parliament. Maseres proposed a parish-based annuity scheme, where laborers in the manufacturing districts could purchase an annuity to secure themselves against indigence in old age.[54] He expected poor rates to decrease in parishes granting annuities because

per week, each would receive an annuity of £5 beginning at age 64, increasing every year by £1 until age 75 when it would be set at £12 for life, as well as 12 s per week during illness. In the second plan, paying 7 pence per week would increase the life annuity to £20 after age 79 and the sick pay to 15s per week. (Price, *Observations on Reversionary Payments on Schemes for Providing Annuities for Widows, and for Persons in Old Age; the Method of Calculating the Values of Assurance on Lives; and on the National Debt, 1772*, 120–121.)

[52] Price calculated sickness tables based on the data collected from the bills of mortality in the county of Northampton. He published them in the 5th edition (1792) of his *Observations*. He assumed that sickness increased uniformly throughout a person's life. Later actuaries would prove through observation that sickness increased significantly after the age of 60 and then doubled again after the age of 70. (See Chapter 5 for a more detailed history of actuarial science as it related to sickness.)

[53] The cost of Price's scheme was well beyond what any laborer could afford at this time and the sick pay was well beyond what most lived on – by almost double. After collecting weekly budgets from laborers all over England, Sir Frederick Eden calculated the average weekly wage between 8 and 9s and the average sick pay friendly societies offered was 7s per week, reduced to 5s if the person was sick longer than a year. Most friendly societies did not provide annuities at this early date; the majority of their funds went to sick pay and the lump sum of £5 at death.

[54] Instead of simple interest on individual funds, Maseres's plan promised compound interest on the combined funds of any member of a parish interested in purchasing one. Overseers would collect the money bi-annually and invest it in bank annuities with a guaranteed 3 percent return. Ratable property in the parish would act as security for the fund. (Francis Maseres, *A Proposal for Establishing Life-Annuities in Parishes for the Benefit of the Industrious Poor* (London, 1772), 6.)

the money paid into them would supplement the poor rates. And the people purchasing them, who would otherwise be recipients of relief in their old age, "would now be maintained. . .by annuities paid to them out of a fund of their own raising."[55] Beyond reducing rates, and what would turn out to be far more important for thinking on poverty, Maseres's scheme suggested the possibility of decoupling labor from necessary poverty.[56] Instead of the spiraling road from occasional relief to idleness, profligacy, disease, and finally pauperism, annuity-owning able-bodied laborers would look down a straight and narrow path to "the comforts they might procure to themselves in their time of sickness or old age."[57] And the property these laborers would own in an annuity would act as "an incitement to get more."[58]

Maseres went beyond Price by offering an incentive structure that could make the separation between labor and poverty a permanent one. For Maseres, a laborer's future did not have to be a picture of assured poverty; it could be an assurance of relative prosperity. His approach, giving laborers a propertied stake in their society as the key to social order, was more forward thinking than many subsequent friendly society schemes that tended to rely on some form of paternalism to do that work. Practically speaking, Maseres's proposal came to nothing. The bill based on Maseres's plan was eventually thrown out by the House of Lords, but "the effect of the discussion was to awake considerable interest in the subject of friendly societies."[59] In the course of that discussion, insurance principles that promised to transform current problems into future possibilities were matched with friendly society principles that mitigated individual vulnerabilities with mutual aid. The result was both a great proliferation of friendly societies schemes and an expansion of the types of problems friendly societies were thought capable of solving.

---

[55] Ibid., 13.

[56] Maseres's scheme even had implications for the high-wage low-wage debate. The high wages that many contemporaries still thought dangerous to a laborer's moral health, would be captured in annuities and be put to use against future indigence.

[57] Maseres, *A Proposal for Establishing Life-Annuities in Parishes for the Benefit of the Industrious Poor*, 7–8.

[58] Francis Maseres, *Considerations on the Bill Now Depending in the House of Commons, for Enabling Parishes to Grant Life-Annuities to Poor Persons, upon Purchase* ... (London, 1773), 15.

[59] The fact that ratable property was expected to act as security for the annuity fund was apparently the point on which it failed. Lord Camden objected to putting landed interests at double risk for poverty. On this point, see Walford, *The Insurance Cyclopáedia*, 285; and Eden, *The State of the Poor*, 1:355. Also, see "Abridgement of Abstract of Answers and Returns Relative to Expense and Maintenance of Poor in England and Wales" XIX. 1 (1818). The 1817 Poor Law Committee members were otherwise very much in favor of Maseres's scheme.

Revd. John Acland, a magistrate for Devon, was particularly inspired by Maseres's formulation. He expanded on Price's and Maseres's insurance idea by combining it with the actual workings of the laborer's box club. Acland began with an actuarially sound version of the local club, but then instead of just offsetting the future liabilities of the able-bodied with their own current assets, he proposed to use the mutuality principle already found in box clubs to offset the vulnerabilities of each individual in the parish against the strengths of the combined force of the whole nation. His plan is important to consider because it used friendly societies to treat poverty socially rather than simply as an insurance problem. In doing so, it brought friendly societies into the debates over poverty in a way that could deal both with rising rates and with fears about social trust. Acland's proposal for a parish-based but nationally-funded friendly society introduced a new criterion for belonging, one that was capable of policing the line between the deserving and undeserving poor without relying on local or moral knowledge of the relief recipient.

In Acland's scheme, eligibility for relief was based on one's contribution to the parish friendly society fund. That membership earned a person the right to relief. Because everyone, rich and poor, men and women, had liabilities of various sorts, everyone who *could* would contribute. Acland also recognized that not everyone had the same ability to pay for their liabilities. So he created a series of inverse relationships between certain types of liabilities and the minimum contributions required from different classes of people.[60] On one end of the spectrum, he proposed that those with monied property would be taxed alongside landed property because it is "more liable to accident, and bears no proportional share of the public burthens …"[61] On the other end, because women were customarily paid lower wages, for example, they paid lower contribution rates – ½ d. less than males in the same class. In general, for every 1½ d. paid in per week, members would be eligible for 3s. weekly when illness or some other contingency rendered them unable to work. Members were free to subscribe more than the minimum for higher benefits, but no more than 1s per week.[62] In addition to offsetting

---

[60] Where liabilities were great and ability to pay for them were low, as among the "Stations of Low-Life," Acland set a minimum contribution. And where the ability to pay was great but the liability to poverty low as it was among the higher stations, Acland set a maximum contribution. Acland's justification for charging the higher stations more even though their chances of future poverty were small was two-fold: first, they would no longer have to pay for poor relief, and second, freed from poverty, the nation's workforce would continue to make the nation rich. (Acland, *A Plan for Rendering the Poor Independent on Public Contribution*, 12.)

[61] Ibid., 13–14.   [62] Ibid., 10–11, 14.

liabilities with the ability to pay, the power of combining all the funds beyond the parish would offset the liabilities of those who had no ability to pay at all. Married laborers with one or more children would receive benefits without contributing; although if they could afford it, they could opt in to a higher class of payments/benefits. Sailors and soldiers would be eligible for relief in recompense for their service. The helpless poor would all be subsidized out of the funds.

Although Acland relied on actuarial tables produced by Richard Price, the foundation for his friendly society was not strictly actuarial. His approach might best be described as actuarial paternalism. Acland used actuarial principles to offset the liabilities of one class of people against the abilities to absorb those losses by another. He also created such relationships between regions of the country. Funds collected locally, for example, would be deposited into countywide funds, which would be invested in public securities. The interest earned on these funds would be enough to make up for the liabilities of those classes of society who were physically, or by virtue of their occupation, unable to contribute, as well as those parts of the country hit by unusual deprivation. As he put it, "in case it should happen, that one particular County should be insolvent, at the same Time that the general Fund should remain rich," that county would be relieved out of the surplus of the general funds. He even included the differing liabilities of being poor in cities like London as opposed to being poor in the countryside and calculated higher benefits for city dwellers to compensate for their higher costs of provisions and rent – the difference to be made up by the higher proportion of "gratuitous Contributors" to be found in cities.[63] Where actuarial science fell short, both Acland and Price, whose letter was published in the preface to the pamphlet, were sure that the higher classes would more than make up for the deficit. In this way, the combined and compounded sum of their own contributions, as well as the surpluses provided by wealthy contributors, would secure labor; earned interest on these funds would support the impotent poor; and national prosperity would overcome temporary local poverty, whether urban or rural.

Yet, Acland's harmonious vision of belonging – where each contributed according to ability and received according to liability – was made possible by a powerful exclusionary principle. It was similar to the one used by Quakers in the late seventeenth and early eighteenth century. The opprobrium Acland reserved for those who refused to join the parish friendly society is startling after the cool appeal to interests and warm rushes of humanity that characterize the bulk of his treatise. The implementation of the plan was to be gradual, recognizing the difficulty some

---

[63] Ibid., 38–40.

people would initially have in contributing – but after a few years, there would be no mercy on those who refused to join. " ... [A]ll Persons so refusing," he railed, "whether Male or Female, forasmuch as they determine to live on others Labours, shall be badged ... with the Word Drone, in large Letters of Red Cloth ... "[64] Badging, though legal, was increasingly looked down upon as inhumane in the late eighteenth century.[65] Acland was sure that "drones" would be numerically insignificant, but his explanation for why these people would be treated so harshly reveals the moral dilemma at the heart of the debates over poverty in the late eighteenth century.[66] In Acland's mind, refusing to join one of his parish friendly societies would entail a moral choice,

for who but a person of so worthless a Character, as must be lost to all the Feelings of a Man, as well as to all Sense of Shame, could be so brutish as not only to deprive both himself and his Family of so many great Advantages, but expose himself also to such public Scorn and Disgrace, merely to save the Payment of 4s. 8d. a Year...[67]

By coupling a powerful incentive for joining a parish friendly society, on the one hand, with a harsh punishment for refusing to join, on the other, Acland discovered what he thought was a foolproof method for distinguishing between the deserving and undeserving, the trustworthy and the untrustworthy. Friendly society membership itself rendered one deserving of relief because members paid contributions for this purpose. From Acland's perspective, refusing to contribute rendered one's moral deprivation clear for all to see.

The impact Acland had on poor law discussions was less a matter of the practicability of his scheme and more a function of the way he emphasized how friendly society membership could be read as a sign of a laborer's moral health. His only critic, Revd. John Howlett, the vicar of Great Dunmow and Badow in Essex, called Acland's plan a "*baseless fabric of a vision.*"[68] Howlett did not believe that the poor laws pauperized the poor. He saw the disparity between the cost of provisions and the wages of laborers as the real problem. And he thought the claim that poor

[64] Ibid., 42.

[65] Badging the poor was outlawed in 1810. Even though the practice of badging the deserving poor in the late medieval period was seen as an honorable distinction used both by monasteries and parish administered charitable trusts, it acquired a negative connotation in the seventeenth and eighteenth century. See Steve Hindle, "Dependency, Shame and Belonging: Badging the Deserving Poor, c.1550–1750," *Cultural and Social History* 1, no. 1 (January 2004): 6–35.

[66] Acland, *A Plan for Rendering the Poor Independent on Public Contribution*, 43.

[67] Ibid., 57.

[68] John Howlett, *The Insufficiency of the Causes to Which the Increase of Our Poor, and of the Poor's Rates Have Been Commonly Ascribed* (London, 1788), 117.

relief demoralized the poor absurd, "Shall I be vicious and profligate," he asked, "because I know that after a long course of contempt and infamy, of rags and wretchedness, of infirmity, sickness and disease, the parish will provide me a doctor to protract the wretched remains of my life?"[69] After citing evidence from his longitudinal study comparing the price of provisions to average wages earned during previous poor rate increases, Howlett concluded that Acland's plan failed on the "fundamentally erroneous conception, namely, that the present earnings of the Poor, if properly managed, are perfectly adequate to their comfortable maintenance."[70] Nevertheless, even Howlett saw the moral power of friendly societies; not for the destitute rural laborer who could not afford membership in any case, but for the urban laborer whose "great wages," he believed, led to idleness, profligacy and destitution. Taking a cue from Maseres's plan, Howlett proposed to discipline the urban worker by earmarking his surplus wages for investment in a friendly society.[71]

Although not everyone agreed as to whose morals were in need of reforming or why, by the early 1790s, friendly societies became a powerful resource for shaping them regardless of the rationale or desired goal. Howlett's proposal to use friendly societies to constrain the immoral impulses of high-wage laborers became very popular but was only the negative, and rather unoriginal, side of the equation. Disciplining laborers by taking away their pay, as Howlett proposed, was only different in method from artificially reducing wages to match the price of bread – the "low wage" approach that had been around for well over a century. What was new was the idea that in addition to their disciplinary function, friendly societies could also have a liberating effect, decoupling labor from the necessity of life-cycle poverty. Price had made it possible to

---

[69] John Howlett, *Examination of Mr. Pitt's Speech in the House of Commons on Friday February 12, 1796 Relative to the Condition of the Poor* (London, 1796), 6.

[70] Howlett, *The Insufficiency of the Causes to Which the Increase of Our Poor, and of the Poor's Rates Have Been Commonly Ascribed*, 110.

[71] Maseres first introduced the moralizing potential of friendly societies in his annuity scheme, answering a common fear about the immoral effects of the high wages of urban workers. "Numbers of ['labouring men that live in towns and cities'] are known to get so much by their labour, that they can maintain themselves the whole week upon the earnings of the three first days of it; and often do so, spending half of their time in idleness and pleasure; whilst others, who are more industrious, spend the whole of their gettings, which are much more than sufficient for their maintenance, in drunkenness and debauchery." Their debauchery was "prejudicial both to the public and themselves" because "the public loses the benefit of their labour… and they themselves lose the benefit of the wages they might earn by that labour … " Investing their extra money in annuities rather than drinking would kill both birds with one stone. This view would become quite common as concerns about urban instability grew in the first decades of the nineteenth century. (Maseres, *A Proposal for Establishing Life-Annuities in Parishes for the Benefit of the Industrious Poor*, 6.)

imagine a cost-effective way of separating the relief of the able-bodied from that of the ordinary poor and thus keeping the poor laws from demoralizing able-bodied laborers. Maseres further elaborated that separation by making it self-sustaining, giving laborers the hope of a proper-tied stake in society. And, Acland contributed a comprehensive vision of belonging, albeit patriarchal in nature, where membership in a friendly society marked a person as morally sound without requiring personal knowledge of her character. Howlett's practical critique notwithstanding, the conceptual possibility through which friendly societies would enable the poor to contribute to their own maintenance – that is, to "belong" on the same terms as everyone else – changed the way in which many reformers thought about poverty. This new way of thinking about poverty, in turn, changed the way in which reformers thought about the poor and social organization more broadly.

★★★

Friendly societies made it possible to imagine decoupling labor from necessary poverty. In particular, they opened up the possibility for the "laboring poor" to be thought of instead as "industrious laborers."[72] At the same time, these societies provided the means with which to effect that transformation. Like Maseres's bill, the bill based on Acland's plan failed to become law. But in this case, it was because critics worried it would be too comprehensive and too radical a change. His idea that membership in a friendly society provided a meaningful way to distinguish between the deserving and undeserving lived on, however, and informed all subsequent poor law reform – including legislation on friendly societies.

The first Friendly Society Act, passed in 1793, acknowledged and rewarded the moral distinction of friendly society membership, thus giving that distinction legal sanction. One of the most important rewards in this respect was freeing friendly society members from the laws of settlement. As we saw earlier in this chapter, the poor laws and settlement laws worked in conjunction, the former attaching responsibility of caring for the poor to the parish, the latter assigned the poor to a particular parish.[73] But as the expense of relief and the number of people

---

[72] For the early history of the material conditions that made it possible to conceptualize industriousness as an attribute of laborers, see Craig Muldrew, *Food, Energy and the Creation of Industriousness: Work and Material Culture in Agrarian England, 1550–1780* (Cambridge: Cambridge University Press, 2011).

[73] The laws of settlement were "an integral corollary of the parish poor law, which would have had great difficulty functioning without it." (Snell, "Settlement, Poor Law and the Rural Historian," 146.)

migrating increased at the end of the eighteenth century, the settlement laws also came under attack for the presumed effect they had on a laborer's ability to "take his labor to the best market." Poor law historians think that Adam Smith exaggerated the prison-like effect the laws had on economic migration in this respect. But the cost of removing paupers back to their home parish could be ruinous to already precarious parish resources. Certificates, which assured the destination parish that the parish of settlement would pay for the relief of the migrant should he or she become chargeable, were thus restricted to people considered industrious enough to prove a good bet.[74]

The Friendly Society Act explicitly stated that friendly society members were necessarily industrious enough to prove a good bet. A member's industry was demonstrated by the fact that he had worked hard enough to save enough money to join a friendly society in the first place. Membership proved his willingness to work, which rendered him deserving, but also proved that he was never likely to become "chargeable." Instead of going to the parish for relief when sick, a friendly society member would go to his club to receive the benefits of membership. As George Rose, the parliamentarian responsible for the first Friendly Society Act, explained, the legislature extended "its care and attention to the industrious" by granting friendly society members an automatic right to a certificate for themselves as well as their families.[75] Jeremy Bentham later described this exemption as a "boon" granted by the legislature "to this privileged part of its subjects in the shape of a reward for virtue . . . "[76] By rewarding the industrious friendly society member, Rose hoped "the Principle, once established, the Measure would soon become general."[77] Friendly society members would become the example for all laborers. And indeed, they did. The path blazed by friendly society members was opened to everyone in the new Settlement Act of 1795.[78]

So optimistic were legislators about the industrious character of friendly society members, in fact, they also increased the number of ways by which a friendly society member could acquire a legal settlement in the 1793 Act. Unlike laborers traveling on an ordinary certificate,

---

[74] Landau, "The Regulation of Immigration, Economic Structures and Definitions of the Poor in Eighteenth-Century England," 558–560; Snell, "Settlement, Poor Law and the Rural Historian."

[75] George Rose, "Observations on the Above Act by the Gentlemen Who Framed the Bill," *Annals of Agriculture and Other Useful Arts* XXI (1794): 17.

[76] Jeremy Bentham, *Pauper Management Improved: Particularly by Means of an Application of the Panopticon Principle of Construction* (London, 1812), 206.

[77] George Rose, *Observations on Banks for Savings* (London, 1816), 29.

[78] 35 Geo. 3. c. 101. (1795)

friendly society members could gain a legal settlement "by hiring and service, or by apprenticeship, with a settled inhabitant of the parish."[79] These avenues of gaining a settlement had been cut off for holders of ordinary certificates in the early eighteenth-century settlement statutes and were not extended to everyone even under the 1795 Settlement Act. Considering the amount of time and money spent determining, disputing, and deposing issues surrounding settlement, and the growing jealousy with which parish officers guarded access to settlement as the eighteenth century wore on, increasing a friendly society member's access to new settlements was high praise indeed.[80] It demonstrates that legislators saw laborers who joined friendly societies in a different moral light than they saw non-members.

While the Friendly Society Act legally equated friendly society membership with industriousness, Frederick Eden reinforced that equivalence with empirical evidence. Eden was first introduced to the theoretical power of friendly societies through his study of John Acland's and Thomas Gilbert's writings in the 1780s. But he discovered the practical importance of these organizations on his own during the course of his investigation into *The State of the Poor* in the mid-1790s. His research was quite vast, encompassing Parochial Returns from every county in England and Wales. The kind of information he sought from parishes was wide-ranging, including the geographic extent and population of parishes, the number of houses that pay the house or window tax, and the number of houses exempted; the occupations of parishioners, whether in agriculture, commerce, or manufactures; the price of provisions and wages of labor; the usual diet and rent of land; the different religious sects and tithes, the number of inns or alehouses; the size of commons, and the number of acres enclosed in the last forty years; and finally, minute queries about how the poor were maintained, including the number and state of friendly societies.[81] He wanted to gather a quantitative sense of the "present state of the Labouring part of the community, as well as the actual Poor."[82] The distinction he made here between the laboring part of the community and the poor presages both his findings

---

[79] Rose, "Observations on the Above Act by the Gentlemen Who Framed the Bill," 16.

[80] Landau, "The Regulation of Immigration, Economic Structures and Definitions of the Poor in Eighteenth-Century England," 567–568. Also see Taylor, *Poverty, Migration, and Settlement in the Industrial Revolution.*

[81] These categories have been drawn from his query form, which he fashioned based on the one John Sinclair used in his *Statistical Account of Scotland.* (Eden, *The State of the Poor,* 1:ii–iv.)

[82] Ibid., 1:i.

and his hope that the laborer need not necessarily be included among the ranks of the poor.

Upon examining the returns, Eden claimed that the difference between those laborers who got by without parish relief and those who relied on it for survival turned on the practice of domestic economy. The distinction was particularly evident when he compared the amount of earnings the northern laborer spent on food, clothing, and fuel with the larger amount spent on those same items by the laborer in the south.[83] He conceded that this disparity was due, in part, to cultural differences, or as he called them, "customary" differences, but he did not see that as an impediment to the lessons southern laborers could learn from their northern counterparts. In contrast to Howlett's findings, Eden concluded, "the miseries of the labouring Poor arose, less from the scantiness of their income ... than from their own improvidence and unthriftiness."[84] And from his point of view, improvidence had been fostered because of the principle behind the poor laws. For Eden, the practice of "allowances in aid of wages" (later known as the controversial "Speenhamland system"), which he found to be widespread in southern England during the 1795 grain scarcity, had merely exaggerated, and therefore brought into relief, the negative effects of what a compulsory system of relief did in general. Receiving part of their wages as "extorted charity" rather than as a just recompense for "their own well exerted industry" was "most prejudicial to their moral interests," he warned.[85] Eden claimed to have encountered enough cases of northern laborers who lived through the scarcity without recourse to poor relief to convince him that "there is more difference, comparatively, in the mode of living from economy than from income; the deficiency in income may possibly be made up by increase of work or wages, but the want of economy is irremediable."[86]

---

[83] Whereas southern laborers "are habituated to the unvarying meal of dry bread and cheese from week's end to week's end," in the north they "regale themselves with a variety of dishes unknown in the south." He goes on to give recipes for Hasty pudding, Crowdie, pease-kail, lobscouse, and the like. The variety of food and the ways in which it was differently prepared depending on what was available struck Eden as an ingenious antidote to the scarcity of any one thing. The economy of the northern laborer extended to the way in which they made their own clothes and even wore clogs rather than shoes, because they "keep the feet remarkably warm and comfortable, and entirely exclude all damp" and were cheaper too. He did not recommend their use in the North of Scotland because "in a country where there is so much walking up and down hill, they would not answer." (Ibid., 1:496, 556, 558.)

[84] His conclusions on this point are summarized in ibid., 1:495, 410–589.

[85] Ibid., 1:583.   [86] Ibid., 1:587.

If the lack of economy exhibited by southern laborers proved for Eden the pauperizing effects of the poor laws, the members of friendly societies he met convinced him that these organizations had the potential to change the face of the laboring classes. Wherever he went in the course of his investigations, Eden thought the friendly society member stood out most distinctly as the example of how a laborer should live – indeed how he should look. He reported observing a stark and uniform difference between the appearance of members and non-members. Laborers who belonged to a friendly society were "in general, comparatively cleanly, orderly, and sober, and consequently happy and good members of society." Whereas those "who are contented to rely on the parish for relief" are

living in filth, and wretchedness, and are often, from the pressure of a casual sickness, or accident, which incapacitates them from working, tempted to the commission of improper acts, (not to say crimes,) against which the sure resource of a Benefit Club would have been the best preservative.[87]

Cleanliness and dirt formed a legible social binary between the friendly society member and the non-member, which for Eden and his contemporaries corresponded directly to moral character.[88]

For Eden, the ability to read the moral character of a laborer through his membership and the extent to which friendly societies had already proliferated was enough evidence to convince him that friendly societies were the antidote to the demoralizing effects of the poor laws. The "industrious laborer" was not only a theoretical possibility, then. For Eden, such a laborer already existed. And if friendly societies were properly facilitated, all laborers could become industrious laborers. Eden was unequivocal when he stated as much in his *Observations on Friendly Societies* (1801),

---

[87] Ibid., 1:615.

[88] Eden's claim that the morality of a laborer was visible on his body became a truism by the first quarter of the nineteenth century. In her popular popularization of the principles and problems of political economy, *Conversations on Political Economy* (1816), Jane Marcet rehearsed the same correspondence between morality and hygiene, though she pushed it further. Members of friendly societies, she instructed Caroline, "are comparatively cleanly, industrious, sober, frugal, respecting themselves, and respected by others . . . ," while non-members "become a prey to dirt and wretchedness; and being dissatisfied with the scantiness of parish relief, they are often driven to the commission of crimes." (Jane Marcet, *Conversations on Political Economy* (London, 1816), 160.) Revd. Richard Vivian made the same point, "You may know a [friendly society member] by his gait. He who demands or knows he may demand twelve shillings a week from the steward of his club in case of disaster, is a different being from the pauper who teases the overseer for parish pay." (Richard Vivian, *A Letter on Friendly Societies and Savings Banks* (London, 1816), 7.)

Friendly societies have now established, on the broad basis of experience, one great and fundamental truth, of infinite national importance; viz. that, with very few exceptions, the people, in general, of all characters, and under all circumstances, with good management, are perfectly competent to their own maintenance.[89]

For without any prompting from Parliament or private benevolence, friendly society members had "rejected" the gratuitous provisions of poor relief "which was to cost them nothing." Instead, "they chose to be indebted for relief ... to their own industry and frugality."[90] The final testimony of the "infinite national importance" of friendly societies was that over the course of his very extensive investigations – even during the grain scarcity – he did not find that "any parish had been burthened with the maintenance of a member of any Friendly Society."[91] Consequently, Eden advocated a turn away from revising the poor laws and toward facilitating the natural inclinations of "the great mass of the people," who, through their membership, proved themselves capable "to legislate for themselves."[92]

Emphasizing the sharp, and purportedly, visible contrasts between members of friendly societies with those who were willing to accept poor relief, Eden's work reinforced the social distinctions introduced in Acland's friendly society scheme and which were instantiated in the 1793 Friendly Society Act. The attributes displayed by members of friendly societies – industriousness, frugality, and cleanliness – were those appropriate to laborers in a commercial society. Those attributes displayed by people "content to rely on parish relief" – a lack of thrift, improvidence, and slothfulness – were more than inappropriate – they were the marks of those on the criminal margins. If friendly societies "promote[d] a higher spirit of independence and better habits of industry and frugality than are usually found among the labouring classes," poor relief took away a person's ability to sustain himself and so made him more susceptible to immoral, which by the early nineteenth century had shaded into criminal, acts.[93] Not surprisingly, the "criminal" acquired the dimensions of a "social archetype" as a concomitant to the process wherein the "industrious labourer" acquired the same.[94] And while

---

[89] Eden, *Observations on Friendly Societies for the Maintenance of the Industrious Classes during Sickness, Infirmity, Old Age and Other Exigencies*, 10.

[90] Eden, *The State of the Poor*, 1:xxiv.   [91] Ibid., 1:xxiv, xxv.   [92] Ibid., 1:615.

[93] Eden, *Observations on Friendly Societies for the Maintenance of the Industrious Classes during Sickness, Infirmity, Old Age and Other Exigencies*, 10–11.

[94] V. A. C. Gatrell, "Crime, Authority, and the Policeman State," In *The Cambridge Social History of Britain 1750–1950*, F. M. L. Thompson, ed., vol. 3 (Cambridge: Cambridge University Press, 1990), 248.

people like Patrick Colquhoun and Jeremy Bentham zealously took to the task of policing the line where the indigent became the criminal, Eden and other friendly society promoters focused on encouraging the indigent to become the "industrious."[95]

There is no doubt that Eden exaggerated these distinctions. But whether or not Eden's findings were accurate is not the point here. His interpretation of what friendly societies meant for poverty, and for the future of British labor, was compelling in those harrowing years because it gave reformers hope for a stable, prosperous world without what they saw as the potentially degrading effects of the poor laws. His discovery of the great good that friendly societies were doing – even through times of extreme economic hardship – obviated for him the need to pursue any further the practical question of whether or not the poor – even the rural poor – could afford to join friendly societies.[96] In his mind, some quite clearly did afford membership, so under the proper conditions, the rest could too. His own calculations regarding existing membership was the most compelling evidence from his perspective. He discovered that friendly society membership was already far more extensive than anyone had imagined, with an estimated 7,200 societies, comprising 648,000 members, which provided mutual aid to nearly a quarter of the population of England and Wales.[97]

By the 1810s, the belief that friendly society membership was in the reach of all able-bodied laborers had become commonplace, "It is notorious that the economical class of laborers now annually deposit in friendly societies," one observer noted, " ... and that the less frugal have the power of doing the same, did they possess the inclination."[98] Even Thomas

---

[95] See Patrick Colquhoun, *A Treatise on the Police of the Metropolis; Containing a Detail of the Various Crimes and Misdemeanors by Which Public and Private Property...*, 6th ed. (London, 1800); Bentham, *Pauper Management Improved: Particularly by Means of an Application of the Panopticon Principle of Construction.*

[96] As John Sinclair put it in 1813, " ... there is no doubt, that [the 'peasantry'] could easily afford small weekly payments, that would be sufficient to secure them a comfortable and independent subsistence when advanced in life. Nothing therefore is wanted, to complete the comfortable situation of this most deserving class of the community, but the institution of Benefit Societies ... " (John Sinclair, *An Account of the Systems of Husbandry Adopted in the More Improved Districts of Scotland...*, 2nd ed., vol. II (Edinburgh, 1813), 271.)

[97] Eden made this estimate based on the number of societies registered under the 1793 Friendly Society Act and the average number of members in those societies. He then raised that number by a third based on responses he received from queries to town clerks about the number of unregistered friendly societies. (Eden, *Observations on Friendly Societies for the Maintenance of the Industrious Classes during Sickness, Infirmity, Old Age and Other Exigencies*, 6–8.)

[98] William Hanning, *A Letter to the Members of the Select Committees of the Two Houses of Parliament, Appointed to Examine and Report on the Poor Laws* (Taunton, 1818), 34.

Malthus, the man who put the dismal in the "dismal science" of political economy, came to see the proliferation of friendly societies as evidence of "the growth of the desire to become independent of parish assistance … "[99] Even more optimistically, James Scarlett, MP for Peterborough, argued that the "numerous" friendly societies proved that there was no "general disposition in the laboring classes to rely for subsistence on the poor rates."[100] What was left for reformers to do was to create the proper conditions for the further proliferation of friendly societies.

After Eden's intervention, interest in friendly societies shifted from speculating about them and their virtues to experimenting with various ways of making them a universal reality. Eden provided the raw materials for patronizing friendly societies by including in his three volume *State of the Poor* the rules and regulations of clubs from all over the country "with a view of enabling those, whose practical experience in matters of this nature authorize them to legislate for Friendly Societies, to construct such approved regulations, as might, … be adopted by almost every Society."[101]

Many philanthropically inclined and reform-minded people followed Eden's advice, especially evangelicals. At the end of 1796, Thomas Barnard, the manufacturer turned philanthropist who co-founded the moderate-evangelical Society for the Bettering of the Condition of the Poor (SBCP), for example, gave the promotion of friendly societies top billing in his first annual report.[102] The goal of the Society was to investigate means for improving the condition of the poor both materially and morally.[103] From Bernard's point of view, this was precisely what friendly societies did. "When legally and properly established," he explained, friendly societies "are sure and unvaried in promoting industry, economy, philanthropy, and every virtue, among the poor."[104] The Irish branch of the Society, founded in Cork in 1800, followed suit, naming the encouragement of friendly societies its first priority. The founders reasoned, "Of all the schemes that have been devised for the

---

[99] Thomas Malthus, *An Essay on the Principle of Population*, 5th ed., vol. 3 (London, 1817), 279.

[100] "House of Commons," *The Derby Mercury*, June 27, 1821.

[101] Eden, *The State of the Poor*, 1:615–616.

[102] He cites Eden's work in the preface to the first set of Reports. Thomas Barnard, *The Reports of the Society: Society for Bettering the Condition and Increasing the Comforts of the Poor*, vol. I, 1797, viii. The other founders were William Wilberforce and Bishop Barrington. For more on their evangelical attitudes, see Hilton, *Age of Atonement: The Influence of Evangelicalism on Social and Economic Thought, 1785–1865*, 98–100.

[103] Barnard, *The Reports of the Society: Society for Bettering the Condition and Increasing the Comforts of the Poor, 1797*, 1:iv.

[104] Thomas Barnard, *The Reports of the Society: Society for Bettering the Condition and Increasing the Comforts of the Poor*, vol. II, 1799, 21.

relief of the poor, and for combining with that relief, the general improvement of their morals and condition, none seem to hold out fairer prospects of advantage, than the institution of Friendly Societies."[105]

Individual philanthropists responded to the call for action as well, sometimes advertising their methods in the reports of the SBCP but just as often publishing their friendly society models on their own. The details and rationale behind each of these private ventures were quite varied and the virtues they sought to inculcate ranged from independence, frugality, and industriousness, to "a sense of social duties" and "operating as a security against ... habits of unreasonable expense ... "[106] One of the SBCP's favorite success stories, for example, was the Castle Eden Friendly Society, whose rules it printed verbatim as a guide for those who wanted to form friendly societies "on prudent and equitable terms." The SBCP reports brought special attention to the fact that when deciding the proportion between subscriptions and benefits, attention should be given "to the circumstances and local situation of the subscribers," charging fees according to the ability to pay.[107] They even appended updated tables from Richard Price to help promoters determine how much to charge members. Large employers in manufacturing, industry, agriculture, and even large estates also began subsidizing or paying in full the membership dues of their employees.[108] Members of the local gentry also founded and patronized friendly societies.[109] And the

---

[105] *The First Number of the Reports: Reports of the Society for Promoting the Comforts of the Poor* (Cork, 1800), Preliminary Address, appendix 1.

[106] William Marshall, *The Rural Economy of the West of England* (Dublin, 1797), 21. The second quote comes from Andrew Whyte, *General View of the Agriculture of the County of Dumbarton with Observations on the Means of Its Improvement* (Glasgow, 1811), 291.

[107] *Reports of the Society: Society for Promoting the Comforts of the Poor* (Dublin, 1800), appendix, No. III, 52.

[108] See Edward Wakefield, *An Account of Ireland, Statistical and Political*, vol. II (London, 1812), 812. For instances of masters paying for servants, see Vivian, *A Letter on Friendly Societies and Savings Banks*, 22. For farmers paying for their "loyal labourers," see William Otter, *A Sermon upon the Influence of the Clergy in Improving the Condition of the Poor ...* (Shrewsbury, 1818), n. 48. For an example of an early industrialist instituting a friendly society, see Samuel Smiles on the Soho Friendly Society at Matthew Boulton and James Watt's factory. (Samuel Smiles, *Lives of Boulton and Watt: Principally from the Original Soho Mss. Comprising Also a History of the Invention and Introduction of the Steam Engine* (London: John Murray, 1865), 480–482. And also, Eric Roll, *An Early Experiment in Industrial Organisation: Being a History of the Firm of Boulton & Watt, 1775–1805* (London: Cass, 1968), 225–236.)

[109] William Bleamire, a philanthropic member of the gentry in Hampstead, started a friendly society in 1802, superintended and subsidized by the "principle inhabitants" of the town, the goal of which was to "place charity on the basis of industry." (*Plan of the Parochial Benefit Society, Established at Hampstead, on Tuesday the Ninth Day of February 1802, under the Patronage and Protection of the Principal Inhabitants; for the Benefit of the Sober and Industrious of All Descriptions* (London, 1802), 15.)

list goes on.[110] The belief common to all these various versions was that friendly societies would keep members safe from the negative effects of poor relief and also create new ties connecting the upper and lower classes.

The agriculturalist, mine owner, and parliamentarian, John Christian Curwen was responsible for a rather impressive success story in this respect – which also became one of the most important impetuses to subsequent poor law reform. He started six friendly societies for the colliers who worked in his mines in Workington, a mining town on the coast of Cumberland, which included a female friendly society. Curwen contributed three tenths of the members' total contributions and made up deficiencies whenever there were any. Between 1796–1816, he contributed £30,000 for the relief of the sick, injured, and aged.[111] In the spring of 1816, Curwen gave a speech in Parliament calling for a select committee to investigate the state of the poor laws and specifically the possibility of implementing a national benefit society on the basis of his experience in Workington so as to "to relieve the poor, independently of the existing statutes."[112] Curwen felt that not only his own successes but also those of other employers in almost every county in Great Britain – all during a time of war – justified such a measure.[113] He was convinced that the new system of mutuality in the National Benefit Society would prevent poverty and produce a "union ... between the higher and lower orders."[114]

The committee he moved for became the House of Commons Select Committee on the Poor Laws. It convened in 1817 and produced a bill encompassing the spirit of Curwen's plan if not all of the particulars. The bill called for parish friendly societies that would initially be funded by

---

[110] Eighteenth-century employer-subsidized sick funds were versions of seventeenth century sick funds in mines and ironworks. For more on these earlier examples, see Waddell, *God, Duty and Community in English Economic Life, 1660–1720*, 117. For other examples see, David Levine and Keith Wrightson, *The Making of an Industrial Society: Whickham, 1560–1765* (Oxford: Clarendon Press, 1991), 365–366.

[111] J. C. Curwen, *Sketch of a Plan ... for Bettering the Condition of the Labouring Classes of the Community, and for Equalizing and Reducing the Amount of The ...* (London, 1817). For the first iteration of the plan, see J. C. Curwen, *Hints on the Economy of Feeding Stock and Bettering the Condition of the Poor* (London, 1808).

[112] "ART. VI. An Essay on the Nature and Advantages of Parish Banks for the Savings of the Industrious, &c. with Remarks on the Propriety of Uniting These Institutions with Friendly Societies; Together with an Appendix, Containing the Rules of the Dumfries Parish Bank, &c. &c," *Quarterly Review* 16, no. 31 (October 1816): 96.

[113] Curwen, *Sketch of a Plan ... for Bettering the Condition of the Labouring Classes of the Community, and for Equalizing and Reducing the Amount of The ...*, 23.

[114] Curwen from the Minutes of Evidence taken before a House of Commons Select Committee on the Poor Laws quoted in "Post Script," *The Ipswich Journal*, April 19, 1817.

the poor rates, supplementing the contributions of the poorest members of the parish (but not those who could afford to pay their own dues), gradually reducing that amount until all the poor were able to fund their own membership.[115] The Committee members explained that "it is chiefly by the gradual restoration of a feeling of reliance upon their own industry, rather than upon the parochial assessments, that the transition to a more wholesome system can be effected."[116] Yet, the poor laws were seen as so demoralizing to the able-bodied by the mid-1810s, as we will see more specifically in the next chapter, that connecting a friendly society plan to the existing system of relief doomed the bill.[117] Although it was read in different forms several times before Parliament between 1817 and 1819, it ultimately failed on the basis that it might serve to prop up the very system reformers were trying to destroy.[118] The growing popularity of Malthus's criticism of compulsory alternatives, including compulsory friendly societies, ensured that if friendly societies were the solution,[119] they would have to form a distinct and separate system from the poor laws "or Poor-law dependence will only change its name, and but slightly abate of its malignant influence."[120] Consequently, after 1819, even though friendly societies continued to be the alternative social policy of choice for poor law reformers, they were legislated for

[115] *Bill for Further Protection and Encouragement of Friendly Societies, and for Authorizing Establishment of Parochial Benefit Societies,* P.P., 1819 (223) i.

[116] *Report from the Select Committee on the Poor Laws; with the Minutes of Evidence Taken before the Committee,* P.P., 1817 (462) vi, 24.

[117] *Report from the Select Committee on the Poor Laws,* 1817, 24.

[118] As John Davison, the influential poor law thinker, put it in his letter to Sturges-Bourne, "A mixed contribution from rich and poor together, would be liable, as I have endeavored to shew, to the greatest objection of all, if it is to create a fund for general purposes, open to the same forms of demand as now subsist." (John Davison, *Considerations on the Poor Laws* (Oxford, 1817), 22.) Explaining why friendly societies should be kept distinct from the parish funds, one witness before the Committee said, "The goodness of every plan may be tested by this unamalgamating mixture of independence and beggary." (Richard Vivian, *Thoughts on the Causes and Cures of Excessive Poor Rates . . .* (London, 1817), 26.)

[119] Because most early friendly society schemes had included subsidies for large families and because Malthus's belief that preventing improvident marriages was more important than paying for the results of them, he dropped his support of friendly societies from editions of his *Essay* after 1803. But while Malthus was not the most enthusiastic supporter of friendly societies, he was only opposed to compulsory friendly societies. Compulsory schemes like Courtenay's would put a "direct tax on labor," and would be "merely a different mode of collecting parish rates." (Thomas Malthus, *An Essay on the Principle of Population,* 2nd ed. (London, 1803), 230–33.)

[120] John Farey, *General View of the Agriculture of Derbyshire with Observations on the Means of Its Improvement. . .,* vol. 3 (London, 1811), 575.

separately.[121] If friendly societies were going to make the poor laws obsolete for able-bodied poverty, they could not be attached to them in any way. But they also had to be more secure than they seemed to be when left to the voluntary devices of laborers. To this end, the government appointed two select committees, one in 1825 and one in 1827, to investigate the state of friendly societies and to figure out how to make them more financially sound.

As the importance of friendly societies to social policy grew in the late 1810s and throughout the 1820s, criticism of the laborer's friendly society increased apace. The most important critiques centered on the friendly society's potential for supporting strikes, fostering political radicalism, the alcohol consumed at their meetings, and the actuarial mismatch between the contributions they asked for and the benefits they seemed to promise. These critiques, and the temporary preference given to a new idea – savings banks – is, however, its own story and will be treated as such in Chapter 3. The policy goal of using friendly societies as the key means through which the poor laws would be gradually abolished remained consistent throughout the period.[122] The preamble to the 1819 Bill for the further Protection and Encouragement of Friendly Societies, which was drawn directly from the language used in the 1817 Select Committee on the Poor Laws, makes this clear,

... it is desirable, with a view to the reduction of the assessments made for the relief of the Poor, as to the gradual introduction of a better feeling among the people, that special encouragement and facility should be afforded to meritorious and industrious persons, for rescuing themselves from the necessity of a resort to parochial relief...[123]

Thus, the rationale that gave friendly societies a significant role in the making of social policy in this period, and in relation to the New Poor

---

[121] Between 1800 and 1819, several Friendly Society Acts were passed in an effort to encourage friendly societies to adopt a more financially sound foundation without also undermining the voluntary nature of their membership. In addition to their exemption from settlement and the legal protection of their funds, the printed documents of friendly societies were exempted from the Stamp Act. The most important new legal benefit was the protection offered to the trustees of friendly societies so that if one of them went bankrupt, the friendly society funds would not be lost. Only after the friendly society funds had been repaired could the rest of the trustee's creditors have their share.

[122] See Thomas Peregrine Courtenay, *Copy of a Letter to the Rt. Hon. William Sturges Bourne, Chairman of the Select Committee of the House of Commons Appointed for the Consideration ...* (London, 1817), 19.

[123] *Bill for further Protection and Encouragement of Friendly Societies, and for authorizing Establishment of Parochial Benefit Societies*, 1819, 1. The 1817 Poor Law Report made this claim with the exact same language. See *Report from the Select Committee on the Poor Laws*, 1817, 11.

Law in particular, was already in place by the early 1820s. In these years when poverty threatened the entire basis of their society, reformers believed friendly societies could produce a "transition, from the present system of relief to one founded upon better principles ... "[124] But it was to be gradual and humane. As the Liberal MP for Shrewsbury Robert Slaney explained in 1828, "the goal was to increase the wages of labour, bring into wider operation friendly societies and provident institutions, and not harshly, but prospectively and gradually to do away with the claim of able-bodied labourers to parochial relief."[125] The assertion that late eighteenth and early nineteenth-century poor law reformers wanted to subject the poor to the unmitigated forces of the market does not adequately capture the new system reformers were trying to create. In the first place, every friendly society proposal contained some element of paternalism. What contemporary reformers envisioned was a new system of reciprocity more appropriate to their changing society. Friendly societies implied more than a new system of poor relief. They made it possible to conceive of a new basis for social trust. Indeed, because of their preventative potential, friendly societies made it possible to imagine a society whose moral order did not depend on one's relationship to poverty at all. Friendly societies could prevent the assured poverty of the laborer before it happened and would provide mutual aid to those incapable of helping themselves. In this new society, the "laboring poor" had the potential to become "industrious laborers" and all classes would be united by their role in the mutual prevention of poverty.[126]

★★★

Because friendly societies were not stipulated in the New Poor Law, historians have hitherto assumed that the Commissioners dismissed them as nothing more than "frills."[127] As we have seen, friendly societies were so important that legislators did not want to taint them by associating them either financially or in principle with the poor laws. These organizations and the ways in which they had been legally regulated since

---

[124] *Report from the Select Committee on the Poor Laws*, 1817, 26.

[125] "House of Commons," *The Bury and Norwich Post*, April 23, 1828.

[126] As Curwen noted in his National Benefit Society Plan, "Crimes resulting from poverty would be prevented, and the police of the country powerfully assisted in the detection of offenders, not only by the registry of the name and abode of every working individual, but of the habits and general character of each for industry or idleness." (Curwen, *Sketch of a Plan ... for Bettering the Condition of the Labouring Classes of the Community, and for Equalizing and Reducing the Amount of The ...*, 11.)

[127] J. D. Marshall, "The Nottinghamshire Reformers and Their Contribution to the New Poor Law," *The Economic History Review* 13, no. 3 (1961): 393–396.

the 1793 Friendly Society Act nevertheless had a direct impact on the way the New Poor Law itself was written. The two most puzzling aspects of the machinery of the new law for historians, and the most difficult to understand in terms of the debates that preceded it, are the seemingly unprecedented centralization of relief administration and the harsh principle of "less eligibility." Here again, friendly societies gave the Commission the precedents and the rationales they needed to justify such a radical shift in policy.

The precedent for centralized control of poor relief was actually set in the early nineteenth century Friendly Society Acts. The provisions of these laws had been oriented toward encouraging voluntary participation in friendly societies. Yet, in order to facilitate this process and to ensure that those voluntary societies were financially sound, the offices of government concerned with these problems grew significantly over the first quarter of the nineteenth century. Unlike poor law administration where local vested interests entrenched over many years made any changes in the regulation of relief difficult to make, the regulation of friendly societies was of very recent origin and was encumbered only by the members' resistance. While that resistance did in several notable cases succeed in reducing local interference in friendly society matters, the national organ, concerned to make friendly societies more financially sound, grew in proportion as local measures failed.[128] When it became clear that local persons were not "skilled in calculation" to the extent necessary to certify sickness and mortality tables called for in the 1819 Act, for example, the job was given first to the Accountant to the Commissioners for the Reduction of the National Debt and then to the Offices in charge of registering savings banks in England, Scotland, and Ireland.[129] These offices were ultimately consolidated through the 1834 Friendly Society

---

[128] The protests from the old friendly societies – specifically, against "the misguided philanthropy of others, in interfering in the pecuniary concerns of the noblest Institutions that ever graced civilized Society" – eventually made itself heard. (G. R. Cotter, *An Address to the Members of Benefit Societies, throughout the Kingdom; with an Abstract of Mr. Courtenay's Bill and Comments on the Obnoxious Clauses Therein Contained* ... (London, 1828), 21.) Several old, established societies were rumored to have divided their funds and dissolved their societies preemptively rather than submit to such outside interference. And the rumor that had been afoot since the days of Eden's investigations, indeed since the first Friendly Society Act was passed in 1793, that the government was going to confiscate the money of friendly societies, was said to be responsible for the dissolution of still others. Faced with such a powerful and negative response, Thomas Courtenay, the bill's author, was forced to rewrite his bill. The bill that eventually passed in 1829 reduced outside interference, as we will see in Chapter 3.

[129] The anxiety that reformers expressed about the ability to calculate the liabilities of sickness and death among friendly society members will be addressed more fully in Chapter 5.

Act into one central Registrar for Friendly Societies for Great Britain, with John Tidd Pratt, the former registrar for England, at the helm. The centralization of this office paved the way for the centralization of the administration of the poor laws.

Taking the administration of the poor laws out of the hands of purportedly incompetent parish officers and placing it in the hands of local magistrates or a centralized commission of professional men had been the desire of many poor law reformers for some time.[130] The centralization of friendly society regulation under the 1829 Friendly Society Act and the further consolidation under the 1834 Friendly Society Act was the precedent cited to support a similar reorganization of poor law administration. As the Commissioners explained,

> The course of proceeding which we recommend for adoption, is in principle that which the legislature adopted for the management of the savings' banks, the friendly societies, and the annuity societies throughout the country. Having prescribed the outline and general principles on which those institutions should be conducted, a special agency (which, in this instance, was constituted by one barrister only) was appointed to see that their rules and detailed regulations conformed to the intention of the law. This agency, we believe, has accomplished the object effectually.[131]

In addition to the precedent set by the centralization of friendly society regulation, the Commissioners also learned during the course of their investigation that friendly society members themselves preferred national to local regulation of friendly societies. The Commissioners claimed that friendly society members objected to local interference, but not to the reasoned guidance of the national government "made on extended information derived from all similar institutions throughout the kingdom."[132] Dr. James Mitchell, who was a key figure in the successful resistance to the increased local interference proposed in the 1829 Friendly Society Act, agreed. He affirmed the preference the Commissioners attributed to regular members,

> In order to prevent the capricious control of the various local authorities, ... the working men thought it would be very beneficial to get one person appointed to revise the rules of all the societies throughout the country, in order that their administration might be rendered uniform, and that the detailed regulations might be the result of more extended information. The chief object of the

---

[130] For an especially good example of this critique, see Richard Burn, *The History of the Poor Laws* (London, 1764), 284–286.

[131] *Report from His Majesty's Commissioners for Inquiry into the Administration and Practical Operation of the Poor Laws with Evidence and Appendices*, PP, 1834 (44) xxvii, 167.

[132] Ibid.

labouring men was to prevent capricious local interference, which might often be the interference of employers.[133]

In this way, the precedent set by friendly society law, and the preferences evidently stated by friendly society members themselves, helped the Commissioners to justify in turn the centralization of poor law administration.

The other major change that came out of the 1834 Poor Law Report and on which friendly societies had an important bearing was the principle of "less eligibility." Very simply, "less eligibility" was the idea that poor relief should be made less generous than what the lowest paid laborer could earn by working in the open market. In conjunction with the shift to indoor relief, the purpose of this principle was to make poor relief an extremely unattractive prospect. But, as we saw with Townsend's and many other friendly society schemes, ungenerous poor relief was never meant to affect this separation on its own. The only thing a "less eligible," system of poor relief could do was to repel all but the most destitute from asking for relief. The necessary and countervailing corollary of meager relief was the private and public promotion of friendly societies.

This carrot-stick or push-pull relationship was a central mechanism in the friendly societies schemes proposed throughout the 1780s and 1790s.[134] We began with Townsend's extreme version of it: in order "to drive them into these societies," he railed, "no man should be entitled to relief from the parochial fund who did not belong to one of these."[135] Yet, even David Davies, the one reformer singled out by posterity for his consistent humanitarian approach to the poor, thought that for the young and single or for families with only a few small children, wages were sufficient but often carelessly husbanded; therefore, "a line of separation" should be drawn "between such as are deserving and undeserving

---

[133] Ibid., 164.

[134] Richard Pew, who thought his friendly society would make "the lower orders of the community" full members of society because "instead of being a burthen, [they] would become, in every sense of the word beneficial to the nation" also thought that "the indolent man, not contributing his quota, would be equally obnoxious to the squire and to the peasant; and as from his deficiency he would be immediately detected, so his idleness should inevitably meet its proper antidotes, confinement and labour." (Richard Pew, "Twenty Minutes Observations on a Better Mode of Providing for the Poor," In *Letters and Papers on Agriculture, Planting, &c. Selected from the Correspondence of the Bath and West of England Society*, (Bath, 1792), 228, 235.)

[135] Joseph Townsend, *A Dissertation on the Poor Laws* (Republished, London: Printed for Ridgways, 1817), 90.

of parochial assistance."[136] Davies proposed that before their family encumbrances became too great, day-laborers should be encouraged to save and join friendly societies – and that those who refused should be refused parish relief.[137] Thomas Courtenay, a leading member of the 1817 Select Committee appointed for the Consideration of the Poor Laws, repeated what was by then a commonplace when he explained to Committee Chairman William Sturges-Bourne in 1817 that it is through friendly society membership, "rather than by any certificates or badges, that I would make and note the distinction between the innocent and the criminal poor" recommending "harsher treatment...for those who neglect the opportunity of belonging to a Society ... "[138] At the same time, he went on, "[b]ut I would *not* consider or treat as Paupers in this sense, either those who labour under permanent natural incapacities, or those who have contributed a fair portion of their earnings to a Friendly [Society]."[139]

The 1834 Commissioners found that this theoretical push-pull relationship also had what appeared to be empirical grounding. Among the witnesses called to testify, more than a few gave examples demonstrating its effect. For example, Mr. Gordon, a cooper and ship owner with forty to fifty men in his employ, a resident for thirty years, and parish officer for All Saints, Poplar, testified before the Commission that "where stricter management of the able-bodied paupers has been established," the effect had been "very beneficial" to the laborers "in inducing them to rely more on their own resources than they did formerly." He explained what he meant by beneficial by adding, "they contribute more regularly and largely to savings' banks and benefit societies ... "[140] Another witness, Launcelot Snowden, a member of a comparatively generous parish, affirmed this sentiment by making the counterpoint, saying that liberal parish relief made men "very careless of work and of their money ever afterwards. It has also acted very mischievously on the benefit societies,

---

[136] David Davies, *The Case of Labourers in Husbandry Stated and Considered, in Three Parts ... A View of Their Distressed Conditions ... The Principal Causes Of ...* (Bath: 1795), 130.

[137] Ibid., 130.

[138] Courtenay, *Copy of a Letter to the Rt. Hon. William Sturges Bourne, Chairman of the Select Committee of the House of Commons Appointed for the Consideration ...*, 34. When asked what the effect would be if friendly societies became general, one parish officer interviewed before the 1817 Committee answered, "there would be no occasion for this Committee." (*Report from the Select Committee on the Poor Laws*, 1817, 92.)

[139] Courtenay, *Copy of a Letter to the Rt. Hon. William Sturges Bourne, Chairman of the Select Committee of the House of Commons Appointed for the Consideration ...*, 20.

[140] *Report from His Majesty's Commissioners for Inquiry into the Administration and Practical Operation of the Poor Laws*, 1834, 133.

as these men would never contribute to them." He was convinced that indiscriminate parish relief had caused the local friendly society of which he had been a member to fail. "But for the parish, [it] would have stood firm."[141] Such evidence confirmed for the Commissioners what they deeply desired to be true: Harsh poor relief increased friendly societies; generous poor relief undermined them.

The Commissioners also discovered, to their great delight, that members of friendly societies practiced less eligibility on themselves, further verifying its validity as a principle for general social policy.

On this point, as on many others, the independent labourers may be our best teachers. We have seen, that in the administration of the funds of their friendly societies, they have long acted on the principle of rendering the condition of a person receiving their relief less eligible than that of an independent labourer.[142]

Tidd Pratt confirmed the generality of this practice in his capacity as Friendly Society Registrar. In answer to the question "is the condition of a [friendly society] member receiving relief, or living without work, ever allowed to be as eligible on the whole, as the condition of a member living by his work," he replied,

In most cases the allowances made by the societies are so adjusted as to make it the interest of every member not to receive relief from the society so long as he can earn his usual wages. The average allowance which they make is about one-third of what a member can earn.[143]

But it was Revd. John Becher, one of the so-called Nottinghamshire Reformers, a group that also included George Nicholls who was a leading member of the Commission, who provided the most compelling evidence on the importance of combining the repellent aspect of workhouses with the attractive draw of friendly societies. If Townsend had the first word on making a deterrent system of relief, the Commissioners gave Becher something like the last word. Becher had been intimately involved in poor law matters privately since the late 1790s and publicly since 1816 in his capacity as long-time Chairman of the Quarter Sessions of the Newark Division of the County of Nottingham. Becher is best known to poor law historians for the model deterrent workhouse he designed in Southwell and for the influence it had on the 1834 report.[144] He explained to the Commission that when he first came

---

[141] *Report from His Majesty's Commissioners for Inquiry into the Administration and Practical Operation of the Poor Laws*, 1834, 189.
[142] Ibid., 153.   [143] Ibid., 130.
[144] See Marshall, "The Nottinghamshire Reformers and Their Contribution to the New Poor Law"; Brundage, *The English Poor Laws, 1700–1930*.

into his position as magistrate, poor relief was administered liberally; and yet rates kept rising. The parish officers had to take several special subscriptions to supplement the rates because of the rising demand for relief. So, in 1806, he built a workhouse where relief was made "less eligible," indeed, where the living conditions bordered on inhumane. Becher justified these conditions by explaining that the benefits of the workhouse arose "not from keeping the poor in the house, but from keeping them out of it."[145] He did not trust the market or hunger to do the work of keeping them out. Instead, he wanted to draw them out by the attraction to his Friendly Institution at Southwell, which combined friendly society, saving bank, and annuity scheme into one organization. (I examine Becher's role in creating what contemporaries called the New Friendly Society in the next chapter.) Historians give Becher a great deal of credit for influencing the Commission specifically on the point of less eligibility, while failing to mention the Commission's keen interest in the alternative relief system he created in the New Friendly Society.

Charles Dickens was certainly right when he said that each Commissioner sifted "for the odds and ends he wanted, and...throwing the dust about into the eyes of other people who wanted other odds and ends."[146] My claim is not that the arguments that the Commissioners made based on the evidence that they carefully cherry-picked were correct. Rather, in the very act of picking the particular "odds and ends" they did, the Poor Law Commissioners demonstrated that friendly societies were no mere frills. They were a critical resource, both conceptually and practically, for making social policy in this period, and for producing a new basis for social trust.

Social policy is not social reality, however. The harsh New Poor Law in conjunction with the promise of friendly societies did not make poverty or poor relief obsolete. Although poor relief continued to be given out of doors for some time after the law went into effect, by the 1840s, workhouses proliferated and made poverty even more painful for those forced to enter them.[147] But, friendly societies proliferated, too. There was a significant increase in the number of friendly societies founded in the wake of the law.[148] And in 1874, the Friendly Societies Commission estimated that friendly societies had saved ratepayers 2 million pounds

---

[145] *Reports from the Select Committee of the House of Lords Appointed to Consider of the Poor Laws; with the Minutes of Evidence Taken before the Committee, and an Appendix and Index,* 1831, 219.

[146] Charles Dickens, *Hard Times* quoted in Lees, *The Solidarities of Strangers,* 122.

[147] Derek Fraser, *The Evolution of the British Welfare State: A History of Social Policy since the Industrial Revolution,* 4th ed., (Basingstoke: Palgrave Macmillan, 2009), 63–64.

[148] Gosden, *The Friendly Societies in England, 1815–1875,* 207–210.

annually.[149] These facts continued to provide legislators with hope that a new system of reciprocity might gradually emerge. But the importance of friendly societies as increasingly critical to the social welfare of hundreds of thousands of laborers raised the stakes for their long-term stability. The next chapter will look more closely at how friendly societies fared during two of the most acute years of social and economic crisis in the early nineteenth century.

---

[149] *Fourth Report of the Commissioners Appointed to Inquire into Friendly and Benefit Building Societies*, 1874, xvii.

3   The Battle between Savings Banks and Friendly Societies

A savings bank not only "connects, by a new link, the different orders of society. It tends to cement those ties between the government and the people, which are equally essential to the prosperity of both, but which, in these ominous times, so many attempts have been made to weaken."[1]   Hertfordshire Saving Bank Report, 1818

The [savings bank] is selfish; the [friendly society] is generous – the one is solitary the other is public – the one fits a man for a cell; the other for a nation – the one sets a man to dig a pond in his own garden; the other prompts him to form a canal for the common benefit of mankind.[2]   J. W. Cunningham, 1817

Whereas every penny in a savings bank is directed towards the social enjoyments of the domestic circle ... [that of] the friendly society all tend towards the alehouse.[3]   John Weyland, 1816

The selfish principles, which actuate the depositors in a savings bank, can never stand in competition with the social benevolence of a [friendly] society, united for the purposes of mutual support, cemented by the principles of reciprocal attachment, and drawn together by the bonds of brotherly love.[4]   John T. Becher, 1828

If friendly societies were an important means through which Britons grappled with the problem of poverty over the entire period from 1780s–1830s, there were two years between 1815 and 1817, when they went out of favor. Indeed, in these years "all the rank and fortune of the country [formed] into committees, for the purpose of bringing forward

---

[1] Hertfordshire Saving Bank Report quoted in Francis Burdett Sir, ed., *Annals of Banks for Savings* (London, 1818), 38.
[2] J. W. Cunningham, *A Few Observations on Friendly Societies, and Their Influence on Public Morals* (London, 1817), 6.
[3] John Weyland, *The Principles of Population and Production* (London, 1816), 380.
[4] John T. Becher, *The Antipauper System: Exemplifying the Positive and Practical Good, Realized by the Relievers and the Relieved, under the Frugal, Beneficial, ...* (London: 1828), 31.

savings banks and throwing benefit societies into the background."[5] More than simply adding savings banks to the mix of proposals for alleviating poverty, however, patrons wanted to "erect them on the ruins of Friendly Societies."[6] In addition to the "rank and fortune," moreover, the most important social thinkers of the day made this about-face in favor of savings banks. The Provident Institution for Savings (1816) in London, for example, attracted the patronage of the Duke of Somerset and twenty peers. Its managing board was also a who's who of early nineteenth century politicians and social reformers – including Malthus, Ricardo, Wilberforce, Rose, Colquhoun, Bernard, Hume, and Vansittart.[7] These influential people committed impressive financial resources and devoted significant time to these banks. The subscription collected at the meeting proposing to create the Devon and Exeter Savings Bank, for example, totaled £468.[8] And that was just for startup costs. Beyond that, patrons funded the management and subsidized above-market rates of return.[9] These kinds of financial layouts were taking place all over Britain, in towns and the countryside, as well as in the colonies.[10] By 1818, there were a total of 256 savings banks in England alone, and 465 in the British Isles.[11] To be sure, the experiment with using savings banks as a solution to poverty was short-lived. The most enthusiastic proponents quickly realized that these banks were utterly incapable of

---

[5] Vivian, *A Letter on Friendly Societies and Savings Banks*, 8.

[6] Cunningham, *A Few Observations on Friendly Societies, and Their Influence on Public Morals*, 12.

[7] For an account of this bank, see Joseph Hume, *An Account of the Provident Institution for Savings, Established in the Western Part of the Metropolis; with Observations upon Different* (London, 1816).

[8] Oliver Horne, *A History of Savings Banks* (London: Oxford University Press, 1947), 66.

[9] After the Savings Bank Act was passed in 1817, the state took over paying these subsidies. Joseph Hume reported to Parliament that the "uneconomical" rate granted to savings banks cost the state £40,000 to £50,000 annually, which savings banks historian Oliver Horne found was actually "an understatement, for the excess of interest paid to trustees [of savings banks] between 1818 and 1828 over that received from investments was £744,363 or over £67,000 a year." (Ibid., 100.)

[10] For a map of the geographic distribution of savings banks, see Ibid., foldout between 90 and 91. The East India Company introduced a savings bank for its army in Calcutta in 1820. For more on the way the EIC used savings banks to promote discipline among its soldiers, see Dawn Burton, "Discipline, Self-Discipline and Legacy: Military and Regimental Savings Banks in India," *The Journal of Imperial and Commonwealth History* 44, no. 1 (2016): 1–22. Reformers brought them to the West Indies in the 1830s as a means of promoting thrift among the soon to be liberated former slaves. See, for example, "Savings Banks and Benefit or Mutual Insurance Societies," *Antigua Herald and Gazette*, January 11, 1834.

[11] Horne, *A History of Savings Banks*, 81. For a catalogue of the savings banks in the United Kingdom by 1830, see John Tidd Pratt, *The History of Savings Banks in England, Wales and Ireland* (London, 1830).

keeping even the most industrious and most frugal laborer out of poverty for long. After the 1817 *Report from the Select Committee on the Poor Laws*, friendly societies once again took center stage as the key alternative to the poor laws.

But the question of what was suddenly so wrong with friendly societies in these years and so right with savings banks is important. If there was a single moment in the entire period where the perception of social and economic crisis was universal, the period from 1815 to 1817 was it. The wartime economy had been hard on everyone. The "Luddites" smashed machines and the government's troops smashed them. But when the war ended, things got much worse. Fractures were apparent nearly everywhere. Tens of thousands of sailors and soldiers were demobilized into a depressed economy and glutted labor market.[12] The Corn Laws were a victory for the landed elite, but they also raised the price of bread and registered the fragility of their authority. Foreign trade fell, and the national debt reached a staggering £792 million, more than 250 percent of national income, suggesting that the "monied interests" were in danger as well.[13] Meanwhile, just as population mobility and urbanization intensified, so too did the poor rates, reaching the highest level they would ever attain in the nineteenth century. The distress was so great that, in 1815, for the first time the "fundamental disapproval of a legal provision for the poor (and especially for the able-bodied) became sufficiently widespread to be regarded as orthodox . . . "[14] In other words, the poor laws, the very link that was supposed to produce "mutual confidence between the two orders," had itself come to be seen as a major part of the problem.[15]

Given this terrifying context, it might not seem particularly difficult to account for the sudden shift away from friendly societies and toward savings banks in these years. The radical politician William Cobbett certainly had no trouble explaining it. The ruling classes abandoned friendly societies, the only association where it was legal for working-class people to meet, because, as he put it, they wanted "to avoid the[ir] *congregating* evil." In a savings bank, where no meetings were required,

---

[12] Page, *Britain and the Seventy Years War, 1744–1815*, 137.
[13] J. F. Wright, "British Government Borrowing in Wartime, 1750–1815," *The Economic History Review* 52, no. 2 (May 1, 1999): 355.
[14] Poynter, *Society and Pauperism*, 224.
[15] Anon., *The Poor Enriched! To the Magistrates of the Borough-upon-Tweed, . . . the Following Letter, on the Utility of Parish, or Savings-Banks* (Berwick, 1815), 8.

"it is intended to *collect* the money, *without collecting the people.*"[16] For friendly societies "*drew men together*; and, when assembled together, they TALKED! Wicked rogues!"[17]

Even without their potential for fostering radicalism in these ominous years, however, support for friendly societies had never been unqualified. These associations had many critics, even among their most ardent advocates. For example, after singing the praises of friendly societies in his *State of the Poor* (1796) and *Observations on Friendly Societies* (1801), Frederick Eden went on at length about their shortcomings. Membership in local clubs was exclusive and could be revoked at any time; there was no relationship at all between contributions and benefits, much less an actuarial one; and regardless of differing circumstances or needs, contributions and benefits were the same for everyone. He also criticized the universal practice of holding club nights at pubs, paying "wet rent" (purchasing a set amount of alcohol in lieu of paying for the use of the club room) to the publican, and using the benefit funds to pay for annual feasts. But Eden, like most everyone else before 1815, excused these failings by explaining that even though friendly societies had some unsavory characteristics, they at least "convert a vicious propensity into an *useful instrument.*"[18] The principle was sound, even if the methods were sometimes less than optimal.

But the criticism in 1815 was different. It was less tolerant of friendly societies' shortcomings and more disapproving of their strengths. Critics found their convivial practices only slightly less egregious than the principle on which they were based. Specifically, when a member of a friendly society paid his periodic contributions, the money went into a common fund. The common fund was used to relieve distress caused by sickness, accident, or death. If a member was lucky enough not to require relief, his dues helped someone who was not so fortunate. Savings bank advocates took issue with friendly societies on this very point. One of the managers of the savings bank at Bath explained the essence of the complaint in this way,

Our desire is that every man, by timely saving, may enjoy the fruits of his *own* industry, when his wants shall require; but [friendly societies] are a sort of

---

[16] William Cobbett, "To the People of the United States of America, Letter XIII," *Cobbett's Weekly Political Register*, May 18, 1816, 617.

[17] Ibid., 615.

[18] Eden, *The State of the Poor*, 1:631–632. Also see Whyte, *General View of the Agriculture of the County of Dumbarton with Observations on the Means of Its Improvement Drawn up for the Board of Agriculture, and Internal Improvement*, 291.

benevolent lottery, by which the Contributor may or may not receive the benefit of his contributions.[19] (emphasis in the original)

In other words, this critique was directed toward the very principle that had made friendly societies such an attractive solution to life-cycle poverty in the first place – mutuality.

So, in 1815, not only did critics want to discard an organization whose principles were so well suited to alleviating poverty (even if its methods were sometimes suspect), they also wanted to replace it with an organization predicated on the individual accumulation of wealth. While there were important differences between the types of savings banks on offer, as we will see, these institutions were at base what their name suggests, nothing more than a safe place for laborers to deposit and earn interest on their surplus wages. While it is conceivable that individual savings might keep a few, relatively affluent laborers from becoming paupers, it was not a realistic solution to life-cycle poverty and certainly could not be expected to have an immediate effect on the 1815 poverty crisis. Why, then, at the very moment when distress was greatest and the poor laws considered defunct, would reformers abandon their best alternative in the friendly society, and put in its stead a bank?

The answer to this question goes deeper than the problem of poverty and right to the heart of social order itself. In the last chapter, we saw how the poor laws had always been much more than a system of poor relief. They delineated the parameters of the community and set the conditions of belonging in the parish. They stipulated the obligations and reciprocities between the rich and the poor, and thus served as a key conduit for the maintenance and reinforcement of social trust.[20] The German sociologist, Niklas Luhmann, argues that the reason social trust is so important in complex societies is that it helps to reduce that complexity. Trust enables people to act in the face of uncertainty.[21] The obverse also holds true. In moments of breakdown, when the bases for social trust are delegitimized, untenable levels of complexity are uncomfortably exposed. Crisis brings to the surface the paralyzing fears that trust makes

[19] William Davis, *Friendly Advice to Industrious and Frugal Persons, Recommending Provident Institutions, or Savings Banks*, 4th ed. (London, 1817), 19.

[20] In short, "the poor law was the key nexus of the paternal system" and had long been "the arena where the reciprocities of paternal social relations were displayed to most social and political effect." Richard Price, *British Society, 1680–1880: Dynamism, Containment, and Change* (Cambridge: Cambridge University Press, 1999), 323.

[21] Niklas Luhmann, "Familiarity, Confidence, Trust: Problems and Alternatives," In *Trust: Making and Breaking Cooperative Relations*, Diego Gambetta, ed., (Oxford: Basil Blackwell, 2000).

bearable. In these moments, the most basic assumptions of social order, those that go unspoken in peaceful times, are suddenly open to debate.

In the contest between savings banks and friendly societies, then, we have access to a rare discussion about rebuilding social trust in a society that felt itself on the brink of collapse. Savings banks were a genuinely new form of reciprocity. Their origins date back to the late eighteenth century, but not before.[22] So, when advocates designed them, they explicitly discussed the effects of the social arrangements and the new kinds of obligations that the rich and the poor could expect from each other. They were just as explicit about the ways friendly societies no longer seemed capable of producing such cross-class solidarity.

The fact that the savings bank approach failed is not surprising. But the failure taught these reformers a lesson they were able to learn once the immediate crisis had passed. In fact, they used the lessons they learned in this episode to create a new kind of friendly society; they called it the New Friendly Society. It was an organization that combined the savings bank principle of accumulation with the friendly society's structure of mutuality; it was made safe with a thick blanket of patronage and paternalism. The New Friendly Society then became the model that poor law reformers subsequently used to imagine a social order appropriate to the conditions of the urban, industrial society that rural, agricultural Britain was rapidly becoming.

***

So, what was really so wrong with friendly societies in 1815? While advocates of savings banks occasionally mentioned the danger of political radicalism inherent in the frequent meetings of working classes on their club nights, they focused the bulk of their critique on a more complex set of social dangers.[23] The great rise in poverty that had contemporaries so worried about the fate of their society was largely a rural phenomenon. Urban poverty would not be seen as a key social problem until the 1840s. And yet, when savings bank advocates attacked friendly societies, it was the condition of the urban laborer that provided much of their ammunition. Rather than the centuries old material deprivation and threat

---

[22] The feminist, Quaker, and philanthropist Priscilla Wakefield started the first savings bank in Tottenham in 1798. (William Robinson, *The History and Antiquities of the Parish of Tottenham High Cross...* (Coventry, 1818), 237.)

[23] George Rose, the MP who did so much to promote friendly societies, argued that "though he has sought anxiously for information" suggesting political radicalism, he "has not been able to discover a single instance where those consequences have followed in the case of a society, whose rules were registered according to law." (Rose quoted in Burdett, *Annals of Banks for Savings*, 6.)

of demoralization dynamic that characterized the rural problem of poverty, in newly formed urban centers, it was the lack of material deprivation that seemed to demoralize laborers. They simply had too much money and not enough (or the right kind) of moral restraint to spend it in a socially beneficial manner. The laborer's friendly society, which made it possible to imagine new ways of reestablishing a traditional social order if only the ruling classes were allowed to manage them properly, became in 1815 a synecdoche for a world they may not be able to manage at all.

What savings bank promoters worried about in rapidly growing urban centers was a lack of a clear mechanism for establishing and maintaining any kind of social order. To many observers, the increasing population density that characterized the 1810s and 1820s seemed to dilute the effect of traditional social constraints. A common refrain found in both the moral reform movement and poor law reform literature was that urbanization decreased the power of social vigilance over the behavior of city dwellers. As a commentator in the *Edinburgh Review* explained,

In the density of such a compact and crowded mass, individuals and families are scarcely within sight of each other; and the power which lies in that nearer and more intimate observation which is exercised by those few who are familiar with him who is just standing on the brink of pauperism, is in a great measure diluted . . .[24]

The report issued by the House of Commons Committee on Mendicity and Vagrancy (1816), much quoted in the savings bank literature, also added to the picture of urban disorder by detailing the free rein vagrants and beggars had gained in the metropolis.[25]

In an attempt to account for these conditions, promoters of savings banks claimed that laborers who made more than was necessary for subsistence, and who had no safe place to save their money, ended up spending it to the detriment of their own morals.[26] From their

[24] "ART. I. Minutes of the Evidence Taken before the Committee Appointed by the House of Commons, to Inquire into the State of Mendicity and Vagrancy in the Metropolis and Its Neighbourhood," *Edinburgh Review* 28, no. 55 (March 1817): 1–31.

[25] *Report from the Committee to Inquire into the State of Mendicity and Vagrancy in the Metropolis and Its Neighbourhood; Minutes of Evidence to Which Is Added, the Second Report*, P.P., 1816, (396) v, 119. For an example of the way in which this report was used in the savings banks literature see George Rose, *Observations on Banks for Savings. 4th Ed., with Alterations and Additions, in Consequence of the Act Which Was Passed in the Last Session Of . . .*, 4th ed. (London, 1817), 24.

[26] Outside of London and below a certain amount, there was no safe place for a laborer to save money. The Bank of England did not take deposits less than £10. Private or country banks sometimes took notes as low as £5, but unlike Scottish banks, English banks did not offer interest on deposits – and more to the point, they failed at shockingly high rates. No less than 700 private banks were started between 1797–1814 – and a full one third of

perspective, high wages without the proper social constraints led to poverty. Whenever laborers found themselves with a little extra money, they argued, "the slightest invitation to squander [it] is too seldom resisted ... "[27] The very act of spending money on superfluities was thought to have a cascading effect. "When a man gives way to a *little* indulgence," wrote William Davis, an advocate of a Benjamin Franklin-styled savings bank, "he may soon extend it to a *greater*, until the barrier is broken down, and he knows not where to stop."[28] Consuming commercial goods unleashed desire, contemporaries reasoned, and "there was no clear boundary between the sexual kind and that which fuelled consumption."[29] Indeed, one commentator took the relationship between consuming and sexual desire a step further, insisting that " ... servants, who have indulged in extravagance in Dress, are determined to keep up their appearance, become not very scrupulous as to the *means* of continuing it. Some have had recourse to theft, and others to prostitution ... "[30] Cities increased laborers' exposure to such temptations and at the same time imposed no checks on their behavior.

Proponents of savings banks reserved their most impressive scorn for publicans because, they claimed, he abused his position of authority by actively encouraging laborers to abandon both their morals and their money in the pub. In one tract used to popularize savings banks, the publican was dubbed "Tempter, the-tapster."[31] Critics argued that, in addition to converting high wages into dissipation, the publican also converted the poverty resulting from that dissipation into debt. Laborers might borrow money or pawn their tools or other "implements of their

---

them failed by 1815. (Horne, *A History of Savings Banks*, 10.) Those who wanted to save their money had to risk keeping it at home or lending it out to a local tradesman. Both were equally bad options, according to savings bank advocates, because word of hoarded treasure tended to get around and the industrious laborer inevitably lost the money to theft, unscrupulous borrowers, and even honest tradesmen who became insolvent at even higher rates than banks.

[27] J. H. Forbes, *A Short Account of the Edinburgh Savings' Bank, Containing Directions for Establishing Similar Banks, with the Mode of Keeping the Accounts, And ...*, 3rd ed. (Edinburgh, 1815), 4.

[28] Davis, *Friendly Advice to Industrious and Frugal Persons, Recommending Provident Institutions, or Savings Banks*, 27.

[29] Thomas Laqueur, "Sex and Desire in the Industrial Revolution," In *The Industrial Revolution and British Society*, Patrick O'Brien, ed., (Cambridge: Cambridge University Press, 1993), 101.

[30] Davis, *Friendly Advice to Industrious and Frugal Persons, Recommending Provident Institutions, or Savings Banks*, 23.

[31] *The Saving Bank: Part Second. Ralph Ragged & Will Wise* (Saffron Walden, 1818), 8.

trade" as a means of keeping up their new life-style or avoiding pauperism.[32] It did not help that the publican was the main creditor for working people in this period and often served as the local pawnbroker. Indeed, the publican stood at the very center of the "credit nexus" for early nineteenth century communities.[33] This role was critical to the credit networks on which most communities depended and through which early industrialization was funded.[34] Yet, from the perspective of savings bank advocates, instead of using their position for the promotion of social virtue, publicans exacerbated social disorder for their own monetary gain.

Each of the issues that concerned the promoters of savings banks – the loss of social trust through the poor laws, the dilution of social constraints in cities, and the publican's usurpation of social authority for his own gain – were all concentrated in microcosmic form in the friendly society. First, friendly societies reproduced the temptations faced by laborers who earned high wages. And they introduced these temptations to less affluent and also agricultural laborers. Drinking, the archetypical form of dissipation, was built into the very structure of the friendly society organization. As noted earlier in this chapter, in exchange for a meeting room, friendly societies traditionally paid "wet rent," an agreement to purchase a set amount of beer on each club night, regardless of

---

[32] See the section on "Journeymen," George Rose, *Observations on Banks for Savings* (London, 1817), 24–25.

[33] Kenneth Hudson, *Pawnbroking: An Aspect of British Social History* (London: Bodley Head, 1982). Publicans were pawnbrokers until the end of the century, when there was enough of a market for pawnbroking to become a standalone operation. Even then, while pawnbrokers became an important source of small, and usually short-term, loans to laborers, publicans were still the biggest local creditors, and thus, most laborers were dependent upon them. For an analysis of the relationship between credit, pawnbrokers, and poverty later in the nineteenth century, see Johnson, *Saving and Spending: The Working-Class Economy in Britain*; Finn, *The Character of Credit*, 277; Melanie Tebbutt, *Making Ends Meet: Pawnbroking and Working-Class Credit* (New York: St. Martin's Press, 1983).

[34] In the early days of industrialization, publicans held even more local debt than formerly as a result of the common practice of manufacturers who issued private tokens as wages or paid several laborers with a single large note. The publican would agree to give credit for these tokens or to break up large notes and would also take a cut. (L. S. Presnell, *Country Banking in the Industrial Revolution* (Oxford: Oxford University Press, 1956), 16.) "An almost incestuous relationship between the alehouse and employer" obtained throughout the early part of the century. (Finn, *The Character of Credit*, 77.) For the relationship between pawnbroking and poverty in late eighteenth-century York, see Alannah Tomkins, "Pawnbroking and the Survival Strategies of the Urban Poor in 1770s York," In *The Poor in England 1700–1850, An Economy of Makeshifts* (Manchester: Manchester University Press, 2003), 166–198.

the number of members actually in attendance.[35] The result, one critic explained, was that

enough beer is drunk to make them wish for more, and purchase more: and, if not, the man who otherwise would have shunned the public-house, having gone there to do the business of his Club, probably acquires a taste for its company and its habits; and, if he goes to-night for the Society, returns to-morrow for himself.[36]

Patrick Colquhoun, the London Magistrate and creator of the first preventative police force in London, estimated that nearly a half million pounds were "wasted" annually by friendly societies in the alehouse.[37]

Second, on top of the financial benefit the publican received from "wet-rent," he was usually the treasurer of all the clubs that met in his pub. Many critics claimed that publicans even started friendly societies in their pubs as a means of increasing business.[38] One even called friendly societies "Publicans' Clubs" and claimed that in order to attract members they advertised rates and promised benefits "inconsistent with the permanence of any such Institution."[39] It was well known that brewers like Samuel Whitbread, the Parliamentarian famous for his 1807 poor law reform bill, patronized well-managed friendly societies in the pubs he owned. It was also clear that the publican was the most logical person to be the treasurer for friendly societies given his or her role at the center of the parish credit nexus and the lack of other safe repositories for laborers' money. Nevertheless, it was difficult not to suspect the motives of publicans in general because they controlled the majority of friendly society funds in the country. As one especially virulent critic put it, friendly societies seemed to be designed specifically

---

[35] The eleventh rule of the Friendly Society of Millthrop, for example, read "And that on each Club night there shall be spent five shillings if the number [of members present] do not exceed thirty, if above two-pence each." (*Rules and Orders of the Friendly Society of Millthrop, Instituted the 12th Day of May, 1788.*, 2nd ed. (Kendal, 1794), 7.)

[36] Cunningham, *A Few Observations on Friendly Societies, and Their Influence on Public Morals*, 24–25.

[37] His calculation was based on the 1803 Parliamentary returns of registered friendly societies, where there were 9,272 societies comprising 704,350 members. Colquhoun estimated that with one meeting a month at the alehouse, plus four quarterly meetings and one annual feast, each member would spend on average 9d. at the alehouse, totaling £420,000 per year. (Patrick Colquhoun, *A Treatise on Indigence* (London, 1806), 116.) This claim was repeated in other critiques of friendly societies. See, for example, Anon., *The Poor Enriched! To the Magistrates of the Borough-upon-Tweed, … the Following Letter, on the Utility of Parish, or Savings-Banks*, 13.

[38] *Hints to Agriculturists and Others Residing in the Neighbourhood of Colchester upon the Advantages Which May Be Derived from Benefit Societies …* (Colchester, 1827), 25–27.

[39] Farey, *General View of the Agriculture of Derbyshire with Observations on the Means of Its Improvement…*, 3:573.

for the "benefit of the publican" but certainly not for the benefit of "the public."[40] The fact that most friendly societies were considered financially unsound only increased the anxieties about the role the publican played in their financial affairs.[41]

Third, while the working-class members of friendly societies seemed willing to allow publicans "undue" influence over their affairs, they were perfectly hostile to the interference of either the government or benevolent members of the upper classes. In this sense, friendly societies were problematic for one of the key reasons that had previously made them so attractive. As we saw in the last chapter, one of the great virtues of friendly societies was that laborers had founded them on their own accord. Thus, it was possible to use membership as a register of a laborer's "willingness to work" and indeed as a sign of trustworthiness. Friendly society membership implied that a laborer worked harder and earned more than was necessary for mere subsistence and then, instead of spending it, he deposited it in a fund for his own relief. The first Friendly Society Act (1793) had been designed to encourage more laborers to do the same by giving friendly societies legal protection – but, importantly, without destroying the voluntary impulse that gave rise to them. The law even granted legal sanction to their convivial practices by including "fellowship" in the description of the lawful purposes for which a friendly society could be formed. But while the legislation was made permissive in part because of the virtue of limited government and the fragility of voluntarism, it was also because friendly societies threatened to disappear if the government tried to interfere too much.[42] In 1815, this threat began to look both unreasonable and suspicious.

Finally, critics took their greatest umbrage to the way laborers constrained private patronage in their clubs. Friendly societies were generally willing to accept donations from local notables and were rather proud to have them attend their anniversary dinners.[43] But the rules

---

[40] Cunningham, *A Few Observations on Friendly Societies, and Their Influence on Public Morals*, 26.

[41] "ART. VI. An Essay on the Nature and Advantages of Parish Banks for the Savings of the Industrious, &c. with Remarks on the Propriety of Uniting These Institutions with Friendly Societies; Together with an Appendix, Containing the Rules of the Dumfries Parish Bank, &c. &c," 94.

[42] Cordery, *British Friendly Societies, 1750–1914*, 65.

[43] The anniversary account in *Jackson's Oxford Journal* was typical in this respect. After the details of the procession and the subject of the divine service, an account of the dinner was given. "After dinner, many healths were drank; The King – Queen and Family – Lord Abingdon, and the rest of the Honorary Members – The Rev Mr. Canninford, and thanks to him for his sermon – The mayor, and thanks to him for the use of the Hall." ("Oxford, Saturday, July 9," *Jackson's Oxford Journal*, July 9, 1814.)

common to most friendly societies in this period ensured that patrons would only ever have a very limited role in the actual management of the club. If patrons wanted to be "honorary" members, they were allowed to contribute to the fund of a friendly society but not to its management. The way friendly societies were managed was, of course, thought to be the problem. If, instead, patrons wanted to be considered full members and thereby have a role in management, they would have to submit to the regulations and fines stipulated in the rules of the society and have no more say than any other member. In other words, a patron would have to become an ordinary member and have his influence diluted by the democratic provisions of the club. Whether honorary or ordinary, the influence of the upper classes on friendly societies was circumscribed, and any charitable contributions they did make only added to the possible dissipations in which members could indulge.

If friendly societies restricted the role patronage played in the management of their clubs, their principle of mutuality threatened to nullify the meaning of upper-class charity altogether. The attack made on mutuality can only be fully explained by looking at the individualist replacement developed in the savings banks, which we will examine in the next section. But an important part of that explanation is that a relationship of mutuality restricted to laborers left no room for the upper classes. The way John Davison, an important poor law thinker, characterized the problem makes this clear, "It is not fit that the poor should subscribe for the relief of one another. Pecuniary charity is not their duty: it is out of their province. Their own real wants forbid it."[44] Friendly societies were a bad model for alleviating poverty, then, because they tried to do it without the help of those for whom charity was a primary duty – a class of people whose charity was supposed to make the unequal distribution of wealth socially acceptable to other classes.[45]

Given the allegedly vast power friendly societies granted to publicans, the limits they set on the influence of the upper classes, and the dissipation and financial ruin that seemed to follow, friendly societies provided contemporary social thinkers with a taste of what society would look like if laborers were left to their own devices. Friendly societies replicated the temptations facing high wage laborers in cities, exposed less affluent and even agricultural laborers to the same dangerous influences, all of which

[44] Davison, *Considerations on the Poor Laws*, 18.
[45] The importance of charitable giving for both the rich and the poor was given new emphasis with the rise of Evangelical Economics in the early nineteenth century. For more on the evangelical impact on social thought, see Hilton, *Age of Atonement: The Influence of Evangelicalism on Social and Economic Thought, 1785–1865*, chapter 3.

introduced "habits that accelerate the period at which the members will become a charge upon" the rates.[46] Thus even the claims friendly societies had on the potential to prevent poverty were undermined. When critics further took into

account the waste of time and loss of principles, necessarily resulting from such frequent conviviality, we behold with regret the benevolent intentions of parliament perverted and counteracted by moral and political evils of baneful tendency, and of more than ordinary magnitude.[47]

In a friendly society, as in the vastly expanding urban cityscapes, money was thought to have the paradoxical effect of making its owner poorer while perverting the benevolent intentions of the public and private patrons toward socially destructive ends. Friendly societies did not actually have to engage in political radicalism, then, to give the upper classes a glimpse of what the world would look like without them in it.

$$\star\star\star$$

The attraction to savings banks in 1815 was certainly due in part to the fact that they "collected the money without collecting the people," as Cobbett had it. More significant, however, savings banks looked capable of fixing what was broken both in friendly societies and in rapidly growing urban centers. The great boast of the savings bank was that it alone could render the laborer independent. But in a rapidly changing world, just how that independence would look and what exactly it meant was unclear. Everyone agreed that first and foremost it should involve freedom from poor relief.[48] Beyond that, ideas about independence diverged significantly. In Poynter's words,

Old-fashioned paternalists, and many cold rational employers, wanted the laborer to be dependent only on his social superiors; political economists sought his independence in a free economic system which alone could improve his situation in the long run; moralists wished him to be the guardian

---

[46] "The frequent meetings at the public-house for monthly payments, the annual feast, and the funerals of members, if they do not tend to exhaust the funds, undoubtedly introduce habits that accelerate the period at which the members will become a charge upon them. It is certainly true that the landlord of the public house is the person who thinks himself principally interested in the maintenance of the club ... " (Weyland, *The Principles of Population and Production*, 366–367.)

[47] John T. Becher, *The Constitution of Friendly Societies upon Legal and Scientific Principles*, 2nd ed. (London, 1824), 49.

[48] As Poynter put it, "The desire to see the laborer independent of public relief was a common point of agreement, the more deep-rooted because it seemed consistent with even violently opposed social and political philosophies." (Poynter, *Society and Pauperism*, 280.)

of his own virtue; and radicals deplored that he be dependent on any man, or any institution.[49]

The savings bank literature echoed these different viewpoints. By 1817, advocates worked out a kind of independence that garnered consensus. The kind of independence envisioned in a savings bank would align the interests of the laborer with those of the bank patron, which was ultimately the state, through the principle of accumulation.

Advocates of savings banks were convinced that this new independence would emerge from the simple act of saving itself. Saving even a little money required self-discipline and sacrifice from the laborer, whether working harder if wages were low or resisting the urge to spend if wages were high. But that initial act of economy would then produce a whole host of other virtues, which would automatically accrue to the laborer. As one advocate put it,

> To the artisan and the labourer economy never comes alone: she is ever attended on either hand by a throng of "kindred virtues" and he who admits her to his abode, and submits himself to her government, in learning to command his appetites, improves in virtue as well as circumstances ... [50]

What reformers considered wasteful spending (on either superfluities or dissipations) could thus be avoided. At the same time, putting aside present surpluses for future want would focus a laborer's attention always on the future when that frugality would be repaid with comfort during sickness or old age. Connecting current actions with their future consequences would guarantee a laborer's honesty because "he who forms himself into the habit of looking at remote consequences will not readily incur the guilt or deserve the punishment of crime ... "[51] In the minds of savings bank advocates, then, the independence that saving produced would not just eliminate poverty and poor relief, but also debauchery, dishonesty, and even crime. In a word, saving made men moral and thus trustworthy: "Generally, men in whom such habits are inculcated may be trusted ... ," as one advocate put it.[52]

While the initial act of saving would require sacrifice, the continuation of the habit would be practically self-sustaining. Accumulation aided by

---

49 Ibid., 280.
50 Peter Bayley, *Observations on the Plan of an Institution for the Promotion of Industry and Provident Economy among the Manufacturing and Labouring Classes* ... (London, 1819), 13.
51 Ibid., 13. Nicoll also noted that saving prevented crime. (S. W. Nicoll, *An Account of the York Saving Bank* (York, 1817), 39–40.)
52 John Thomas Barber Beaumont, *An Essay on Provident or Parish Banks, for the Security and Improvement of the Savings of Tradesmen, Artificers, Servants, &c.* (London, 1816), 43.

guaranteed interest, whether compounded or simple, would increase the desire to save more because it would make the money appear "to be gradually increasing under their eyes," and consequently, "the same system which held out to them encouragements for saving at first, still retains its influence over their minds."[53] As Colquhoun reported to the House of Commons Committee on Mendicity and Vagrancy, it took "a very slight knowledge of human nature" to realize that "when a man gets on a little in the world, he is desirous of getting on a little further; and once established a little fund in this bank, he would be desirous... to increase it by every possible means."[54]

Laborers themselves provided some of the most compelling evidence that simply having a savings account was inspiration enough to fill it with money. After one laborer had been given his blank deposit sheet, covered with empty squares, one for each week of the year, he exclaimed, "Oh, how tempting this ticket is. I cannot bear to see any of the *lozens* unfilled up. It is as uncomfortable as a window without glass."[55] Social pressures would also add to this effect, promoters thought. The savings of one depositor would spark competition between others, accord social status to the winner, and inspire non-depositors to emulate them.[56] In other words, saving would tempt laborers to save more in the same way that spending had tempted them to spend more. As S.W. Nicoll of the York Savings Bank put it, "the temptation to indolence may be great, but the temptation to save is greater."[57]

Some observers worried that encouraging laborers to become obsessed with saving would make them selfish and anti-social. But savings banks advocates interpreted this potential obsession as a virtue. They were united in the belief that strict saving without the "the more generous

---

[53] Henry Duncan, *An Essay on the Nature and Advantages of Parish Banks, for the Savings of the Industrious*, 2nd ed. (Edinburgh, 1816), 21. Weyland also pointed out the power that a growing savings account would have over the behavior of the depositor. "The spirit of accumulation is also a growing principle, and the poor man who has saved five pounds will much more probably exercise industry, sobriety, and self-denial to add to it other five pounds than he who has yet received no practical proof of his power of saving or of the advantages attending it." (Weyland, *The Principles of Population and Production*, 380.)

[54] *Report from the Committee to Inquire into the State of Mendicity and Vagrancy in the Metropolis and Its Neighbourhood; Minutes of Evidence to Which Is Added, the Second Report*, 1816, 120.

[55] Horne, *A History of Savings Banks*, 45.

[56] Competition could not be completely open because publicizing the names of the depositor alongside the amount in his account might induce his friends to ask for loans, putting the laborer back into his original position of the credit-debt cycle. But advocates reasoned that numbers could be assigned to accounts and then published publicly to create the same effect. See Duncan, *An Essay on the Nature and Advantages of Parish Banks, for the Savings of the Industrious*, 15–16.

[57] Nicoll, *An Account of the York Saving Bank*, 41.

and public spirited art of *spending* " would be selfish in the rich but that it was the absolute embodiment of social virtue in the poor.[58] John Weyland, an evangelical, major critic of Malthus, and an influential poor law thinker, argued that worrying about too much saving was like complaining "lest a tradesman should be too scrupulously honest, a clergyman too pious, a woman too modest or a magistrate too firm; lest society, in short, should be cursed with too much of a good thing."[59] Revd. Henry Duncan, founder of one of the first savings banks, agreed. In any other class of people, he noted, parsimony would be a "vice of selfish niggardliness." But in the poor, by laying "up a provision for the exigencies of his family, he exhibits a pattern of prudence and manly resolution, which would do honour to the highest station."[60] What was selfish, they countered, was when a poor man gave into the "indulgence of his indolence or his passions," which then "robs those, whom nature teaches to look to him for support, of the aid they have a right to expect at his hands."[61] In other words, the reason a miserly fixation on accumulation was a virtue in the poor was because it would enable them to perform the duty the poor law had taken from them, "the one virtue of a poor man," the single responsibility of his station: "the honest support of himself and his family."[62]

Given the powerful moral properties contemporaries attributed to saving at a time of social unrest, the attack on the principle of mutuality in a friendly society makes sense. In contrast to the moral discipline that came with saving, friendly society mutuality reduced the moral effect of saving to the point of non-existence. Paying into a friendly society without the guarantee of receiving, (and, critics added, that there was no hope of receiving), kept a friendly society member focused primarily on his fellow members and their present pleasure – not his own future, much

---

[58] Weyland, *The Principles of Population and Production*, 381. Nicoll made a similar point. Accumulation "become an object in the mind and imagination of the contributor – it is like the strong box of the miser of old – it assumes a value beyond it's worth – it is loved for it's own sake. This state, so advantageous to the poor, so dangerous to the rich, once attained – a never ceasing influence accompanies the poor man in all his actions … " (Nicoll, *An Account of the York Saving Bank*, 41.)

[59] Weyland, *The Principles of Population and Production*, 381.

[60] Duncan, *An Essay on the Nature and Advantages of Parish Banks, for the Savings of the Industrious*, 64.

[61] Charles Thorp, *Economy, a Duty of Natural and Revealed Religion, with Thoughts on Friendly Societies, and Savings' Banks* (Newcastle, 1818), 14. For a similar argument, see Duncan, *An Essay on the Nature and Advantages of Parish Banks, for the Savings of the Industrious*, 64; Otter, *A Sermon upon the Influence of the Clergy in Improving the Condition of the Poor …* , 25.

[62] Nicoll, *An Account of the York Saving Bank*, 40.

less that of his family.[63] A story designed to explain savings banks in simple terms to a popular audience illustrated the deficiencies of mutuality very clearly: in a friendly society, "you keep paying and paying as long as you live; and unless you happen to be ill yourself, there's your money all gone for the advantage of other people."[64] Weyland concurred and added, "a poor man *must* practice economy before he has the power of being generous to *others*."[65] Practicing economy, or becoming one's *"own FRIEND,"* as another savings bank promoter put it, was superior to the principle of mutuality because its moral hold on the saver was much more powerful.[66]

While savings bank advocates were agreed on the importance of individual saving, they had more difficulty deciding how best to configure the relationship between the patron/managers and the laborer/depositors, which could make or break the laborer's hard earned independence. The problem was that the savings bank was a very peculiar form of charity. The idea behind the savings bank was in some ways similar to that captured in the adage that it is better to teach a man to fish for a lifetime of sustenance than it is to give him a single fish to feed him for a day. Patrons wanted laborers to feel like the money they were saving was due to their own hard work and sacrifice. But a bank is a more complex tool than a fishing pole. In the first place, there were structural and legal limitations on how savings banks were organized that necessitated intervention beyond the initial opening of the account. In Scotland, where savings banks first proliferated, regular banks were able to pay interest on deposits, but did not accept anything less than £10. So Scottish savings banks were designed to help depositors to accumulate the first £10, which could then be transferred to a regular bank and earn interest like anyone else. In England, by contrast, banks did not normally offer interest on deposits and so a laborer's funds had to be deposited in government notes or public stocks. The English patron protected the laborer's deposits until they were sufficient to purchase stocks.

The question of how to intervene was even more complex than the structural limitations governing that intervention. How much and what

---

[63] Whereas every penny in a savings bank "is directed towards the social enjoyments of the domestic circle...[that of] the friendly society all tend towards the alehouse." (Weyland, *The Principles of Population and Production*, 380.)

[64] Member of the Provisional Committee for the Establishment of a Savings Bank at Buckingham, *The Savings' Bank: A Dialogue Intended to Illustrate the Nature and Advantages of Those Institutions* (London, 1818), 8.

[65] Weyland, *The Principles of Population and Production*, 382.

[66] Davis, *Friendly Advice to Industrious and Frugal Persons, Recommending Provident Institutions, or Savings Banks*, 8–9.

kind of paternalism would produce the right kind of independence? Too much superintendence would destroy the very independence they were trying to inculcate. And the wrong kind would excite the suspicions of the people it was meant to help. The problem with which early patrons struggled, then, was to find the right proportion of paternalism-to-independence without recreating the dependence of pauperism or exacerbating the distrust that was already thought to be marring social relationships.

Savings bank patrons fell into two camps on this problem, those who wanted depositors to be attached to the specific patron and those who wanted depositors to feel attached to the upper classes and "the system" more generally. Revd. Henry Duncan's Ruthwell Bank (1810), in the parish of Dumfrieshire (Scotland), was firmly in the first camp. And in the end, his bank became an important case study for what not to do for this very reason. Duncan had wanted depositors to feel a personal attachment to him. He believed that personal solicitousness was required in order to get laborers to save and thought it was necessary "to bribe [the lower orders] to attend to their own interests." From his perspective, it would help to "speed virtue on its way."[67] His bribes came in the form of offering premiums to those who contributed something weekly and assigning a fine to members who did not contribute a certain amount in a year; giving higher rates of interest to those who reached a certain principle or a certain period of time as a member; establishing a waiting period of thirty days before withdrawals could be made; and in the meantime, inquiring into the morality, necessity, and utility of the purpose of the withdrawal.[68] But it was a delicate balance. Duncan found that too much solicitousness could backfire. When he first opened his bank, he offered 5 percent interest on deposits. He soon found that the liberality "which was expected to be so favourable to the success of the plan, had at first a contrary effect with some, by operating on their ... distrust." The laborers in his parish imagined that he might "have some private end to serve."[69]

---

[67] Duncan, *An Essay on the Nature and Advantages of Parish Banks, for the Savings of the Industrious*, 27. The characterization of Duncan's method as speeding virtue on its way comes from Horne, *A History of Savings Banks*, 45.

[68] Duncan, *An Essay on the Nature and Advantages of Parish Banks, for the Savings of the Industrious*, 45. For a survey of the different methods employed see Edward Christian, *A Plan for a County Provident Bank with Observations upon Provident Institutions Already Established* (London, 1816).

[69] Duncan, *An Essay on the Nature and Advantages of Parish Banks, for the Savings of the Industrious*, 9.

The Scottish banker John Hay Forbes created a commercially minded corrective to Duncan's brand of paternalism in the form of the Edinburgh Savings Bank (1813), which became the model for the savings banks that began proliferating in England in 1815. He wanted to avoid the kind of distrust that Duncan's "inquisitorial power" and "paternal vigilance" caused.[70] The Edinburgh Bank was designed simply as a safe place for laborers to deposit their money and would act like an "ordinary bank." Depositors retained full control over their own property and could withdraw their funds as they saw fit. In this way, Forbes reasoned, the funds rather than the patron would retain full control over the morals of depositors. The Provident Institution for Savings (1816) introduced earlier followed this logic. The stated goal of the Provident Institution was simply

to afford the laboring classes...a secure investment in the Public Funds for such sums of money as they may be able to save, and may wish to deposit at interest; leaving them at liberty to withdraw the whole, or part, whenever they require it.[71]

Duncan's interventionist approach was too reminiscent of the untenable relationships between parish officers and paupers. John Beaumont, who started a savings bank in Covent Garden, explained that laborers who had made the sacrifice necessary to save in the first place

may be trusted; they must be the best judges of the wants they feel; and are likely to be the best economists in their difficulties; but should a man be determined to relapse into extravagance, he cannot be stopt (sic) while he has property...

He concluded by saying, "the prudence, like chastity, which requires continual watching, is not worth the watchman."[72]

Considering the social instability marking the post-war years, the dizzying variety of radical social programs on offer, and the unsustainable rise of the poor rates, it is easy to see why the savings bank view of society was so attractive. It may have used money to forge relationships between the classes, but it was no cash nexus. Individual savings were clearly thought to have profound moral and social effects. While friendly societies seemed to make a mockery of government protection and private charity in addition to engendering distrust between the upper and lower

---

[70] "ART. VI. An Essay on the Nature and Advantages of Parish Banks...by Henry Duncan, A Short Account of the Edinburgh Savings Bank..., and Report of the Committee Appointed by the Highland Society of Scotland ...," *Edinburgh Review* 25, no. 29 (June 1815): 145.

[71] Hume, *An Account of the Provident Institution for Savings, Established in the Western Part of the Metropolis; with Observations upon Different*, 8.

[72] Beaumont, *An Essay on Provident or Parish Banks, for the Security and Improvement of the Savings of Tradesmen, Artificers, Servants, &c.*, 43. Also see Burdett, *Annals of Banks for Savings*, 48.

classes, the savings bank promised to draw the classes closer together on the basis of their mutual financial interests. Laborers handed their money to the patron, who invested it in the funds and provided security for any market fluctuations; those increasing funds gave all parties a stake in the stability, credit, and security of the nation. This propertied stake in society would not just make the laborer "interested in the stability of the administration for the time being, but in the *perpetual stability of universal order and good government* . . . "[73]

What promoters of the commercial savings bank failed to appreciate, however, was that by appealing to the economic self-interest of laborers when promoting these banks, laborers began to suspect patrons of having self-interested motives. Patrons like Beaumont might feel that the great sacrifice involved in saving might make a laborer trustworthy, but what reason did the laborer have to trust the patron to keep those savings safe? What was to stop patrons or the government from spending their hard-earned savings to pay off the national debt rather than invest in it? Indeed, laborers were right to be suspicious, as the savings banks frauds of the mid-1840s would later demonstrate. But the point I want to emphasize is that a model of reciprocity based on mutual self-interest solved the stranger problem but exacerbated the trust problem. Just as important, however, savings bank advocates and legislators then responded directly to the way laborers articulated their suspicions. When Parliament passed the Savings Bank Act in 1817, legislators made clear what they thought would engender the laborer's trust in these new institutions. The law stipulated that depositors would retain full control over their property to dispose of it as they saw fit without any questions asked.[74] Local patrons would still act as trustees and wield moral influence through their management of the banks, but the government would absorb all the risk for guaranteeing the "unfluctuating" and "uneconomical" rate of return of 4.5 percent on deposits.[75] The state would become the disinterested benefactor. Government intervention was kept to a minimum and local trustees also had to stipulate in the bank rules that they stood to gain nothing from their position as patrons.[76] This

---

[73] Article from the *Quarterly Review* (1814) quoted in Burdett, *Annals of Banks for Savings*, 37.

[74] Rose, *Observations on Banks for Savings*, 22.

[75] It was reduced to 3.75 percent in 1828.

[76] James Taylor makes a similar point about the apparent shift to *laissez-faire* from the 1844 Companies Act to the one passed in 1856. Rather than restricting the role of government for ideological reasons, he argues that the government was trying to get shareholders to take on a greater role in determining the trustworthiness of a company's board of directors. (Taylor, "Company Fraud in Victorian Britain.")

stipulation would act as a statement of their trustworthiness. This stance was considered so important, that the exact verbiage appeared in the rules of every savings bank after 1817. That language was also highlighted in a short address to depositors printed on the back of the model deposit book circulated after the law was passed, the very first sentence of which stated that the managers "are prohibited from deriving any *benefit* whatsoever either directly or indirectly, from the deposits, or the produce of them..."[77] We do not know how laborers read such statements, but the fact that the state felt compelled to include it shows that they were sensitive to emergent problems of trust.

By the end of 1817, even as poor rates continued to rise, savings bank advocates had some indications that their efforts to replace poor law dependence with savings bank independence was a success. The alacrity with which people deposited their money in the new banks seemed to suggest that patrons had convinced laborers that accumulation was preferable to a life of dissipation. When records were first taken under the auspices of the Savings Bank Act in 1817, £231,028 had already been deposited in the 151 banks in England. Just one year later, that amount increased seven-fold, totaling £1,697,853. The rise continued to be remarkable throughout the century.[78]

However, it soon became clear that there were two problems with the apparent success of savings banks. First, they were successful among the wrong class of people. Savings banks did not attract low wage laborers or even the occasionally highly paid laborer.[79] They drew deposits only from the very top layer of the laboring classes. Depositors were overwhelmingly servants, followed by "mechanics, journeymen, clerks, little tradesmen and very small farmers."[80] Worse still, the government

---

[77] Burdett, *Annals of Banks for Savings*, 86. Revd. Charles Thorp emphasized this point in a sermon he preached in 1818 to members of the friendly society with which he was associated in order to show them that they could trust their money in a savings bank. He said, savings banks "are conducted by persons, who have no private interest to answer, no individual gain to make; whose characters, generally speaking, are a guarantee of the propriety of their management, and who are restrained by legal provisions from any abuse of confidence." (Thorp, *Economy, a Duty of Natural and Revealed Religion, with Thoughts on Friendly Societies, and Savings' Banks*, 28.)

[78] These totals include savings banks from England and Wales only; Scotland was not brought under the Savings Banks Acts until 1835. For the increases in deposits throughout the century, see Horne, *A History of Savings Banks*, 386–387.

[79] Notwithstanding the rare and likely exaggerated cases where instances of extraordinary thrift, under the most adverse circumstances, led to substantial savings among the once very poor, most depositors saved only modest amounts. For examples of the outlandish success stories advocates repeated as gospel, see Rose, *Observations on Banks for Savings*, 1816, 21–22, note(*); Duncan, *An Essay on the Nature and Advantages of Parish Banks, for the Savings of the Industrious*, 19–20, 43–45.

[80] Horne, *A History of Savings Banks*, 95–98.

learned that an even higher class of people was depositing their money in savings banks, under various pretenses, in order to secure the "uneconomical" rate of return.[81] Poor law thinker Revd. Vivian pointed out, "Men in elevated stations imagine that they see the lowest order, when they see but the *lower*."[82] In a savings bank, Vivian explained, "a butler may lay up enough money to keep a public house. But there must be a Benefit Society to keep a ploughman and his family from the workhouse."[83] For the vast majority of laborers, saving was simply out of the question. In his public letter to the 1817 Poor Law Commission, Thomas Courtenay put it plainly; most laborers could not afford to save, "because there are no savings."[84]

Second, and more devastating in the context of rising poverty, was the fact that even for those manufacturing laborers who occasionally had money to save, the savings banks provided no protection against the contingencies of the life-cycle or trade-cycles. In a word, savings banks could not keep the laborer independent of poor relief. Many critics made this point, but Vivian said it best. Subscribing to a savings bank at the same rate as a friendly society "will not carry [a laborer] through a long illness; and in old age it will make him independent for a few years, and then leave him to a workhouse."[85] The *Report from the Select Committee on Friendly Societies* (1825) later concluded that the real speculator was not the member of the friendly society, as savings bank advocates had claimed. The laborers at greatest risk of losing everything were those who put all their money in savings banks. "If sickness attacks him during his years of strength and activity, and he *dies* before he is past labour, he has been successful in his speculation." But if he should fall sick along the way, "he is a great loser; for his savings, with their accumulations, will support him but for a short time in sickness."[86] Those manufacturing laborers who "won" the sickness or old age gamble could just as easily have their savings depleted by a bankrupt manufacturer or an arbitrary change in fashion. The economy of the individual laborer was no match for the liabilities of sickness or accident, or the caprice of the

---

[81] This led to a cap on how much could be invested each year and overall. The amount changed several times, starting before the 1817 Act, some banks limited deposits to £10, the minimum necessary to invest in the public funds. After legislation was passed guaranteeing funds, caps were £50 per year and £200 overall; in 1844, it was reduced to £20 annually and £120 overall. (Ibid., 103.)

[82] Vivian, *A Letter on Friendly Societies and Savings Banks*, 13.   [83] Ibid., 14.

[84] Courtenay, *Copy of a Letter to the Rt. Hon. William Sturges Bourne, Chairman of the Select Committee of the House of Commons Appointed for the Consideration . . .*, 33.

[85] Vivian, *A Letter on Friendly Societies and Savings Banks*, 24.

[86] *Report from the Select Committee of the House of Commons on the Laws Respecting Friendly Societies*, P.P., 1825 (522) iv., 9.

market – even when these risks were secured by a patron as powerful as the British state.

Regardless of the social and financial limitations of savings banks, however, the practical and intellectual experiment with them proved extremely productive. It helped reformers develop principles that made a new social order imaginable while obviating the twin dangers of "poor-law dependence," on the one side, and the distrust that self-interested individualism threatened to introduce between the classes, on the other. And, it turned out that those principles, the disinterested superintendence of the upper classes and the self-disciplining properties of ownership, could easily be reconfigured for a new kind of friendly society.

★★★

The turn back to friendly societies in 1817 did not entail a simultaneous turn away from savings banks. Some reformers put greater emphasis on the one, and some on the other.[87] With few exceptions, most reformers and legislators saw the two institutions as mutually compatible, because as one observer put it, "the savings bank enables a man to rise; the friendly society prevents him from falling."[88] From then on, the priority was to ensure that the base of this new welfare superstructure was secure. The principles developed in savings banks seemed perfectly capable of making friendly society mutuality economically effective. But more than that, by reconstituting friendly societies with upper-class leadership, it became possible to imagine both commercially appropriate and socially meaningful relationships between the classes.

Thomas Courtenay, Chair of the 1817 Committee on the Poor Laws and author of the Parochial Benefit Societies Bill (1819), and Revd. J. T. Becher, magistrate at Southwell and inventor of the famous "Anti-Pauper system" made much of by the 1834 Poor Law Commission, were the key figures behind the effort to reform friendly societies on the new principles. Because friendly societies had regained a critical role in poor

---

[87] Revd. Cunningham was a harsh critic of unreformed friendly societies but came down decidedly on the side of the mutuality of a friendly society over the individualism of a savings bank. "The one is selfish; the other is generous – the one is solitary the other is public – the one fits a man for a cell; the other for a nation – the one sets a man to dig a pond in his own garden; the other prompts him to form a canal for the common benefit of mankind." (Cunningham, *A Few Observations on Friendly Societies, and Their Influence on Public Morals*, 6.) Revd. Thorp actually made the Christian case for the "worldly prudence" of a savings bank, though he did not go so far as to undermine friendly societies. See Thorp, *Economy, a Duty of Natural and Revealed Religion, with Thoughts on Friendly Societies, and Savings' Banks*, 27–32.

[88] Hector D. Morgan, *The Expedience and Method of Providing Assurances for the Poor and of Adopting the Improved Constitution of Friendly Societies ...* (Oxford, 1830), 22.

law reform, Courtenay's main concern was to make them secure. He justified the legal intervention of the upper classes on this basis. Becher created the Southwell Friendly Institution in conformity with the new law, but he put at least as much effort into making upper-class superintendence acceptable to potential members. If the laborer's club generated what became known as the "friendly society movement," Becher's Friendly Institution spawned the "New Friendly Society movement" (sometimes referred to as "Mr. Becher's system" or "Becher Clubs").[89] Drawing on some of the experiments with patronized friendly societies that we saw in the last chapter and combining them with the lessons learned in savings banks, Becher systematized a paternalized and "rationalized" friendly society.[90] His method was imitated by patrons all over Britain and became the basis of the 1829 Friendly Society Act.[91] While the efforts of Courtenay and Becher did not make a significant impact on the way the old clubs practiced mutuality, they succeeded in reanimating friendly societies as an important model for both social welfare and social relationships.

When Courtenay wrote the 1819 Friendly Society Act, he had the 1817 Savings Bank Act in the front of his mind, and indeed cited that law as precedent. The goal of the new law, Courtenay made clear, was to make these associations financially secure by protecting members "from the effects of fraud or miscalculation." As we saw above, the perpetrators of fraud and miscalculation were thought to be self-interested publicans and ignorant members.[92] The law systematically circumscribed the influence that a publican could legally have in a registered friendly society. First, it required that every legally registered society appoint at least three trustees, the majority of whom had to own property rated at no less than £50. This requirement did not absolutely preclude the publican from being a trustee but, even if one were to be selected, he would wield only a minority influence over funds. Second, the power of appointing the treasurer was taken from the members themselves and given to these

---

[89] The New Friendly Society based on Becher's system in Stratford-on Avon was named in his honor, "The Becher Club." (Richard Seymour, *Old and New Friendly Societies, The Comparisons between Them, with an Account of the Becher and Victoria Clubs* (London, 1839), 6, 12.)

[90] For an explanation of "Becher's system," see John Hodgson, *Proposed Improvements in Friendly Societies, upon the Southwell System* ... (London, 1830), 8.

[91] Exact numbers are not known, and any approximation would require a systematic survey of the rules of friendly societies that registered after the publication of his "Anti-Pauper system" in 1828 to see how closely they conformed to Becher's model.

[92] See "Friendly Societies and Parochial Benefit Societies," HC Deb March 25, 1819, Vol 39, cc1159–1161.

same trustees, which meant "publican-clubs" were effectively outlawed in the New Friendly Society movement.

In order to save members from their own ignorance, the new law reduced the number of purposes for which friendly societies could be formed. In contrast to the 1793 Act, which had included fellowship as a lawful purpose of friendly societies, the 1819 Act stated that only contingencies "susceptible by way of calculation" were proper objects. These contingencies had to be calculated by "two professional actuaries or persons skilled in calculations." Legislators did not put much stock in actuarial science and seemed aware of its then-very rudimentary state, especially as it related to sickness and mortality among the laboring classes. (In fact, as we will see in Chapter 5, actuaries did not yet put much faith in it either.) But, this limitation was not seen as an obstacle. Legislators believed that friendly societies could be secured through the "more vigilant and attentive superintendence of the magistrates at the quarter sessions."[93] Thus, the 1819 law also required that even after two actuaries approved the tables, three Justices had to further confirm that the contingencies stipulated were properly provided for.[94] Magistrates, then, would provide the oversight necessary to protect members from their own ignorance and actuaries from any overconfidence.[95]

When Becher created the Southwell Friendly Institution in Nottingham, he was sensitive to the actual expectations that members of registered friendly societies had regarding upper-class patronage. Like Courtenay, he wanted to reproduce the moral economy developed in savings banks, "constituting friendly societies upon the honorary superintendence, and the voluntary contributions arising from the benevolence of the superior orders co-operating with the provident frugality of the working classes ... "[96] But even though he deplored the "old system of Mismanagement and Conviviality" that he thought marked the laborer's club, Becher did not think it was right to force the old societies to register under the new law when the former laws had promised legal protection in spite of these problems.[97] To him this amounted to a "breach of public Faith." He predicted that the old clubs would "progressively expire by their inherent defects," but he did not want to mar

[93] Ibid., cc1159–1161, 1160.   [94] 59 Geo. III. c. 128.
[95] For more on the opposition between traditional paternalism and accounting principles, see Sandra Sherman, *Imagining Poverty: Quantification and the Decline of Paternalism* (Columbus: Ohio State University Press, 2001).
[96] John T. Becher, *Observations upon the Report from the Select Committee of the House of Commons, on the Laws Respecting Friendly Societies* (Newark, 1826), 5.
[97] Becher, *The Constitution of Friendly Societies upon Legal and Scientific Principles*, 11.

his own experiment by engendering their mistrust.[98] Instead of interfering with the old clubs, Becher's strategy for reform was to develop New Friendly Societies all over the country, which would be founded on *legal*, *scientific*, and *equitable principles* and managed by upper-class patrons. He expected to entice members from the old clubs to the new.

Becher shared his contemporaries' prejudices about the importance of upper-class supervision of friendly societies, but he went beyond the law by attempting to make that intervention acceptable to members – the effect of which, he thought, would draw the classes more closely together. In the same way that savings bank patrons had offered their disinterest as a testament of their trustworthiness, Becher explained that the fact that the honorary members "enrich the establishment with their donations and subscriptions; but do not receive any Emoluments in return" should have the same effect.[99] Other patrons who established New Friendly Societies on Becher's model credited him with making this principle standard in the New Friendly Society. As one explained, "Becher made the management *independent,* so that persons of all ages and sexes might make their assurance safely, as with an assurance company, or as they make deposits in a savings bank."[100] Further assurances were given in the form of the four stewards who were chosen annually from among the regular members. The regular members would have no role in the management of the society, but the stewards were given a salary and allowed to attend the monthly meetings "to investigate and ascertain, on [the members'] behalf, the state of the funds and the management of the institution."[101] If they were not satisfied, they could take it up with the board of directors and, failing satisfaction there, invite the scrutiny of the local magistrate.

But more than simply making the New Friendly Society unobjectionable, Becher wanted to make it positively attractive to laborers. Taking a page from the savings bank craze, one of the ways he attracted members was with the enticement of property ownership. Unlike the old clubs where the money paid in no longer belonged to the contributor, members in the New Friendly Societies were "joint proprietors" of the

[98] Becher, *Observations upon the Report from the Select Committee of the House of Commons, on the Laws Respecting Friendly Societies*, 109.

[99] Becher, *The Constitution of Friendly Societies upon Legal and Scientific Principles*, 5.

[100] *Instructions for Establishing Friendly Institutions upon the Improved Principle, and in Conformity with the Act*, 2nd ed. (London, 1830), 3. The idea that a lack of pecuniary interest was evidence of trustworthiness was repeated often. For examples, see Thorp, *Economy, a Duty of Natural and Revealed Religion, with Thoughts on Friendly Societies, and Savings' Banks*, 28–32; Seymour, *Old and New Friendly Societies, The Comparisons between Them, with an Account of the Becher and Victoria Clubs*, 14–15.

[101] Becher, *The Constitution of Friendly Societies upon Legal and Scientific Principles*, 6.

funds. Because insurance is not the same as other forms of property, Becher made some adjustments so that the policies that members purchased in his Southwell Institution simulated property ownership. Sickness insurance was combined with an annuity, for example, so that members could redeem a proportion of their investment if they could not afford to continue their membership.[102] He also let members increase or decrease the amount of insurance they owned without penalty. There were ten classes of benefits; each cost incrementally more but also increased the amount of sick pay and annuity a member would receive. The idea was to get the member to buy into the highest class he or she could afford. But if members could no longer afford the class they were in, they had the option of moving down a class rather than losing their initial investment the way they did in an ordinary friendly society. Likewise, if members wanted to insure for more, they could move up a class by simply paying the higher premium. By using actuarial tables, Becher was able to determine the total value of any class of sick or annuity benefit, so the benefit could either be paid for all at once or in monthly installments. In either case, it was a set amount. Once it was paid for, no further payments were required. The member then "owned" that insurance.

The property a member owned in the New Friendly Society would thereby be continuously enticing to members and would exercise a disciplinary effect on the saver in the same way cash accumulations did in a savings bank. George West, one of Becher's many imitators, explained,

whilst he has been making his monthly contributions on a lower scale . . . will not the conviction be unsuspectingly forced upon him, that he is competent to rise to a higher class; till by the savings of his industry from year to year, during the vigor of youth and manhood, he progressively obtains that which the wealthier commercial man, or the attentive agriculturalist does not secure without a long season of toil and labor, a competency to support him when his work is done.[103]

Like the deposits in a savings bank, ownership in a New Friendly Society would inspire the desire for more, and the desire to acquire more insurance would keep that money from being spent in less productive ways

---

[102] See his explanation before the 1825 Select Committee on Friendly Societies. (*Report from the Select Committee of the House of Commons on the Laws Respecting Friendly Societies*, 1825, 35.)

[103] George West, *A Plan for Bettering the Condition of the Working Classes by the Establishment of Friendly Societies, upon Legal and Scientific Principles Exemplified by Practical Illustrations* (Farnham, 1827), 41.

while it also secured the saver against the contingencies of the life- and trade-cycles.

In addition to property ownership, Becher tried to attract members through a principle that might be called "more eligibility." This concept was first introduced in the 1817 Select Committee on the Poor Laws and detailed in Courtenay's failed Parochial Benefit Societies Bill (1819). The original idea was to supplement the funds of the Parochial Benefit Societies so that they could offer "greater pecuniary advantages than could result from the unaided contributions of the subscribers," as Courtenay explained.[104] Becher and his imitators used upper-class patronage to make the New Friendly Societies "more eligible" than either the old clubs or parish relief. One promoter of Becher's system, for example, recommended that all New Friendly Societies should offer "benefits somewhat higher than the allowance a parish would be compelled to grant" to paupers.[105] Although the amount of contributions required for entry into the New Friendly Societies was generally higher than in the old clubs, the new societies, their founders believed, offered greater and more secure benefits. In this way the New Friendly Society was "more eligible" than either the stinginess of the parish officer or the insecurity of old friendly societies.

Becher also made his clubs attractive to laborers by making the conversion of old friendly societies into new ones remarkably easy. He developed a table that could convert the funds of an old friendly society, providing it was in a solvent condition, so that its members could transfer in immediately. Old friendly societies whose funds were no longer sufficient to meet the demands on them could take their accounts to their magistrates and have their funds apportioned equitably to each member depending on how long that member had contributed. Those members could then use that money to buy insurance in the New Friendly Society at whatever level they were able to afford. Those who could not afford the rates of the lowest class were allowed to purchase a special annuity.[106] One advocate of the new system suggested that in the case of insolvency,

---

[104] *Report from the Select Committee on the Poor Laws*, 1817, 25.

[105] *Hints to Agriculturists and Others Residing in the Neighbourhood of Colchester upon the Advantages Which May Be Derived from Benefit Societies . . .*, 86.

[106] In addition to the special dispensation Becher offered poorer members from the old clubs, a new class of friendly society was developed for members from old clubs whose age precluded them from membership in a New Friendly Society on affordable terms. Called "Victoria Clubs," patrons subsidized the members of old clubs who were born before 1810. For more on Victoria Clubs, see Seymour, *Old and New Friendly Societies, The Comparisons between Them, with an Account of the Becher and Victoria Clubs.*

the principle gentlemen of the town might raise a subscription to enable those members to join a New Friendly Society.[107]

The financial advantages in the New Friendly Society – property ownership, the security of the funds, and easy conversion from the old system to the new – were matched with important social securities. In the New Friendly Society, the upper-class patrons protected members socially and morally, emancipating them from the designs of the publican and the temptations of the pub, from the harsh treatment by parish officers and the degradation of poor relief, and from the incompetence of actuaries and the uncertainty of life-cycle and trade-cycle contingencies.[108] Their charity and social status were made meaningful through the rational patronage of a New Friendly Society. A common feature of all New Friendly Societies was that whenever potential deficiencies presented themselves, for example, the auxiliary fund created by the donations of honorary members (and other benevolent persons) would be called upon.[109] Similarly, when the funds experienced a surplus, the honorary members could offer dividends or purchase cottages for especially virtuous members. Honorary members could also purchase (and continue to pay for) the interest of a member who was no longer able to afford payments. Even though there was no weekly sociable component approximating the "club night" of the laborer's friendly society, honorary members subsidized the annual feast in the New Friendly Society. Thus, Becher's system enabled the upper classes to use their elevated status and benevolent contributions toward financially rational and socially meaningful ends.

From Becher's perspective, the social benefits of the New Friendly Society were a necessary corrective to the exclusiveness of the old clubs. But he also believed they created stronger bonds between the classes than savings banks did. Becher was not opposed to savings banks and, in fact, saw them as a critical auxiliary to a laborer's moral probity. He attached

---

[107] *Advice to Agricultural Labourers, and Others, on Benefit Societies; Shewing the Advantages and Comforts, Which May Be Derived from Them, When Founded on Safe Principles* (London, 1828), 27, 32.

[108] *Instructions for Establishing Friendly Institutions upon the Improved Principle, and in Conformity with the Act*, 15.

[109] For example, one promoter explained, members of the New Friendly Society enjoy greater security because they can rely "with confidence upon the skill of those persons, who have calculated the Tables. And besides this, there is every probability, that, where there are many Honorary Members belonging to one of these societies, they would come forward, and subscribe their money, in case there was any prospect of failure of the funds." (*Advice to Agricultural Labourers, and Others, on Benefit Societies; Shewing the Advantages and Comforts, Which May Be Derived from Them, When Founded on Safe Principles*, 9.)

one to his Friendly Institution in Southwell. But in terms of forging strong social attachments between the classes, the New Friendly Society was the more appropriate institution from Becher's perspective. In his words,

The selfish principles, which actuate the depositors in a savings bank, can never stand in competition with the social benevolence of a [friendly] society, united for the purposes of mutual support, cemented by the principles of reciprocal attachment, and drawn together by the bonds of brotherly love.[110]

In this way, Becher transformed mutuality, which had been a liability under the old system, into an asset in the new.

Becher's Friendly Institution and the New Friendly Society movement it initiated did seem to reduce poor rates wherever they were implemented. As we saw in the last chapter, Becher gave evidence to the 1825 Select Committee on Friendly Societies and again to the 1832 Commission on the Poor Laws, claiming that, in combination with a strict administration of poor relief, the Friendly Institution helped restrict relief so that it went almost exclusively to the aged, disabled, and other cases of chronic poverty. Between 1821 and 1822, rates in his parish and the surrounding forty-nine parishes went from £2010 to £1421. Then, when the Friendly Institution was established in 1823, they were further reduced to £589. The following year, the decrease continued.[111] Already in 1826, there were New Friendly Societies on Becher's model in Hampshire, East Devon, North Devon, South Gloucester, Pakefield, Eskdale Ward Cumberland, the County and City of Worcester, and in the County of Dorset.[112] By 1832, other parishes and hundreds followed suit and reported similar results.[113]

But while the New Friendly Societies clearly attracted members, they did not inhibit the creation of additional friendly societies on the "old system." In fact, some advocates of the new system claimed that wherever a New Friendly Society was established, several clubs on the old system were started in retaliation.[114] It is difficult to gauge this

---

[110] Becher, *The Antipauper System: Exemplifying the Positive and Practical Good, Realized by the Relievers and the Relieved, under the Frugal, Beneficial*, 31.

[111] See Becher's evidence in the *Report from the Select Committee of the House of Commons on the Laws Respecting Friendly Societies*, 1825, 31.

[112] Becher, *Observations upon the Report from the Select Committee of the House of Commons, on the Laws Respecting Friendly Societies*, 97.

[113] John T. Becher, *The Antipauper System: Exemplifying the Positive and Practical Good Realized by the Relievers and the Relieved under the Frugal, Beneficent ...* , 2nd ed. (London, 1834), appendix.

[114] Cunningham, *A Few Observations on Friendly Societies, and Their Influence on Public Morals*, 29; *Hints to Agriculturists and Others Residing in the Neighbourhood of Colchester upon the Advantages Which May Be Derived from Benefit Societies ...* , 26–27.

phenomenon in terms of numbers because many of the old clubs did not register. But in 1828, we have very clear evidence that notwithstanding the local success of Becher and his imitators, the principles on which the New Friendly Societies were based were considered anathema to members of the old clubs. That year, Courtenay authored another friendly society bill, this time based on Becher's system. But instead of allowing already registered friendly societies to continue under the protection of the old law without assuming the magisterial supervision of the new, societies would have three years to come under the new law or lose all legal privileges. Members of friendly societies on the old system responded immediately and clearly. They pooled their resources and hired lawyers on their behalf to petition against the bill. Their principle objection was summarized in this way, "we do not wish to have the harmony of our Societies disturbed by a system of coercion and inquisition ... "[115]

The way in which mutuality was practiced in the laborer's friendly society may have looked financially unsound to observers, but members saw it as critical to the security of their organization. Everyone paid in the same amount, received the same benefits and met regularly for group drinking because these measures were critical for fostering trust among people without other means of establishing their *bona fides*. We will explore the internal culture of friendly societies more fully in the next two chapters, but the 1828 petitioners offered some insight when they explained that the purpose of their societies was "mutual assistance and relief in time of illness or affliction, and the engendering, thereby, a friendly, a brotherly feeling in their members."[116] The brotherly feeling, as we will see in Chapter 4, is what made it possible for people with fluctuating incomes to contribute what they were able when one of them was in need. The amount of relief varied with the members' ability to give it. But the bonds between them ensured that each member was guaranteed the mutual support of his brothers when his time came. Upper-class superintendence and a set relationship between contributions and benefits might have provided more certain financial security for friendly societies, but members thought that "doubt and distrust should be engendered amongst us ... " with such interference.[117] In response to

---

[115] Cotter, *An Address to the Members of Benefit Societies*, 5. For similar objections to the 1829 law see James Wright, *A Summary of Objections to Act 10 Geo. IV. c. 56 and of the Grievances Thence Resulting to Benefit Societies: With Propositions for a New Act ...* (London, 1833).
[116] Cotter, *An Address to the Members of Benefit Societies*, 20.   [117] Ibid., 5.

these protests, the 1828 bill was rewritten so that the enforcement clause was eased.[118]

Even though many members of the old clubs rejected the New Friendly Society, social thinkers and reformers continued to see friendly societies managed and patronized by the upper classes as the key to strong social relationships between the classes. In the late 1820s and early 1830s, upper-class interventions in friendly societies were justified on new grounds. At this point, it was "the circumstances of the times and the dreams of a heartless philosophy" that had impaired "the compassionate relation between the rich and poor".[119] Hector Morgan, who was a major fan of Becher's system and who started a savings bank in Essex, claimed that the laboring classes "are not capable of making or appreciating the calculations, ... nor is it probable that such calculations will fall in their way." So, he reasoned that,

in the friendly societies, as in the banks for savings, the rich and the poor, the educated and uneducated classes of the community, should be brought into cooperation with each other, and that with a practical sense of the several relations in which it hath pleased GOD to place them, the one should undertake the expense and trouble of the management and direction, and the other be content to receive the benefit ... [120]

★★★

The battle between savings banks and friendly societies emerged out of a moment of crisis, but through a process of trial and error, it helped contemporaries to create a new kind of cross-class reciprocity. The social aspects of both the savings bank and the New Friendly Society were just as important as the financial security these organizations provided. Even those reformers who saw individual accumulation in a savings bank as the key solution to poverty also believed that the burden of managing these institutions and of protecting the laborer's deposits from market fluctuations belonged to the governing classes. After the 1817 Savings Bank Act, the state spent an enormous amount of money subsidizing the savings of the poor. Between 1818 and 1828, the cost to the government was on the order of £40,000–60,000 per year.[121] When critics suggested that laborers should only receive market rates in the late 1830s, Sir F. T. Baring, the Chancellor of the Exchequer, made it clear

[118] 1829 Friendly Society Act (10 Geo. IV. c. 56).
[119] Morgan, *The Expedience and Method of Providing Assurances for the Poor and of Adopting the Improved Constitution of Friendly Societies* ... , 34.
[120] Ibid., 20–21.   [121] Horne, *A History of Savings Banks*, 100.

in his response that these banks did more than provide a safe place to deposit their funds. The cost of subsidizing them may have represented financial "loss to the public, but a still greater injury to the Community would arise from disturbing the confidence which was felt in the security of Savings Banks."[122] As savings banks became even more central to the economy of the British laborer in the second half of the nineteenth century, so too did the state's commitment to protecting them. By mid-century, there were over a million depositors with investments totaling more than £30 million.[123] When some of the most respected trustees of these banks committed a series of spectacular frauds in the 1840s, the state successfully prosecuted the cases – even when the trustees of railway companies who committed similar frauds "led to no attempts at criminal prosecution."[124] James Taylor argues that the difference in where the state chose to intervene had more to do with who the victims were than with the nature of the crime. In the case of savings banks, the state, as a benefactor to working-class depositors, continued to take its moral and social obligations seriously.

There is no doubt that early savings bank promoters tried to break the social ties that laborers had with each other in their friendly societies and to supplant those ties with a vertical and financial relationship between depositors and bank patrons. But it also seems worth noting that when it turned out that even with guaranteed above-market interest rates that a savings bank could not keep the most industrious laborer from poverty, these same patrons shifted their attention back to friendly societies – and to making a system of welfare that was both financially robust and socially meaningful. The New Poor Law that ultimately got passed in 1834 was an attempt to make the old system of poor relief obsolete. But as it deterred the able-bodied from seeking relief with its harsh strictures, reformers hoped that financially sound and socially secure friendly societies would draw laborers toward a new kind of solidarity with the upper classes.

Just as they had in the late seventeenth century in Defoe's hands, friendly societies once again became an important cultural resource for imagining new social configurations appropriate to a society still in the throes of massive social and economic change. Even though the social conditions in densely populated urban centers and the strain of social relationships under the poor laws first implicated friendly societies as part of the problem, the principles developed in savings banks brought friendly societies back into the realm of social thought as part of the

---

[122] Ibid., 100.   [123] Taylor, *Boardroom Scandal*, 89.   [124] Ibid., 91.

solution. Savings banks promised to reinvigorate the social authority of the upper classes by giving their charity a commercially sound conduit – and by doing so, also offered laborers access to commercial society on a more equitable basis. Becher's translation of commercial paternalism to the peculiarities of a friendly society succeeded in making that financially sound charity socially meaningful as well.

The fact that both savings banks and the New Friendly Societies foundered on different class conceptions of what constituted trustworthiness, however, is significant. The economic disinterestedness that made the propertied classes appear trustworthy to each other was not enough to make them appear trustworthy to those without property. In the next two chapters, we will explore the question of trust among working-class strangers. The legislative attempts to impose upper-class superintendence and actuarial relationships between contributions and benefits, it turns out, conflicted with the very principles through which working-class members relied on each other to provide mutual aid.

4   Trusting Institutions
Making the Independent Order of Odd Fellows, Manchester Unity

> Odd Fellows are they who have certain Particularities founded upon no Reason ... Their Oddnesses are of no signification, nor importance, but to the Owners only; and yet they make these Oddnesses the Standards of Sense and Virtue, and the great Criterion of the Character of Men ...[1]   "Criton," 1723

> The cultivation of friendship, the pleasures of good company, and the improvement of morals are the primary objects – for the attainment of which a number of individuals of the first respectability have formed themselves into a fraternity of Loyal Independent Odd Fellows.[2]
> *Laws and Regulations of the Independent Order of Odd Fellows*, 1820

The efforts of legislators and reformers to use friendly societies to create a system of social welfare that could both shore up social trust between the classes and provide a social safety net to a growing and increasingly mobile population continued throughout the century.[3] At the same time, working men and women had been founding and joining their own friendly societies such that by mid-century somewhere between 2–4 million Britons were members of one.[4] They too were working on the problem of social trust among strangers. And they developed a new kind of friendly society to deal with it. This new type of friendly society came to be called an Affiliated Order, that is, a mutual aid society with multiple branches located beyond the confines of a single town. The Affiliated Orders dominated the friendly society movement from the mid-1830s. There

---

[1] Criton, "To the Author of the British Journal," *British Journal*, October 5, 1723, LV edition.
[2] *Laws and Regulations of the Independent Order of Odd Fellows*, 1820, DDX177/20, Lancashire Record Office, 8–9.
[3] Gosden provides a good overview of these societies from the state's perspective until the 1870s and Cordery gives a much broader overview up to World War I. Gosden, *The Friendly Societies in England, 1815–1875*; Cordery, *British Friendly Societies, 1750–1914.*
[4] HL Deb August 12, 1850, Vol 113 cc1017–1018. Because so many friendly societies were not legally registered, membership estimates vary depending on the source. For different estimates, see Weinbren and James, "Getting a Grip: The Roles of Friendly Societies in Australia and Britain Reappraised," 101 fn. 5.

were a number of Affiliated Orders in Britain with names like Druids, Foresters, Shepherds, and many different denominations of Odd Fellows. But the one that started first, and ultimately provided the model for the others, was the Independent Order of Odd Fellows, Manchester Unity.

Sometimes called the workingman's Freemasons because of the strong family resemblances between their ritualized forms of sociability, the Odd Fellows began with six lodges in Manchester in the early 1810s and, from the early 1820s, began to increase their numbers at a rather impressive rate.[5] By mid-century, the Odd Fellows coordinated mutual relief for some 250,000 members and their families, with lodges located in every county and most towns in Great Britain and Ireland, in the major and emerging metropolises of the United States, and scattered across the new towns of Australia, Van Diemen's Land (later Tasmania), and New Zealand; there were two lodges in Barbados, one in Calcutta, several at the Cape of Good Hope in South Africa, and a few sprang up in eastern Canada. In the 1860s, there would be an Odd Fellow Lodge in Turkey and one in Buenos Aires. By the mid-nineteenth century, then, an Odd Fellow could leave the Social Design Lodge in Halifax, Yorkshire with a "travel card" and migrate to Hobart Town in Tasmania, over 10,000 miles away, where he could "throw his card in" with the brothers of the Southern Star Lodge. If he fell sick en route, he could consult his "list of lodges" and find the nearest pub where an Odd Fellow lodge met and would soon receive relief. If he died, letters would be sent to his home lodge and the expense of his funeral would be forwarded to the lodge that buried him. If he made it all the way to Hobart Town, the brothers of the Southern Star lodge would relieve him until he found work and also help him to find it. Even at its best, the minute books of local lodges show that this was never a perfect system. But the fact that this organization worked at all raises an important question. How did the members of this society manage to forge bonds of trust between people they did not necessarily know across sometimes very great distances?

The story of how the Odd Fellows became an extra-local institution is significant because it gives us a particular case from which to think about what makes an institution trustworthy to different kinds of people. Because the Odd Fellows attracted a largely artisan and working-class membership, they did not have the cultural or material resources that enabled other classes of people to cooperate over great distances in this period. They were not sophisticated men of letters. They came from humble backgrounds and, as the century wore on, members hailed

---

[5] For a critique of the historical lineage of this connection, see Bob James, "Problems with U.K. and U.S. Odd Fellow Literature," 2001, www.takver.com/history/benefit/ofshis.htm.

increasingly from the ranks of the unskilled labor pool. Some members were illiterate, most were under-literate, and, in any case, few were learned in the business of running a local society much less a national organization. Consequently, the standard rules of procedure one might pick up from a professional meeting or club or the shared cultural knowledge one might be familiar with from regional or national print culture might supplement, but could not provide the basis for, their solidarity.[6]

Nor were Odd Fellows from the same trade, which means they did not have the common set of skills, craft language ("mystery"), or shared occupational interests that worked to unify some of the skilled artisan tramping systems.[7] Members did not share the same religion either, and they had a wide range of different political views.[8] While generally concentrated in larger urban or industrial centers, by the mid-1820s, the Odd Fellows were already trying to coordinate relief between urban and rural lodges, as well as domestic and imperial lodges.[9] Finally, the unification of these very diverse parts would take place outside the pale of the law. As we saw in Chapter 2, local friendly societies that registered their rules were protected under the 1793 Friendly Society Act. But the oath an Odd Fellow swore upon his initiation into the brotherhood, the lectures he attended, and the fact that there were multiple branches of Odd Fellows meant that they were technically illegal under the Corresponding Societies and Unlawful Societies Acts (1799/1801). This means that the resources and methods through which the Odd Fellows unified

---

[6] Print culture was of course important for the way middle class people imagined a larger, extra-local community. On this point, see Benedict Anderson, *Imagined Communities: Reflections on the Origins and Spread of Nationalism* (London: Verso Books, 1991).

[7] For more on traveling artisans, see E. J. Hobsbawm, "The Tramping Artisan," *The Economic History Review* 3, no. 3 (1951): 299–320; Peter Clark, "Migrants in the City: The Process of Social Adaptation in English Towns, 1500–1800," In *Migration and Society in Early Modern England, 1987*, 267–291; R. A. Leeson, *Travelling Brothers: The Six Centuries' Road from Craft Fellowship to Trade Unionism* (London: G. Allen & Unwin, 1979); Peter Clark, *The English Alehouse: A Social History, 1200–1830* (London: Longman, 1983). The Masons had access to this type of shared occupational culture, even if their relationship to actual stone masonry was limited. See Mary Ann Clawson, *Constructing Brotherhood: Class, Gender, and Fraternalism* (Princeton, NJ: Princeton University Press, 1989); Jessica Harland-Jacobs, *Builders of Empire: Freemasons and British Imperialism, 1717–1927* (Chapel Hill: University of North Carolina Press, 2007).

[8] For examples of the ways in which family and co-religionists co-operated across distances, see Leanore Davidoff and Catherine Hall, *Family Fortunes: Men and Women of the English Middle Class, 1780–1850* (London: Routledge, 1997); Hancock, *Citizens of the World*; Zahedieh, *The Capital and the Colonies*.

[9] Neave, *Mutual Aid in the Victorian Countryside: Friendly Societies in the Rural East Riding, 1830–1914*, chapter 2; For a study showing the tendency for friendly societies to concentrate in urban centers, see Gorsky, "The Growth and Distribution of English Friendly Societies in the Early Nineteenth Century."

extra-locally were different from the ones we normally associate with the making of modern institutions.

This story about how working men created an institution capable of facilitating trust at a distance is as important for its successes as for its failures. As noted in Chapter 2, questions of trust and belonging also raise questions of distrust and exclusion. In the late eighteenth-century debate over the poor laws, Revd. John Acland and other middle-class reformers, for example, had no trouble including women in their friendly society proposals. For them, solidarity was a function of cross-class reciprocity – in Acland's case, charitable actuarial subsidies in exchange for regular payments according to means.[10] Acland allowed greater subsidies for women due to their generally lower wages. But women were to be considered full members. Belonging was not a matter of how much one paid, but *that* one paid. The only people excluded were those who refused to pay at all. As Acland explained, " ... all Persons so refusing, whether Male or Female forasmuch as they determine to live on others Labours, shall be badged...with the Word Drone, in large Letters of Red Cloth ... "[11] The Affiliated Orders, by contrast, barred women from membership until the very end of the nineteenth century – even though there were definitely women who wanted to join and could afford to pay the cost of membership. At first, the exclusion was due to a kind of cultural default – as membership in late eighteenth-century lodges involved heavy drinking.[12] But later, as we will see, the exclusion of women became critical to the way Odd Fellows designed their extra-local bonds of solidarity.

The working men who created the Independent Order of Odd Fellows may not have had a blueprint to show them how to create trust among strangers, yet their system, flaws and all, became the model for the other Affiliated Orders and other kinds of working-class organizations.[13] In 1874, the House Committee on Friendly Societies were genuinely impressed with the Odd Fellows' pioneer work. Indeed, they felt that the Manchester Unity had earned the right to "speak in the name of the present generation of working men, so far as concerns the largest section

---

[10] For more on Acland's proposal, see Chapter 2.

[11] Acland, *A Plan for Rendering the Poor Independent on Public Contribution; Founded on the Basis of the FRIENDLY SOCIETIES, Commonly Called CLUBS*, 42.

[12] Women frequented pubs alongside men, but heavy drinking in clubs was generally the purview of men. For mixed-gender drinking in the early modern period, see Hailwood, *Alehouses and Good Fellowship in Early Modern England*, 194–203. Anna Clark discusses heavy drinking among male artisans as a way of forging bonds and blowing off steam. (Clark, *The Struggle for the Breeches*, 30–31.)

[13] Simon Cordery, "Mutualism, Friendly Societies, and the Genesis of Railway Trade Unions," *Labour History Review* 67, no. 3 (December 2002): 274.

of the most intelligent among them … " The Committee concluded their assessment by declaring that the Order was "a valuable national possession."[14] While the Freemasons and the longstanding tramping crafts would prove important cultural resources for the Odd Fellows as they forged extra local bonds between members of distant lodges, the Odd Fellows in turn provided the actual experience, the unifying symbols, the specific terminology, and the structural framework for the national trade unions that emerged in the second half of the nineteenth century.[15] Consequently, how six Odd Fellow lodges in Manchester became the Independent Order of Odd Fellows, Manchester Unity, will shed light on how the voluntary societies that scholars claim are so important for producing social trust in modern societies themselves become trustworthy.

★★★

Contrary to what most historians have assumed, the Odd Fellows did not begin their institutional life as a friendly society – instead they began as a convivial club. It is possible that clubs of Odd Fellows existed before the mid-eighteenth century, but documentary evidence of an earlier history does not exist.[16] The records that do exist begin in the 1780s. These late eighteenth- and early nineteenth-century newspaper reports and literary journal references make it clear that the Odd Fellows were very unlikely to become a "valuable national possession" and even less likely to speak on behalf of anyone. They were rarely in shape to speak for themselves. In a case heard at London Guildhall Sessions in 1801, for example, the jury refused to give "credit to some of the witnesses, they having declared themselves Members of a club, called Odd Fellows … "[17] To put it plainly, men joined the Odd Fellows to drink, and like other clubs at the time, to drink heavily.[18]

---

[14] *Fourth Report of the Commissioners Appointed to Inquire into Friendly and Benefit Building Societies*, P.P. 1874, (C 961), xxiii, pt 1, xxxiii.

[15] See the Webb's description of the Builders Union in Sidney Webb, Beatrice Webb, and Robert Alexander Peddie, *The History of Trade Unionism*, (London: Longmans, Green and Co., 1907), 110–117, and notes. For more on this point, see Weinbren and James, "Getting a Grip: The Roles of Friendly Societies in Australia and Britain Reappraised."

[16] A mid-nineteenth-century Odd Fellow apparently saw records from a lodge dating back to 1748, but the documents have not been found by modern historians. For the account of the lodge see Gosden, *The Friendly Societies in England, 1815–1875*, 3–4.

[17] "Guildhall Sessions," *The Morning Chronicle*, November 18, 1801.

[18] In 1802, William Clew, "a genteel young man" who "belonged to a society of Odd Fellows" was convicted of stealing two quart-pots and a measure. In his defense, Clew "lamented his having belonged to the society… in which he spent a great deal of money, and was so much in liquor at the time, that he did not know how the pots got into his pockets, &c." ("Old Bailey," *The Morning Chronicle*, July 20, 1802.)

It is worth emphasizing, however, that the Odd Fellows were not trying to become a friendly society, much less *the* model friendly society for a "generation of workingmen." Early members had enough money to burn; and they reveled in masculine drinking rituals and literary enhancements to those rituals.[19] What transformed them from a convivial club with a questionable reputation into the respectable friendly society they became were two historical contingencies. The first one pushed and the second one pulled the Odd Fellows out of the columns and magazines reserved for humor, wit, and occasionally ridicule and into the eminently respectable subscription lists supporting patriotic causes, and even into the civic processions that reinforced the social order in urban centers all over Britain.[20] Yet, what I will show in this chapter is that it was their convivial origins that gave the Odd Fellows the cultural resources they needed to forge a worldwide system of reciprocity.

By most accounts of their early days, the Odd Fellows were not just a convivial society – they were the quintessential convivial society. In the 1790s, for example, the *Attic Miscellany*, a magazine of wit, published with the express purpose of entertaining its readers by "mirroring" human nature in all of its comical glory, presented a series on the "numerous" convivial clubs of London, beginning with a "club of Odd Fellows."[21] The Odd Fellows were an apt club to begin with because their name was suggestive of the "odd" kinds of people attracted to London's many convivial clubs, which can be seen in the accompanying plate (Figure 4.1). It was also apt because the term "club of odd fellows" in this period was in fact a synonym for any convivial club.[22] John Britton, the author of the piece, was well placed to describe the convivial scene in London because he was a member of several such clubs, including the Odd Fellows. In his youth, when "finances allowed [he] frequented free-and-easy, odd fellows', and spouting clubs." Even though these were indeed different kinds of clubs, he painted them with the same brush – specifically as

---

[19] This kind of masculine sociability was not unique to eighteenth-century London; it was also practiced in early American towns. Rather than "odd fellow," the term used when American men caroused together, drinking, fighting, smoking, and gambling, was "jolly fellows." For more on the moral reform of such jolly fellowship, see Richard Briggs Stott, *Jolly Fellows: Male Milieus in Nineteenth-Century America, Gender Relations in the American Experience* (Baltimore: Johns Hopkins University Press, 2009).

[20] Gunn, *The Public Culture of the Victorian Middle Class: Ritual and Authority in the English Industrial City 1840–1914*; Peter Borsay, "'All the Town's a Stage': Urban Ritual and Ceremony 1660–1800," In *The Transformation of the English Provincial Towns 1600–1800*, Peter Clark, ed., (London: Hutchinson, 1984).

[21] "m," "Convivial Clubs," *The Attic Miscellany; or Characteristic Mirror of Men and Things*, no. 3 (London, 1791): 9.

[22] "NO GENIUS," "Increase of Genius," *St. James's Chronicle or the British Evening Post*, February 19, 1799.

Figure 4.1 "Meeting Night of the Club of Odd Fellows"
by John Barlow, 1789. "m," "Convivial Clubs," frontispiece
© London Metropolitan Archive, London, UK.

"associations of smokers, drinkers, and convivialists."[23] Britton clarified
the convivial nature of the Odd Fellows in the songbook he compiled in
1796, called the *Odd Fellow's Songbook*, which again was intended for use
in any convivial club. In his dedication to the "Man in the Moon," whom
he thanked for the "singular service" of illuminating the path for the many
drunken odd fellows leaving the tavern after club night, Britton wrote,
"the lovers of conviviality are distinguished by the name of Odd
Fellows ... Druids, Free and Easy clubs ... "[24]

The term "Odd Fellow" encapsulated the style of the London convivi-
ial club so well because it alone gave a sense of the wide variety of clubs

[23] John Britton and T. E. Jones, *The Auto-Biography of John Britton* (London, Printed for
the author, as presents to subscribers to "The Britton Testimonial," 1850), 73.
[24] John Britton, ed., *The Odd Fellows Songbook and Merry Medley: Containing a Numerous
Collection of Comical, Tragical, Farcical, Satirical, Pathetic and Convivial Songs...*
(London, 1796), v.

on offer, from the Freemasons at the most elite level to the Kit Kat and Mendicants' Clubs at the most scandalous to the Friends around the Cauliflower and the Club of Ugly Faces at the silliest.[25] Even clubs that were officially titled "Lodge" or "Society of Odd Fellows," used the term odd fellow in this way.[26] Thus, while Odd Fellow clubs most certainly gave occasional relief to necessitous members as most convivial clubs did in this period, they were best known as a drinking club.[27] And they were a popular one. By the late eighteenth century, it is clear that there were individual lodges scattered all over urban Britain, with at least three federations of Odd Fellows concentrated in London. By 1798, the United Order of Odd Fellows, for example, claimed thirty-nine lodges in the metropolis, two in Sheffield and one each in Wolverhampton, Birmingham, Shrewsbury, Windsor, Wandsworth, Canterbury, Liverpool, Richmond in Surrey, and Lewes.[28] We only know about these federations because in this period of revolutionary foment, the radical agitations of the Corresponding Society put all secret societies in a bad light. The elite members of the Freemasons, the king of secret societies, ensured that their organization was exempted from the repressive legislation of the period. The Odd Fellows did not have such political pull. Nevertheless, all clubs in this period were keen to avoid suspicion – even the Freemasons. Scholars suggest that it was at this point that the Freemasons shifted toward a less radical, more patriotic orientation in their organization.[29]

It could be a coincidence that only looks meaningful because of the paucity of sources, but the records that do exist suggest that it was this same moment that the Odd Fellows began to emphasize the more reputable aspects of their society. In 1791, when Britton wrote his piece for the *Attic*, the accompanying illustration openly depicted an Odd Fellow wearing a red cap, the paradigmatic emblem of the Jacobins, those members of the Jacobin Club that radicalized the French Revolution. See Figure 4.1. When describing the character in his image, Britton even joked that the Odd Fellow in the "red night-cap" is giving another

---

[25] Edward Ward, *A Compleat and Humorous Account of All the Remarkable Clubs and Societies in the Cities of London* ... (London, 1745).

[26] "An Arch Wag," *The Festival of Momus, or Complete Cabinet of Wit; Being a Curious Collection of Lively Repartees, Bon-Mots, Choice Puns, and* ... *Selected from the Port-Folios and Other Repositories of Fun, of the Lodge of Odd Fellows* (London, 1800).

[27] For more on the mutual aid provided in eighteenth century clubs, see Clark, *British Clubs and Societies*, 83.

[28] George Smith, *A Sermon, Delivered in the Parish Church of Sheffield, to the Original United Lodge of Odd Fellows, on Monday July 9, 1798* (Sheffield, 1798), 10.

[29] Harland-Jacobs, *Builders of Empire: Freemasons and British Imperialism, 1717–1927*, chapter 4.

Odd Fellow, "a staunch Whig," his views on the "religious revolution in France," much to the latter's secret glee.[30]

Britton was not here claiming that the Odd Fellows were actually a political society. He was writing for a general audience and was merely riffing on the conventional use of the term odd fellow in political satire. Only eight years later, however, with Britain now leading the war against Revolutionary France, the unfortunate association of odd fellow with "odd" politics was no longer inconsequential. In direct response to the shift in political climate, Odd Fellow lodges worked hard to distance themselves from the political connotations suggested by their name. The Original United Lodge in Sheffield of the United Order Odd Fellows, for example, asked Revd. George Smith, Curate of the Parish Church of Sheffield, to preach a public charity sermon specifically to clear them of such associations. The deputies for the lodge explained that "their purpose in coming to the worship of the established church was to convince the world, that [they] were neither associated to encourage antichristian or antimonarchical principles."[31] In the event, Smith took the opportunity to admonish them for their choice in name, which he found to be "equivocal and foolish," for their secrecy, and for the oath they swore which, he warned, made them susceptible to the "guidance and control of UNKNOWN SUPERIORS."[32] Smith thought the fact that the entire Order had subscribed to the relief fund for the widows and orphans left destitute by the war was to their credit. But their coming once to Church was neither "an expression of religion [n]or loyalty."[33]

The "anti-Jacobin" papers agreed. One reviewer wanted to know, given the Odd Fellows' significant membership numbers, "said to be amazingly great and rapidly increasing," what were "their political tenets?" The reviewer referred to the secret societies on the continent that were created to subvert all "the Governments of Europe" and wondered if the Odd Fellows might be formed for similar purposes, concluding that "appearances [were] against them."[34] In 1800, an unfortunate coincidence raised further questions about the Odd Fellows' loyalty. Under the headline "ATTEMPT TO ASSASSINATE HIS MAJESTY!", a correspondent to *Lloyd's Evening Post* related the details of an event, whereby a man

---

[30] "m," "Convivial Clubs," 11.

[31] Smith, *A Sermon, Delivered in the Parish Church of Sheffield, to the Original United Lodge of Odd Fellows, on Monday July 9, 1798*, 5–6.

[32] Ibid., 6.   [33] Ibid., 10.

[34] Urban Sylbanus, "Review of New Publications, No. 233," *The Gentleman's Magazine and Historical Chronicle* 68 (1798): 785–786; "Original Criticism, Art. XV," *Anti-Jacobin Review and Magazine* I, no. 1–6 (1799): 432–434.

called John Hadfield shot a pistol at, but thankfully missed hitting, King George III. When asked if he belonged to a political society, Hadfield said, no; "he belonged to a Club of Odd Fellows and a benefit society."[35] According to his testimony, he had hoped that the King's guards would kill him in an eighteenth-century version of "suicide-by-cop." All of the London and provincial papers carried the story. Whether it was due to the public questioning of their loyalty or the bad press more generally, from then on, when the Odd Fellows appeared in the papers it was most often in a list of subscribers for the "Defence of the Country," the "Patriotic," or one of the many "widows and orphans" funds created to help the families of the soldiers killed in the wars.[36] That is not to say that the Odd Fellows lost their reputation as a convivial society or one with suspicious political views, as Karl Marx had occasion to learn one drunken evening in London in the early 1850s.[37] And the term "odd fellow" did not lose its capacity for political satire. But the Society of Odd Fellows gained a new reputation for being a charitable as well as a loyal convivial society.

If the tense political climate of late eighteenth century pushed the Odd Fellows toward a more respectable appearance, there were demographic factors that pulled them more firmly into the regular practice of mutual aid between lodges. In the early 1800s, all the northern towns that experienced early industrialization, places like Manchester, Leeds, Birmingham, Liverpool, and Sheffield, saw a massive influx of migrants. Manchester, a small, market town at the beginning of the eighteenth century with around 10,000 inhabitants, had already become an important urban center by the end of the century with a population of nearly 90,000. As the cotton industry literally picked up steam, it attracted an amazing number of migrants. In fact, between 1800 and 1820, Manchester's population doubled.[38] One of those migrants brought Odd Fellowship to Manchester, and in the year 1810, he opened a club. There is some dispute about who founded it and whether the first lodge was the

---

[35] "ATTEMPT TO ASSASSINATE HIS MAJESTY!," *London Packet or New Lloyd's Evening Post*, May 14, 1800.

[36] "Voluntary Contributions at the Bank, for the Defence of the Country," *True Briton*, October 31, 1798; "Patriotic Fund," *Lloyd's Evening Post*, March 12, 1804; "Patriotic Fund," *The Morning Chronicle*, January 3, 1806.

[37] In his *Biographical Memoirs*, Wilhelm Liebknecht recounts an evening when he, Edgar Bauer, and Marx were "making a beer trip" on Tottenham Court Road when they encountered "loud singing" issuing from a public house; they "entered and learned that a club of Odd Fellows were celebrating a festival." They were invited in, got into a heated discussion with some Odd Fellows about politics, from which they barely escaped unbeaten. (Wilhelm Liebknecht, *Karl Marx: Biographical Memoirs*, trans. Ernest Untermann (Chicago: C.H. Kerr & Company, 1901), 146–150.)

[38] Alan J. Kidd, *Manchester* (Keele, Staffordshire: Ryburn, 1993), 22.

Abercrombie or the Victory Lodge.[39] Whatever the case, one thing is certain. Like the Odd Fellow clubs in London, the lodges of Odd Fellows in Manchester were popular, convivial clubs, so much so that a single lodge was not enough to accommodate all of the Mancunians who wanted to dress in costumes, sing songs, and drink together. As a result, the overflowing members dispersed themselves into five more lodges, which were opened in nearby pubs over the next few years.

There was clearly some relationship between the lodges in the early days but whether it was more than social in nature, involving the right to visit on club night, to join in each other's annual feasts, or to march in each other's processions is not clear. Each lodge controlled its own finances, and the fees that members paid were directed toward the social aspects of the club. As noted above, mutual aid was part of club life, as it was in most clubs of the day, but such relief was an outgrowth of the friendship between members rather than a regular feature of the club.[40] As they put it, the Odd Fellows "regard[ed] their Lodge as a Family of Brethren … " and bound themselves "under the most solemn obligation firmly to unite, sincerely to love, and inflexibly to stand by each other in sickness or in health; in poverty or in competence; in prosperity or in affliction."[41] "Mirth and Harmony," the term the Odd Fellows used as shorthand for creating and maintaining friendships, took the form of rituals, lectures, and recitations, all of which were interspersed with set toasts where the health of the lodge, its senior officers, and friendship itself were drunk. If one of these friends came into distress, help was certainly offered. But the emphasis for the early Odd Fellows was on the pleasurable aspects of friendship, especially ritualized drinking, as we have seen. When an Odd Fellow was in distress, help was "voluntarily bestowed," usually by subscription, and only when a member was "necessitous." Even then, he was "assisted [only] as far as circumstances will admit."[42]

Whether it was the pressure of increased necessity among members, the desire (or need) to become more respectable, or both, representatives

---

[39] For an account of the competing claims, see James Spry, *The History of Odd-Fellowship; Its Origin, Tradition, and Objects; with a General Review of the Results Arising from Its Adoption by the Branch Known as the Manchester Unity from the Year 1810 to the Present Time* (London: Fred Pitman, 1867), 4–5.

[40] Weinbren and James, "Getting a Grip: The Roles of Friendly Societies in Australia and Britain Reappraised," 88, 101.

[41] *Laws and Regulations of the Independent Order of Odd Fellows*, 1820, introduction.

[42] *Laws and Regulations of the Independent Order of Odd Fellows*, 1820, preface, Law # 1, 32. Lodges were at liberty to arrange their own financial situations. A lodge in York took a subscription any time a member asked for assistance. (*Laws & Regulations to Be Observed by the Brethren of the Loyal Lodge of the Ancient and Honorable Order of Independent Odd-Fellows, Held at … York* (York, 1821), See Rule # 11.)

from the six lodges in Manchester met in January of 1814 to figure out how to afford "each other mutual support, protection and advice and to consider the propriety of passing general laws."[43] This meeting would eventually mark the origin of what came to be the Independent Order of Odd Fellows, Manchester Unity. Yet, it was hardly apparent at the time. Examining the processes, both the successes and failures, through which six convivial lodges in Manchester accidentally became the head of an international organization will give a sense of the kinds of contingencies involved in its making.

★ ★ ★

The first thing the representatives did was to form a committee; they called it the Grand Lodge Committee. Everything the Grand Lodge Committee did in those early days was based on the assumption that they were already part of a larger, "Independent Order" and that they were merely bringing all the lodges into compliance with the rules and rituals of that Order.[44] The secretary used the term "Manchester District" when referring to their place in the structure of this Order. Their terminology for offices matched that used by the federations of Freemasons and the London Odd Fellows of the eighteenth century. The district offices they created were Grand Master, Deputy Grand Master, and Corresponding Secretary, which, in turn, mirrored the three highest offices in each lodge, that of Noble Grand, Vice Grand, and Secretary. The first man to hold the office of district Grand Master was John Christie and the fact that he quickly proved to be an unfortunate choice resulted in a surprising revelation. While there were many other Odd Fellow lodges operating throughout Britain, and perhaps some of them also referred to themselves as members of an "Independent Order," there were no meaningful connections between them, and there was definitely no one in charge of it. The committee only learned that

---

[43] *Minutes, and Other Documents of the Grand Committees of the Independent Order of Odd Fellows: Connected with the Manchester Unity, from January, 1814, to December, 1828, Inclusive* (Manchester: G. M. Mark Wardle, 1829), i. Weinbren and James argue that labor migration has always been "a major driver of fraternal association." (Weinbren and James, "Getting a Grip: The Roles of Friendly Societies in Australia and Britain Reappraised," 93.)

[44] See the entry for Feb. 4, 1814 in *Minutes, and Other Documents . . .* ,11. Late nineteenth century Odd Fellows believed that in 1813 the Manchester Unity had split from the United Order discussed above. There is no surviving documentary evidence that I know of, but since each lodge was self-instituted and grand lodges exercised no authority beyond local bounds in this period, it is entirely possible that such an affiliation existed. (Charles H. Brooks, *The Official History and Manual of the Grand United Order of Odd Fellows in America* (Philadelphia: Grand United Order of Odd Fellows, 1902), 7–10.)

their organization had no head because of Christie's autocratic leadership style and his propensity for using "abusive language" during meetings. It frustrated the other members enough to write to the entity they assumed to be the head of the Order. The letter went to the Mermaid Tap Lodge in London, the lodge that had apparently granted the original dispensation to open the Victory Lodge, one of those first six Manchester lodges. There is no record of any return correspondence from the Mermaid Tap, but its members very likely expressed some surprise upon receiving the inquiry. For just a few years later, the secretary of the Mermaid Tap wrote to Manchester asking if they could get copies of the general laws and lectures that had been printed by the Manchester committee so that they might sell them to other lodges in London. In other words, three years after the Manchester Grand Lodge Committee wrote to London thinking that the Mermaid Tap was the head of the Order, the Mermaid Tap wrote to the Manchester Grand Committee for the same reason.

The members of the Mermaid Tap got the impression that the Manchester Lodges were in charge in those three intervening years because of Manchester's centripetal demographic force. This boomtown had its most intense rate of growth of any decade in the nineteenth century in the 1820s, the very moment when the Manchester lodges were being looked to as the "head" of the Order.[45] Included in this human flood were people who had been Odd Fellows in their hometowns. They began knocking on lodge doors in and around Manchester, looking for relief and information about employment. From the records that exist, it seems that the Odd Fellows in Manchester were happy to relieve the occasional migrant and did so in the same ad hoc way they gave other forms of relief.[46] But when occasional and apparently legitimate requests turned into continual and sometimes obviously fraudulent claims, the Manchester District attempted to coordinate with distant lodges to create some kind of system to both deter interlopers and to help pay for the relief of travelers. But, again, they took these actions as a district, not as the head of an Order. Specifically, the Manchester district Corresponding Secretary, a man called Isaac Hardman, began writing to the migrants' home lodges to inquire about how they conducted their lodges and to suggest methods for safeguarding all Odd Fellows from imposters.[47] The fallout from the

---

[45] Asa Briggs, *Victorian Cities* (Harmondsworth: Penguin, 1977), 89.

[46] There were no specially designated funds for travel relief. For example, the Duke of York Lodge in Preston, whose minute book is the earliest extant record of a local lodge, simply notes the amount they had agreed to give (1s. and a bed for the night) and who the relieving officer would be for a given month. (Minute Book, Duke of York Lodge, No. 17, Nov. 29, 1820, DDX433/1, Lancashire Record Office.)

[47] See *Minutes, and Other Documents . . .*, (Sep 7, 1820) 97.

wave of migrating Odd Fellows seeking relief and Hardman's prolific letter writing was that the various Odd Fellow lodges that existed in Britain began hearing about an "Order" in Manchester and then acting, in turn, as though it existed. As word spread about the lodges in Manchester, lodges from all over Britain did what the Mermaid Tap had done. They wrote to the Grand Lodge Committee in Manchester asking them for instructions, for dispensations, and for copies of their general laws, lectures, and rituals.

But the Manchester Committee was not interested in being the head of a national Order and suggested that other lodges simply do what they had done in 1814 and set up their own districts with their own Grand Lodge Committees.[48] Because all roads seemed to lead to Manchester in these years, however, they were essentially forced into a leadership position, to which they eventually, albeit reluctantly, acceded.[49] They only did so because the steady stream of Odd Fellows migrating to Manchester had become a very real problem. Someone had to figure out how to ensure travel relief for legitimate Odd Fellows, on the one hand, and how to guard this system against fraud, on the other. The Committee could not simply divide the cost among the Manchester lodges because it would have left the Manchester Odd Fellows footing an enormous bill. And, because the Odd Fellows were not a legal society, they could not simply bring suit in court against parties trying to defraud them. The new system, then, would have to solve the problem of trust at a distance and trust between strangers simultaneously.

The key questions they would need to address in order to create this new system were: How could they distinguish true Odd Fellows from frauds? How would the migrant's relief be compensated and by whom? Did the receiving lodge have to pay for every traveler who knocked on its door? Would all the lodges in the Order pay a small amount periodically to equalize the cost the way the Freemasons did through the auspices of their Grand Lodge? Or, alternatively, would the cost be fully covered by the lodge that had sent the traveler, in the way poor relief was? Obviously, the upfront costs would be far higher in the lodges of northern industrial towns than elsewhere given the general direction of migration flows in this period. The potential for fraud was not restricted to northwestern, urban lodges, however. The Odd Fellows may have been a "secret society" but it was not

---

[48] In the summer of 1821, for example, the Caledonian Lodge in Leeds wrote asking for a dispensation from Manchester. The Committee responded with a letter addressed to all the lodges in Leeds announcing that the Manchester lodges had no intention of granting dispensations to lodges in Leeds, because they "believ[ed] the Leeds lodges competent to settle their own affairs, in a grand committee of the various lodges in their district." The very next entry in the minutes records a similar response given to similar letters from the lodges in Leicester. (*Minutes, and Other Documents* . . ., June 16, 1821.)

[49] Briggs, *Victorian Cities*, 96.

difficult to become a member and thus gain access to its secrets. Indeed, some unscrupulous people began joining lodges in one part of the country for the purpose of traveling to another at the expense of the Order.[50]

The Manchester Committee instituted some new practices in the hopes of preventing this and other kinds of frauds. As a first step, they tried to control more carefully the kind of people who were admitted, passing new rules stipulating that all new members had to be proposed by two current members of an existing lodge. After he was proposed, the Noble Grand, the leading officer of the lodge, and one of his supporting officers would conduct an inspection of the candidate's "character." This inspection involved traveling to his home, talking with his friends, neighbors, and employer. If the candidate had a good "character," his membership would be put to a vote of the lodge. If more than three members objected, he would be turned away without explanation. If accepted, a new member could not receive a travel certificate until he had been an Odd Fellow for twelve months. And even then, the Noble Grand of each lodge was instructed to be certain that the reason for travel was absolutely essential. The background investigation and probationary period would enable lodges to continue to admit strangers but would ensure that they were strangers of good character. After a year, they would no longer be strangers. These measures, it was hoped, would go some way in protecting each lodge against imposition.[51]

In addition to developing an extra-legal system that could guard against fraud – and as an important part of that system – the Manchester district faced the task of organizing the ever-increasing number of lodges seeking membership in the fledgling Order. By the early 1820s, there were more than eighty lodges seeking to be part of the system, now dispersed widely in Yorkshire, Hertfordshire, Nottinghamshire, Worcestershire, London, Scotland, and already one in America. By 1825, there were nearly 200 lodges associated with the original six, which added more than ten counties to the mix. (See Map 4.1) The distances between lodges are important to keep in mind because communication either by mail or in person was limited by the time it took a coach or boat to travel. In the early 1800s, for example, it took a mail coach twenty-eight hours to travel one-way from Manchester to London.[52] But it also

---

[50] *Minutes, and Other Documents ...*, 148. This problem became even more pronounced between the lodges in England and America, contributing to the split between the two branches. (Thomas Wildey, "Correspondence with America," *The Odd Fellows Magazine, New Series*, no. 11 (1830): 258.)

[51] "Character," as Margot Finn shows, was essential for policing the nineteenth-century credit economy, as well. (Margot C. Finn, *The Character of Credit: Personal Debt in English Culture, 1740–1914* (Cambridge: Cambridge University Press, 2003).)

[52] Kirstin Olsen, *Daily Life in 18th-Century England* (Westport, CT: Greenwood Press, 1999), 182.

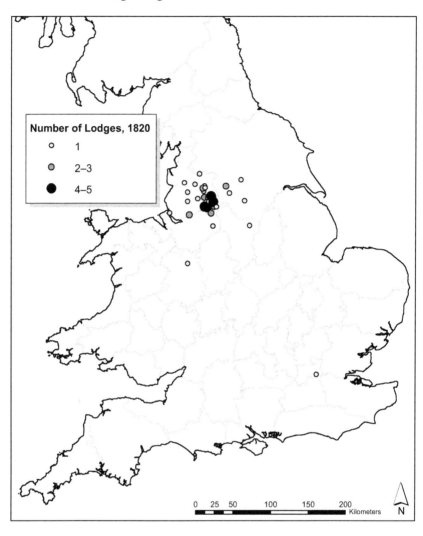

Map 4.1 Comparative Odd Fellow lodge distribution between 1820 and 1825.[53]

meant that the Manchester Grand Lodge Committee had to figure out how to run an organization encompassing great distances with people they only knew through letters. And they had to get all of these strangers

---

[53] Maps designed by Dr. Christine Bertoglio, October 15, 2017. Data drawn from *Minutes, and Other Documents* ..., throughout.

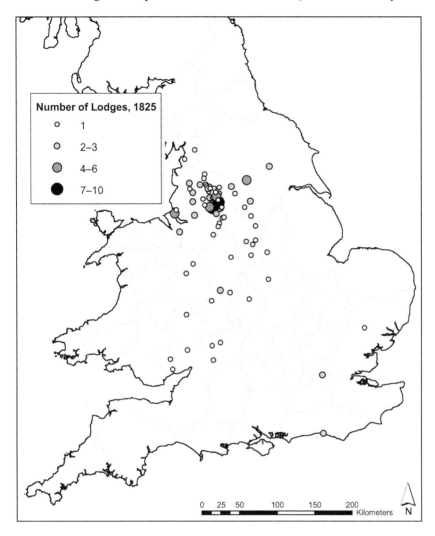

Map 4.1 (*cont.*)

to agree on common practices that would keep imposters from defrauding lodges.

At this point the Freemasons had already established a highly successful model for creating an international system of reciprocity.[54] The hierarchical Grand Lodge system, using travel cards, passwords, and

[54] Clark, *British Clubs and Societies*, 348–349.

arcane knowledge to distinguish true Masons from frauds acted as a kind of "passport," giving members access to mutual aid "in all parts of the empire."[55] The Odd Fellows in Manchester were familiar with this system and used aspects of it when creating their district. But their early efforts to subordinate all the lodges in Britain to this same hierarchical structure ended in an attempted coup by one of their own Manchester lodges.[56] Coordinating a national system of travel relief proved far more challenging than simply asserting authority and instituting a uniform set of rules and practices. It required a moral commitment on the part of Odd Fellows all over the country to act in compliance with a system that was still in the process of being created. The minutes from the early days of this organization reveal outright distrust on the part of member lodges. From their perspective, Manchester had no more claim to authority over the Order than any other lodge.

Because top down solutions ended in failure, the Manchester Committee tried working from the bottom up. Between the reluctance on the part of Manchester to take charge and the insistence on the part of other regions that they have a say in things, rule by committee became a permanent feature of the Order. There would be no executive and, in particular, no Grand Lodge. In their own words, "that the name grand lodge be no more encouraged in Manchester, the late [events] ... having brought the title of grand lodge into contempt among us."[57] A committee of all the representatives would make decisions concerning laws and practices democratically. Any member could bring a grievance or new regulation to be heard by the whole committee. General Laws could even be appealed "where they interfere with ... local circumstances."[58] Rule-by-committee would be made more inclusive by rotating the location of the annual committee meeting. After the first Annual Grand Committee, held in Manchester in 1822, the annual meeting would meet in a different district each year so that it would be more convenient for representatives

---

[55] Harland-Jacobs, *Builders of Empire: Freemasons and British Imperialism, 1717–1927*, 3.

[56] A similar instance illustrating their lack of authority came after Corresponding Secretary Hardman wrote a very reasonably worded letter to the London lodges asking for ideas about protecting the Order against fraud. He suggested that perhaps lodges in close proximity break themselves into districts like the Manchester lodges had and then coordinate their efforts through a Grand Lodge for each district. In response, the London lodges declared themselves the "Grand Lodge of England." (*Minutes, and Other Documents ...*, (Sept. 7, 1820) 101.)

[57] *Minutes, and Other Documents ...*, (May 30, 1822) 145.

[58] *Minutes, and Other Documents ...*, (June 5, 1823) 157. This rule enabled a great deal of local latitude for dealing with issues throughout the nineteenth century that would have been contentious if national conformity had been required. Welsh lodges used it to justify their translation of the Order's literature into Welsh, for example, and to hold lodge nights in their own language. It was also used to enable clubs with a preponderance of Jewish members to hold meetings on Sundays rather than Saturdays.

Table 4.1. Locations of Annual Movable Committees
(1822–1845)

1822	Manchester	1834	Hull
1823	Hanley	1835	Kendal
1824	Haslingden	1836	Derby
1825	Huddersfield	1837	London
1826	Manchester	1838	Rochdale
1827	Nottingham	1839	Birmingham
1828	Dudley	1840	York
1829	Sheffield	1841	Isle of Man
1830	Leeds	1842	Wigan
1831	Liverpool	1843	Bradford
1832	Monmouth	1844	Newcastle
1833	Bury	1845	Glasgow

from lodges outside of Manchester to attend. And beginning in 1823, its name was officially changed from the Annual Grand Committee to the Annual Moveable Committee (AMC). (See Table 4.1 for a list of the cities in which the AMC was held.)

The resultant cellular structure and government-by-committee did have the effect of soothing "conflicting passions," as the Committee members had hoped.[59] But it failed to create active unity between the lodges. Given the lack of a strong central authority, much depended on the willingness of the lodges to comply with the rules. The Manchester Grand Lodge Committee had learned that they could suspend benefits with some effect. But their ultimate disciplinary mechanism was expulsion, which, of course, did little to promote cooperation. For their part, individual lodges had different reasons for wanting to be a part of an Order, but few of these reasons were particularly conducive to solidarity on a national level. Some lodges were keen to be a part of the Order so that they could have the benefits of travel relief as well as visiting rights.[60] And they were happy to comply with whatever decisions were made there as long as their members were relieved when tramping. Others preferred to be left alone once they had their own copy of the Order's literature. On the other extreme, some lodges were offended by the new system. As we will see, certain lodges in London and Leeds bristled, and finally rebelled, against the Order because they wanted more power.

---

[59] *Minutes, and Other Documents . . .* , (Dec. 1, 1821) 120.
[60] J. Burn, *An Historical Sketch of the Independent Order of Oddfellows M.U.* (Manchester: John Heywood, 1845), 29; "Biography: Robert Naylor, P. G. M.," *The Odd Fellows' Magazine* (1840–1841), 394.

Figure 4.2 Graph showing the number of lodges opened by publicans[61]

Still others wanted the connection as an enticement to build local lodge membership and, thus, custom in their pubs. Publicans opened a large proportion of new lodges seeking to join the Order. In 1822, for example, publicans opened over half of the new lodges recorded in the Committee minute book. This trend continued into the late 1820s (Figure 4.2). This is not to say that the motives of these publicans when opening new lodges were exclusively profit driven. As we saw in Chapter 3, publicans were well positioned to take on such a role because of the place they occupied in the credit nexus. Instead, I want to emphasize that their reasons for belonging to the Order did not necessarily include a strong allegiance to Manchester or to the emergent Order.

The success of the new travel relief procedures depended heavily on the bond the individual lodge and the individual member felt toward the Order. As we have seen, these bonds were not uniformly strong. Not surprisingly, frauds continued unabated, leaving the Committee at a loss for how to proceed. They even resorted to requiring a representative from each lodge to "take an obligation from the grand committee...not to deliver the quarterly pass word to any officer or brother, except belonging to his own lodge, and not unto them, unless they are clear on the books ... "[62] The minute entry concludes by threatening

---

[61] Data drawn from *Minutes, and Other Documents* ... , throughout.
[62] *Minutes, and Other Documents* ..., (Dec. 12, 1822) 152.

expulsion to lodges or brothers who did not comply. Manchester's solution to their lack of strong central control or strong bonds to hold the Order together, in other words, was to direct members to report to Manchester in person to swear an oath that they would comply by the rules of the Order of which they were already sworn members. And if they refused to make this journey and this oath, they were to be expelled.

At the end of 1822, then, the Manchester district had developed the structural elements needed to govern a national institution, and yet the institution, as such, could hardly be said to exist. They had extended their district structure to include the entire Order; they had weathered their first coup and applied the lessons learned; they had developed common practices; and they had a monopoly on the printing of the Order's literature. And while some lodges complied with some things, most complied with none. Even lodges in Manchester refused to adopt the travel certificates designed and printed by Manchester, or to pay toward the expenses of running the district, much less the Order.[63] Other lodges continued to give the password out in open lodge; some lodges refused to contribute toward the travel relief of distant strangers; some even refused to relieve the migrants who showed up at their doors; and still others relieved expelled brothers in spite of repeated warnings from Manchester. Uniformity without the authority to enforce it was meaningless.

Things began to change, however, when the representatives from all the lodges met at the newly instituted Annual Moveable Committee (AMC) in 1823. The members attending this first AMC gathered in a pub centrally located in the West Midland town of Hanley. Instead of a few officers circumscribed by their local vision of how to proceed and making decisions for other people they did not know, ninety-eight deputies from lodges all over the country sat in a room together, listening and responding to each other's concerns. Slowly, in fits and starts, they began to figure out how to make the Order work. Ironically, the committee structure, which had made it impossible to garner compliance when it was the exclusive purview of Mancunians, became the mechanism through which the deputies slowly developed allegiance to the Order. In the context of this Annual Moveable Committee meeting, which for lack of a workable alternative resembled a lodge room more than anything else, the efforts to create a unity that was binding on all the members shifted away from developing uniform practices and penalties and toward forging a brotherhood and the moral bonds that would make

---

[63] *Minutes, and Other Documents ...*, (Dec. 12, 1822) 153.

it meaningful. In other words, they would make the Odd Fellows a friendly society in the more capacious sense of the term.

★★★

The shift from structuring the Order institutionally toward unifying a brotherhood morally and socially is clearly discernable in the Committee minutes from the early 1820s. Although nothing but these minutes remain from these early AMCs, John Elsom, the Corresponding Secretary for the Nottingham District, explained the rationale behind the new ethos. "A faithful adherence to our Order at present," he wrote, "depends chiefly upon the honour of those who compose its numbers, and although we consider this motive as a most sacred tie, yet so varied are our notions respecting it...that it is utterly impossible it can with like verity be by all regarded."[64] Instead of simply insisting on uniformity of their very diverse parts, which had failed over and over again, the solution the deputies adopted at the AMCs between 1823–1825 was to take the ultimate goal of unity as their guiding principle. More specifically, with the local lodge as their model, they enlarged its moral precepts and ritual life to encompass the entire Order. Cooperation within a lodge was maintained through conviviality and mutual charity.[65] Unity in the Order would be promoted through reoriented and slightly moralized versions of the same methods.

The most important unifying ritual in the lodge was the initiation ceremony. In these early days, Odd Fellows called for an elaborate scene where the initiate, arms bound behind his back and stripped completely naked except for his blindfold was led into the lodge room, which had been darkened for the ceremony. The room was kept completely silent. The other members were "masked in some strange mask, such as a wolf, a pig a horse, a nondescript, &c."[66] The officers were outfitted in the elaborate regalia appropriate to their office, long robes trimmed with the color of the degree to which they had been initiated. The candidate was made to travel an imaginary road strewn with dangers. The obstacles included a (simulated) rockslide, dark forest, trial by fire, and a tempest. The conductors traveled with the initiate "to prevent fatal injuries

---

[64] John Elsom, "To the Editor," *The Odd Fellows' Magazine* (1828–1831), 8.

[65] This was true for individual friendly societies as well. For more on this point, see Gosden, *The Friendly Societies in England, 1815–1875*, 115–137; Cordery, *British Friendly Societies, 1750–1914*, 181; Green and Cromwell, *Mutual Aid or Welfare State: Australia's Friendly Societies*, 38–49.

[66] *The Complete Manual of Oddfellowship: Being a Practical Guide to Its History, ... Ceremonies, Etc.* (London: Privately printed for A. Lewis, 1879), 278.

befalling" him. After each turn of the circuit where the conductors made sure he was exposed to the danger, they quickly protected him from it. When the blindfold was removed, "the first object that caught his visual organ was the point of a naked sword close to his seat of love." A "death scene" with a coffin and skeleton were also pushed into his view. Following the ceremony, "each member pledged the newly initiated brother in a flowing glass, for which he had the honour of paying."[67]

Before the reforms enacted during the Annual Moveable Committees in the 1820s, the manner in which this ceremony was carried out varied from lodge to lodge.[68] And since "Mirth and Harmony" were the stated goals of the society, the ritual seems to have been carried out to maximize the discomfort of the initiate and also the amusement of the other brothers. In some lodges, they actually came close to burning the initiate with the fire and many doused the candidate with a tub of water to "symbolize" the tempest. In some unfortunate cases, initiations were given in a kind of physical shorthand. In 1809, for example, six London Odd Fellows were indicted and fined £10 in a London court for beating a new initiate "unmercifully with pieces of rope, knotted hankerchiefs, &c. and the poor fellow being all this time confined in such a manner that he could not perceive who struck him ... "[69] James Burn, an Odd Fellow historian in the 1840s, described the old "making ceremony" as "the most stupid ridiculous nonsense, without anything to recommend it, but it's downright foolery and unmeaning frivolity."[70] Indeed, it was considered so entertaining that the *Dictionary of the Vulgar Tongue* recommended becoming an Odd Fellow, if only to witness this ceremony.[71] Momus and Comus, the gods of mockery and revelry, reigned supreme

---

[67] Burn, *An Historical Sketch of the Independent Order of Oddfellows M.U.*, 19. Burn's account matches the description of the initiation ceremony of the Patriotic Order of Odd Fellows from 1797 printed in *The Complete Manual of Oddfellowship: Being a Practical Guide to Its History, ... Ceremonies, Etc.*, 273–289. And the various revisions made to it by the Manchester District Committee (and later the AMCs) suggest that it was the same ceremony. See, for example, *Minutes, and Other Documents ...*, 149. The Duke of York Lodge in Preston conducted a valuation of their "regalia" which included, a "death seen [sic] and all that belong to it," "coffen," chain, and many other symbols associated with the ritual as it is described in *The Complete Manual of Oddfellowship*. See entry for Oct. 10, 1826 in Minute Book, Duke of York Lodge, No. 17, 1816–1838, Lancashire Record Office, DDX 433/1.

[68] Minute Book, Duke of York Lodge, No. 17, 1816–1838.

[69] Reprinted from a London Paper, "Union Hall," *Connecticut Herald*, Nov. 28, 1809, 2.

[70] Burn, *An Historical Sketch of the Independent Order of Oddfellows M.U.*, 18.

[71] See definition for Oddfellows. Francis Grose, *A Dictionary of the Vulgar Tongue; a Dictionary of Buckish Slang, University Wit and Pickpocket Eloquence* (London, 1811).

and the fears of the initiate-now-brother were drowned in "a loud laugh, the rude jest, or the boisterous chorus of a bacchanalian song."[72]

Most initiation ceremonies share a common structure. And certainly, those derived from either the Freemasons or the craft guilds, as this one likely was, had many commonalities.[73] In general, these rites of passage work by exposing the initiate to some sort of humiliation or trial, where he or she is put face-to-face with the perils of the world. The trial might be real or contrived, but in either case, it is meant to mark the transition from outsider to insider, from initiate to full member.[74] For the Odd Fellows, the nature of the trial mattered less than the meaning then given to it.[75] It is not clear if any changes were made to the actual ceremony detailed above when the Odd Fellows began making reforms in the early AMCs. But in an effort to emphasize the solemnity of the obligation new members took after the ritual, the 1823 AMC voted to take the word Momus out of the making song, which was sung right before the initiate took the oath.[76] Although a seemingly slight change, this song acted as the transition from the ritual trial to the oath, and as such set the tone for how the new brother approached his future obligations. In place of Momus, they inserted "true honour's court is here," reflecting John Eslom's comments about the importance of honor above. They also replaced "mirth" with "reason" in a subsequent line, suggesting that the brothers were meant to take the whole ceremony more seriously.

> Brothers attentive stand,
> While our Most Worthy Grand
> Gives you the charge;
> the bonds of society
> are friendship and harmony;
> Honour and secrecy
> Will us unite.

---

[72] Burn, *An Historical Sketch of the Independent Order of Oddfellows M.U.*, 19.

[73] As one of the founding Odd Fellows explained, "The order of Odd Fellows was originally instituted on the Masonic principle, the object of which is to cement more firmly the bonds of social feeling and sympathetic intercourse between man and man." ("Waterloo, Monmouth," *The Odd Fellows' Magazine* (1828–1831), 146.)

[74] Colin Blakemore and Sheila Jennett, *Initiation Rites* (Oxford: Oxford University Press, 2009), www.encyclopedia.com/doc/1O128-initiationrites.html.

[75] In the early part of the century, American Odd Fellows had rituals that were similar to the British Odd Fellows. For more on the American Odd Fellows, see Yoni Appelbaum, "*The Guilded Age: The American Ideal of Association, 1865–1900*" (Waltham, MA: Brandeis University, 2014); Mark C. Carnes, *Secret Ritual and Manhood in Victorian America* (New Haven: Yale University Press, 1989). For some skepticism about the links between freemasonry and friendly societies, see James, "Problems with U.K. and U.S. Odd Fellow Literature."

[76] *Minutes, and Other Documents . . .*, (Mar. 3, 1823) 149.

Brothers you've nought to fear
~~Momus's~~ True honour's court is here,
Love, mirth, and joy;
Loyalty here abounds,
and ~~mirth~~ Reason our ev'ning crowns;
Let ev'ry voice resound
Long live the King.[77]

After the song, the candidate swore an oath to his new brothers.[78] A great deal depended on this obligation. As noted above, the relief the Odd Fellows gave to members in distress was not calculated in advance. It was collected and given ad hoc as an act of mutual charity, a gift from one's brothers and friends. When the axe was passed, Odd Fellows gave according to their means – that is to say, what they could afford at the moment the need arose. In an economy marked by mutual indebtedness and a serial, though usually temporary, lack of liquidity, this could vary from day to day. When the tables were turned, an Odd Fellow who had given would be in a position to receive. Keeping one's word to relieve others also had benefits beyond a return of help in distress. Even in good times, Odd Fellows bound themselves to "prefer an Odd Fellow to any other in all [his] dealings."[79] The Order followed this same ethic, purchasing all of its printed materials, flags, and other regalia from Odd Fellows who specialized in those occupations.

In addition to obligating the new member to his now brothers, the oath taken after initiation also played a role in protecting the lodge against fraud. Because they had no legal rights, the Odd Fellows had to use internal rather than legal means of enforcing the word of a brother. One of the penalties associated with breaking any part of the oath was a form of blacklisting. The brother in question would be excluded from lodges and custom not just in his own town, but wherever Odd Fellow lodges existed. As a member would later explain, "We compel, under pain of *fraternal displeasure*, our members to act justly in their intercourse with the world and each other, in cases where *legal enactments* cannot reach."[80] (First emphasis is mine.) If a brother not only broke his promise to the lodge

---

[77] *Laws and Regulations of the Independent Order of Odd Fellows*, "Admission of a Brother" song appears after the laws. The old making song still appears in *Laws & Regulations to Be Observed by the Brethren of the Loyal Lodge of the Ancient and Honorable Order of Independent Odd-Fellows, Held at ... York*, 10.

[78] The oath was administered after the making ritual until 1834 when the prosecution of the "Tolpuddle Martyrs" motivated the Manchester Unity to replace the oaths with promises. See Spry, *The History of Odd-Fellowship*, 36.

[79] *The Complete Manual of Oddfellowship: Being a Practical Guide to Its History, ... Ceremonies, Etc.*, 282.

[80] Joseph Burrows, "American Correspondence," *The Odd Fellows' Magazine* (1835–1837), 8.

but went further and imposed upon the Order, he would "be branded with infamy such as [his] unworthy conduct would deserve." His name would be sent to every lodge in the Order as someone to shun.[81] This information was even shared with the Freemasons, whose geographic reach was even broader than the Odd Fellows in this period.[82]

Once an initiate became a member, the General Laws of the Order (and the lodge byelaws drawn from them) established the framework for cooperation within the lodge. Rules guiding and fines enforcing lodge etiquette – how to address the officers; referring to each other as brother; when to come and go from the lodge room; not interrupting or reading or sleeping or whispering when someone else was speaking or singing; not talking about politics or religion; not fighting or swearing; and so on – were all geared toward minimizing conflict in the lodge.[83]

While the rules promoted cooperation by delineating what not to do, the different degrees a brother could achieve gave members positive examples of how to relate to each other. Infused with the language of brotherhood and masculine friendship and illustrated through nonsectarian versions of biblical stories, the lectures for each degree explained how the obligations of mutuality worked in different contexts. The White degree, the one all initiates were required to take, used the relationship between Jonathan and David to exemplify the type of loyal friendship to which an Odd Fellow was committing himself. It is worth emphasizing that they did not simply rely on generalized notions of friendship from the broader culture, which, as we have seen, were extremely important. They taught each other the specific duties of the kind of friendship necessary to be an Odd Fellow. The lessons of this degree gave new members a clear method of thinking about the way in which they were expected to act when one of their brothers was in need, and could expect, in turn, to be treated when they were in need.

By contrast, the higher-level Royal Blue Degree, given to more senior brothers, was meant to teach brotherly love not just toward members of the lodge but also to extend that love outward to anyone in need. The Royal Blue degree used the story of the Good Samaritan to teach an Odd

---

[81] For some examples of fraternal displeasure in action, see *Minutes, and Other Documents* . . ., (Sep. 7, 1820) 96, (Dec. 13, 1824).

[82] *Minutes, and Other Documents* . . ., (July 12, 1815) 30–31. The Freemasons shared information with the Odd Fellows in turn. A minute entered in 1815 reads "that in consequence of information received from the Masonic grand lodge, John Wood never be admitted into our order." (*Minutes, and Other Documents* . . ., (Jan. 27, 1815), 21.)

[83] For an 1820 version of the General Laws, see *Laws and Regulations of the Independent Order of Odd Fellows*. For an example of the byelaws used in a lodge see Minute Book, Duke of York Lodge, No. 17, 1816–1838.

Fellow to relieve distress wherever he found it. The Odd Fellows often distinguished themselves from "ordinary" friendly societies or sick clubs in this way. As one Odd Fellow explained to a Magistrate who thought they were a fraudulent organization, "an odd fellow feels himself bound, according to the principles of his Order, ..., to render aid whenever necessity requires it ... ."[84] This was true when the object of charity was a brother, a distressed lodge of brothers, the widow or orphan of a brother – or even a need that was unrelated to the Order. More than just guides for behavior, however, these lectures gave Odd Fellows a fraternal language through which they could and did settle disputes between members, between lodges, and within the Order more generally.[85] Furthermore, when the lectures were standardized at the 1823 AMC, the specialized knowledge contained in them gave members throughout the Order a means of testing strangers in order to distinguish real Odd Fellows from imposters.[86]

When the rules penalizing disagreeable behavior and the lectures promoting brotherly love failed, which they often did, the Odd Fellows relied upon the drinking culture that gave rise to their clubs to restore harmony in the lodge. Indeed, the act of drinking as a group in an Odd Fellow lodge was called "proceeding to harmony." It was this practice in particular that would draw the most sustained criticism from middle class reformers, as well as the wives of members. Writing about how lodge nights were conducted in England, American Odd Fellow Henry Stillson explained, "when any important event took place, or the bickerings and unpleasantness of the times crept into the meetings, and when it looked stormy, the lodge immediately 'proceeded to harmony;' when, after a brief session, quietness was restored."[87] In the late eighteenth and

---

[84] R. Hawkin, "A Dialogue," *The Odd Fellows' Magazine* (1828–1831), 204.

[85] Although the content of the lectures was supposed to be kept secret, contributors to the magazine (beginning in 1824) used phrases taken from the different lectures in their efforts to resolve the various disputes between lodges. See, for example, "To the Independent Order," *The Odd Fellows' Magazine* (1824), 6–12. An example of a full lecture can be seen in "Lecture on the Emblems," *The Odd Fellows' Magazine* (1828–1831), 26–32. I borrowed the insight about the lectures providing the Odd Fellows with a new language for cooperation from Mary-Ann Clawson's work on Freemasonry in the U.S. (Clawson, *Constructing Brotherhood: Class, Gender, and Fraternalism*, 76.)

[86] So critical was the role the lectures played in this respect, the AMC recommended that lodges protect lecture books and passwords in a box with two keys each held by different officers. (*Minutes, and Other Documents ...*, (Mar. 3, 1823) 150.) As we will see later in the chapter, the American and British Orders of Odd Fellows split because they could not agree to use the same set of lectures.

[87] H. L. Stillson, *The Official History and Literature of Odd Fellowship: The Three-Link Fraternity* (Norwood, MA: Norwood Press, 1897), 276.

early nineteenth century, the Odd Fellows were not unique in this respect. In his history of *Drink and the Victorians*, Brian Harrison quotes Lord Shaftesbury to show "how many quarrels and animosities have been made up by meeting at the convivial dinner-table."[88] Peter Clark also argues that rules guiding behavior and group drinking performed important unifying functions in British clubs up and down the social hierarchy.[89]

In the 1820s, however, there was a marked shift in the relationship that respectable British culture had with drinking, as much for what it said about the character of a person as for the behavior to which excessive drinking could lead. The elite clubs proliferating at this time began to adopt rules of "proper decorum" and modeled "an idealized moral self" for members to follow, and by the end of the decade, respectable clubs were doing away with drinking altogether.[90] To be a respectable man in this period meant controlling one's self in public as well as the semi-public space of the club. The American Odd Fellows also made a decided turn toward total abstinence. They saw conviviality as "utterly at variance with the respectability, dignity and consequent usefulness" of Odd Fellowship, and so outlawed drinking altogether while increasing the emphasis they put on the Christian aspects of their lectures and rituals.[91] For the British Odd Fellows, there was certainly room for improvement in this area. As we saw, the predominant goal of an eighteenth century Odd Fellow lodge had been conviviality, with particular emphasis on drinking. This trend continued into the early nineteenth century, as well. It was the reason that the first six lodges in Manchester were opened. And even as those lodges joined together to start providing mutual aid to each other, the early Manchester district minutes attest to fact that liquor continued to be an integral part of being an Odd Fellow.[92]

---

[88] Brian Harrison, *Drink and the Victorians: The Temperance Question in England 1815–1872* (London: Faber and Faber, 1971), 42, 44.

[89] Clark, *British Clubs and Societies*, 225–229. For more on the good relations promoted by drinking together, see Keith Wrightson, "Alehouses, Order and Reformation in Rural England, 1590–1660," In *Popular Culture and Class Conflict, 1590–1914: Explorations in the History of Labour and Leisure*, eds. Eileen Yeo and Stephen Yeo (Atlantic Highlands, NJ: Humanities Press, 1981), 6; Hailwood, *Alehouses and Good Fellowship in Early Modern England*, 114.

[90] Roberts, *Making English Morals: Voluntary Association and Moral Reform in England, 1787–1886*; Gunn, *The Public Culture of the Victorian Middle Class: Ritual and Authority in the English Industrial City 1840–1914*, 77, 95.

[91] A. D. Meacham, Special Deputy Grand Sire quoted In Stillson, *The Official History and Literature of Odd Fellowship: The Three-Link Fraternity*, 524.

[92] Fines were paid in liquor; when the Grand Master visited another lodge, his expenses were paid in liquor; the leading officers of a district were allowed so many quarts of liquor per committee meeting, and so on. (*Minutes, and Other Documents . . .*, (July 11,

Some of the reforms made during the AMCs that took place in the 1820s suggest that Odd Fellows were also part of the more general shift away from alcohol-based conviviality. In 1823, drinking was disallowed during the time when either rituals or the other "business of the lodge" was taking place. The same rules were applied to district committee meetings.[93] In 1822, the Committee had called for a revision to the *Odd Fellows Song Book* (or *Harmonia*), requesting that members send in "any amendment, addition or alteration, new or old song, recitation, toast, sentiment &c, for consideration ... and that it be generally understood, such songs, recitations, etc., be of a moral, chaste, and instructive nature."[94] It makes sense that the Committee would want to introduce a morally upright tone into the lodge as part of the larger effort to improve solidarity and guard against impositions.

And yet a comparison of the *Harmonia* used in 1820, that includes handwritten songs alongside the official songs, with the revised version, suggests that strict temperance does not adequately capture the goal of the changes.[95] Given the Odd Fellows' early convivial reputation and the moral reforms the Committee called for, one might expect to find some boisterous if not indecent songs among at least the handwritten songs of the older edition. Instead, the printed songs in the earlier edition extolled the virtues of friendship, brotherly love, harmony, and Odd Fellowship. Though more general in scope, the handwritten songs were no less innocuous in nature. The new edition, too, contained many morally uplifting songs. Odd Fellowship was praised over and over (and over) again for thirty-seven pages, songs printed two columns to a page. But added to these "Songs of the Order," were eight extra sections that were also uplifting – but in a different way. These sections were titled "Sentimental Songs," "Amatory Songs," "Naval Songs," "Bacchanalian

---

1816) 42.) For example, in 1817, the Grand Master was allotted one shilling for visiting a lodge and it was "to come in in liquor." (*Minutes, and Other Documents* ..., (Apr. 3, 1817) 56.)

[93] *Minutes, and Other Documents* ..., (May 19–20, 1823) 154.

[94] *Minutes, and Other Documents* ..., (Mar. 3, 1823) 151.

[95] The only copy of the earlier edition that I have come across belonged to a shoemaker from the village of Baxenden in Lancashire called James Smith, originally initiated into the Prosperity Lodge in 1820. Smith bound his copy of the printed *Harmonia* with a piece of leather, holding it together with the general laws of the Order, the laws of his local lodge, and a great many blank sheets on which he added more songs, recitations, and anecdotes in his own hand. Therefore, not only can a comparison between the official versions of the songbook be made but also between those versions and the songs one might actually have heard sung in an Odd Fellows lodge. (*The Independent Odd Fellows' Harmonia: Comprising Songs, Epilogues, Dialogues, Prologues, &c., Also a List of Lodges* (Rochdale, 1820), DDX 177/20, Lancashire Record Office.)

Songs," "Sporting Songs," "Comic Songs," "Scotch Songs," and "Irish Songs." The Bacchanalian songs could not truthfully be classed as immoral except by the most extreme teetotalers. But to the extent that they were instructive, they taught members how best to appreciate their drink. "Bacchus, God of rosy wine, / Shed your influence Divine; / Fill to the brim the sprightly bowl, / Nought but wine can cheer the soul" is just one example.[96] The reforms instituted by the 1823 AMC, then, resulted in a renewed emphasis on conviviality rather than the reverse.

The Odd Fellows did not follow the general cultural trend away from drinking because they faced a problem that other organizations did not. Specifically, the Odd Fellows were trying to figure out how to take the social obligations that were so effective within the face-to-face meetings of local lodges and extend them both to the members of distant lodges and to the Order more generally. The problem of travel relief was dependent not only on the internal harmony of a lodge, but also on the ability to extend that harmony to the Order. Because the act of drinking together was "the symbol of human interdependence," the Odd Fellows sought to enhance the role it played in local lodges while at the same time enlarging it to include the larger organization.[97]

Obviously, the entire Order could not literally perform the act of group drinking. But Odd Fellows could perform it symbolically in the same way most associations expressed their local solidarity with the nation – through toasts.[98] The toasts found in the 1820 edition of the Odd Fellows' *Harmonia* were similar to those drunk in most of the clubs of the late eighteenth and early nineteenth centuries.[99] A good number of these toasts expressed the desire for social harmony within the lodge, "May the gentle spirit of love, animate the breast of every Odd Fellow," or "May the hearts of Odd-fellows agree, though their heads may differ," or "May Odd-fellows lodges be distinguished for love, peace and harmony." The rest exalted the virtues of good will in general. "Friendship

---

[96] Note this is from the 1836 edition which had been revised for the second time in 1835. The compilers explained that they sought to "insert such a description of songs as will afford the greatest and most pleasing variety, and at the same time to leave out those of an immodest character." *The Independent Order of Odd Fellows' Harmonia, Being a Choice Collection of Songs, Original and Selected … with an Appendix of Original Toasts and Sentiments for the Use of the Order* (Manchester: 1836), iv.

[97] Harrison, *Drink and the Victorians*, 44.

[98] For a particularly good example of how these toasts to the order were actually conducted, see the description of the Lord Nelson Lodge's anniversary feast in "Anniversary of the Loyal Nelson Lodge, Kendal," *The Odd Fellows' Magazine* (1828–1831), 92.

[99] Clark, *British Clubs and Societies*, 269, 304–305.

to a few and good-will to all," ... "May the hinges of hospitality never grow rusty" ... "A warm house, a snug estate, and an agreeable wife to every Odd-fellow."[100] Yet, while the toasts found in the revised edition also included calls for harmony and good will to all, they added very specific toasts to the Order, its officers, its laws, to specific lodges, and even to specific towns. Thus, at the same time lodge harmony was promoted through singing and drinking, so too was the unity of the entire Order. Its structure was conjured in many of the new toasts, as were the relationships between the different aspects of the Order. For example, one toast reads "The _____ Lodge, and may it blossom as the rose, and its usefulness be appreciated throughout the Order."[101] In this way, the harmony an Odd Fellow felt, and the obligations he took, were extended to incorporate distant Odd Fellows as well. In a very real sense, then, the Order – whose general laws gave it an as yet unenforceable legal framework – was given a social life in the minds of members when they drank to its health.

The bonds established in the lodge were performed publicly in the ceremonies surrounding lodge anniversaries, the opening of new lodges, Odd Fellow funerals, and a great variety of local events in which the Odd Fellows participated.[102] The standard mode of celebrating each of these events was not unique to the Odd Fellows; it involved a procession, a charity sermon, and a dinner.[103] Members would meet in the morning at the pub where their lodge was held. Sometimes, multiple lodges in the area would join in, depending on the occasion. From the lodge, they would all process together – in full regalia and often accompanied by a band – to the chapel to hear a sermon. After the service, a collection would be taken for a local charity and then the members would line up again and march through the principal streets of the town before heading back to the lodge room for the anniversary dinner. Wives and sweethearts were generally invited to these dinners, which were often followed by dancing. Anniversary feasts and processions were a common feature of

---

[100] *The Independent Odd Fellows' Harmonia* (1820), 76–77.
[101] *The Independent Order of Odd Fellows' Harmonia, Being a Choice Collection of Songs, Original and Selected ... with an Appendix of Original Toasts and Sentiments for the Use of the Order,* (1836) 151.
[102] Others included opening a new market, laying the foundation stone for a new chapel, celebrating Whit Monday, a victory on the battlefield, commemorating the coronation of the Queen, or the passing of the Reform Act.
[103] In 1824, for example, the Liverpool lodges organized a procession in honor of the anniversary of the King's coronation. ("Varieties," *Liverpool Mercury*, July 23, 1824.)

most local clubs and societies, and sometimes the main reason for joining one.[104] As one scholar of fraternal societies of the nineteenth century has noted, in general the celebration of a society's anniversary served "to bind the members into a unitary whole, while the procession displayed their public identity as a corporate body existing within a larger community."[105] Processions, charity collections, and dinners became a regular feature of the AMCs beginning in 1823. In this way, the local deputies who attended the AMC each year replicated (and thus actualized) the solidarity of the local lodge on the national level of the Order.[106]

The *Odd Fellow Magazine,* first published in 1824, began to augment the actual performances of the Order's solidarity with textual accounts of them. In the first edition, the editor explained that the magazine was designed "to bring the *great body* of Odd Fellows into closer unity – to cement and knit them together as one band of Brothers – and to exhibit to the world the sublime spectacle of thousands *really* LOVING ONE ANOTHER."[107] The officers in Manchester hoped that the magazine would augment the discussions that took place at the AMCs and make their motives transparent to the Order at large. It was not at first a success. Only after the AMC voted to deposit all the profits of the magazine in a new "Widows and Orphans" fund did it begin to gain traction, as we will see later in this chapter. And once it did, the magazine worked to bring together the local performances of the brotherhood into a single publication where members far and wide could read about the celebrations of their brothers.

More than the good feeling an Odd Fellow felt when drinking to the health of the Order, the magazine made the bond between distant members both visible and dynamic. While, not all Odd Fellows could read, the practice of reading aloud key articles on lodge night helped to incorporate more than just the literate members.[108] In a manner analogous to the role Benedict Anderson assigns to print culture in making

---

[104] Clark, *British Clubs and Societies,* 269.
[105] Clawson, *Constructing Brotherhood: Class, Gender, and Fraternalism,* 43.
[106] An observation made by David Cannadine about urban processions more generally quoted in Gunn, *The Public Culture of the Victorian Middle Class: Ritual and Authority in the English Industrial City 1840–1914,* 163.
[107] "To the Independent Order," 11.
[108] In the preface to the New Series published in 1828, Mark Wardle, the Corresponding Secretary to the Order made this point, "Every lodge ought to be prepared to present every member with a copy that can read – and a time ought to be appointed for those who cannot read, to hear others read, at least, the most important parts of the work." (Mark Wardle, "Preface to the New Series of the I. O. F's Magazine," *The Odd Fellows' Magazine* (1828–1831), 4.)

real the otherwise abstract concept of nation, the magazine demonstrated that however differently it might be practiced locally, Odd Fellows all over Britain shared a common culture.[109] The magazine began as a compilation of reports on anniversaries, the opening of new lodges, accounts of the annual committees, letters written by members on a dizzying variety of subjects, new songs and poems about Odd Fellowship, birth, death, and marriage announcements, and much other literary miscellanea, which together, functioned as a complex, evolving image of what it meant to be an Odd Fellow. Tellingly, the very idiosyncratic reports of local anniversaries and such in the early issues soon became strikingly similar. Thus, the magazine was not only a medium for discussion about what it meant to be an Odd Fellow, the discussions it facilitated influenced the way people talked about themselves as well. Some contributors were critical of one practice or another. But brothers fashioned their critiques with the language and culture of Odd Fellowship. Thus, it gave them a place to air grievances, resolve differences, and engage in or read about discussions others were having. In this way, they gained familiarity with each other. As a result, the magazine helped to establish and maintain meaningful bonds across great distances in the same way that an Odd Fellow felt fellowship when visiting a lodge in a nearby town. "Have we not, in a measure," one contributor asked, "the same scope through our circulating medium to show our familiarity and friendship?"[110] Longtime editor for the magazine, J. B. Rogerson, added that these regular communications "lead us to regard those who were previously strangers in the light of personal friends."[111]

The rituals, lectures, songs, toasts, processions and the magazine all helped to generalize the local feeling of brotherhood in the lodge to include brothers across the nation. Even though the techniques varied greatly – from collective performances, face-to-face interactions, letters and print media – the various reforms set in motion by the AMCs of the early 1820s led to the emergence of a social morality that began to encompass the entire Order. Thus, by the mid-1820s it was possible to say that the Odd Fellows in Manchester along with the Odd Fellows from all over Britain had succeeded in forming a national-level brotherhood.

---

[109] "What would our correspondence be," wondered one contributor to the *Magazine*, "if it was not for this inestimable means of spreading the same through the Order? – a mass of futile letters, labour spent in vain; nor would the worth of some of you correspondents have been known to us." (George Cooke, "For The Odd Fellows' Magazine," *The Odd Fellows' Magazine* (1828–1831), 5.)

[110] J. Newman, "To the Editor," *The Odd Fellows' Magazine* (1831–1834), 225.

[111] John B. Rogerson, "Preface," *The Odd Fellows' Quarterly Magazine* (1842–1843), iv.

A brotherhood, however, is not yet an institution whose life continues regardless of the particular people involved. The finishing touches to the Order as an institution were put into place in 1825.

★★★

The establishment of, and ongoing revisions to, the laws structuring the Order and the process of generalizing the moral bonds reinforcing that structure would continue throughout the century. These processes were critical to the making of the Independent Order of Odd Fellows. But there was one episode that took place in 1825 that brought the structural and the moral components together in a way that gave the brotherhood of Odd Fellowship an institutional life beyond the individuals who comprised it. The event that precipitated this ultimate unity was another coup, that is to say, another breakdown in trust among members. This time, the Leeds district rebelled because, under the existing system, the Manchester district effectively monopolized the leading offices of the Order. The Leeds district resented this and introduced general discontent throughout the Order because of it. Through the personal intervention of Thomas Armitt, a man who had just stepped down from the highest of those offices, the perpetual life of the Order was established. Detailing this final episode will demonstrate not just how complex the process was, but also how critical conviviality and mutual charity were to the structural integrity of the Order.

The coup began at the Huddersfield AMC in 1825, where Grand Master Thomas Armitt was "openly assailed" by some disgruntled representatives from Leeds. The Leeds Odd Fellows ordered the deputies of the Manchester District out of the room, claiming that the deputies from Manchester had unfairly dominated the power of the Order. Although Armitt succeeded in proving his right to preside in a legal sense to everyone else, the defeated parties "retained their sullen feelings."[112] After the meeting broke up, the Leeds lodges sent circulars to the Lodges in the Order and "emissaries to most of the Yorkshire Lodges to create opposition and distrust and succeeded in many instances."[113] A few months later, the Manchester Grand Committee sent Armitt, the then outgoing Grand Master of the Odd Fellows, on a mission to visit every district in the Order. The ostensible purpose of his journey was to explain the intricacies of a newly adopted degree – but coming so quickly after

---

[112] Spry, *The History of Odd-Fellowship*, 11.   [113] Ibid., 9.

the troubles at Huddersfield, it was hoped that it would also be a mission that would promote unity.

The deputies from Leeds may have made such a ruckus at Huddersfield for their own selfish reasons, but as later events would reveal they had discovered a very real defect in the structure of the Order, one that worried all the deputies. The outstanding source of contention, one that could not be institutionalized with uniform procedures or new rituals, was the manner in which the three leading offices of the Order were elected. Though elected by the Order at large (via the AMC), the offices of the Grand Master, the Deputy Grand Master, and the Corresponding Secretary were, at that point, occupied exclusively by members from Manchester lodges.[114] Although this practice was originally an artifact of the Order's origins, at a time when communication and transportation traveled at the same slow pace, the continued reason for it was logistical. These three officers needed to meet weekly in order to conduct the business of the rapidly growing Order, especially the accounting and distribution of the general laws, ritual and lecture books, regalia, and the other goods required to outfit a lodge. The key point of contention, however, was that the people holding these offices were also the sole trustees to the Order, receiving all the fees associated with opening new lodges, quarterage (at least what lodges would pay), and administering a funeral fund (for the district).[115] In 1825, they already controlled hundreds of pounds and it would soon be thousands. In short, all that unified the Order financially rested with three men who were personally unknown to the vast majority of members. The institutional limits on these offices, that they were unpaid and that they had no say in how the monies were spent, could do nothing to contain an officer determined to steal the money.[116]

Thomas Armitt was charged with making the case for why these offices were nevertheless safe in the hands of Mancunians.[117] After more than 1,000 miles of travel over the course of thirty days, Armitt visited twenty-

---

[114] This was only changed in 1844.

[115] Quarterage was a contribution each lodge was supposed to pay quarterly toward defraying the expenses of the Order.

[116] Their fears did not go long unfounded. In 1845, William Ratcliff, the Corresponding Secretary from 1838–1846, absconded with £4,000. Because the Manchester Unity was not a legal organization, their case had no standing in court. For more on this incident see Chapter 5.

[117] For more on this story, see John Frome Wilkinson, *The Friendly Society Movement: Its Origin, Rise, and Growth; Its Social, Moral, and Educational Influences; the Affiliated Orders* (London: Longmans, Green, Co., 1886), 15–17.

two different cities by coach and horseback.[118] From the report he wrote afterward, he seems to have reenacted the same scene in each district. Upon his arrival in a town central to the lodges in a district, he found a party of Odd Fellows awaiting his visit. In towns where advanced notice had not been received, he would announce himself at the pub where one of the lodges in the district met and would soon find himself surrounded by Odd Fellows. In almost every district, these Odd Fellows questioned Armitt about issues they faced in practicing the Manchester version of Odd Fellowship locally. Some lodges worried about how their district should be constituted. Others wondered about the nature of their relationship to the Order. Armitt acted as a neutral arbiter, explaining the legal answers to their questions and giving them insight into the perspective of the leading officers in Manchester. He did the same for questions about the government and authority of the Order, countering the disingenuous claims that the Leeds lodges had made in the pamphlet they had circulated prior to his visit. In some places, members were happy with his legal explanations because it was their distance from Manchester and their general ignorance about how the governance of this fairly new organization worked that had caused their confusion and distrust.[119] When dissatisfaction remained, as it did when he spoke to the members of the Huddersfield District, Armitt shifted to a moral appeal, which generally had good effect.[120]

Yet, proving the legality of his office with documents produced under the system in question and insisting upon the moral imperatives of a still emerging Odd Fellowship accounts for only part of his success. Armitt's personal intervention was also critical. For regardless of how these distant Odd Fellows felt about the Order, and regardless of the financial state of their lodges, the representatives of every district treated Armitt with generous and convivial hospitality. Some were so solicitous, Armitt felt "*almost* glad to escape from their kindness."[121] It is safe to say that a letter from him would not have had the same effect.[122] His success, then, had as much to do with the substance of what he said as the simple fact that he was there to say it.

He was there in his capacity as the former Grand Master of the Order (1823–1825) and before that as the Deputy Grand Master

---

[118] His trip was conducted in two parts, first with a "southern tour" and then in 1826, a "northern tour." See Map 4.2.

[119] Thomas Armitt, "Biography," *The Odd Fellows' Magazine* (1835–1836), 60.

[120] Ibid., 63.   [121] Ibid., 63.

[122] *Minutes, and Other Documents* ..., (July 28, 1820) 97–101.

(1821–1823) – that is to say, as a living representative of the Order and also as a traveling Odd Fellow. By accepting their hospitality as a representative of the Order, he put each lodge into mutual obligation with the Order, and through him, with each other.[123] In turn, as Armitt ate their food, drank their beer, slept in beds they provided, and traveled at their expense, his acceptance of this hospitality put the Order under obligation to each lodge along his way. Because he was acting under this commitment when he explained the legal and moral aspects of Odd Fellowship, the different lodges could accept them without requiring independent confirmation. As proof that these lodges indeed understood what transpired in this way, each one of the lodges he visited gave him assurances of their loyalty to pass on to the Order's Officers in Manchester.[124] With each promise of loyalty, the solidarity of the Order was strengthened.

Armitt's journey marked a turning point, where a regional organization relying on face-to-face mechanisms for achieving solidarity was transformed into an institution that facilitated national level cooperation.[125] His journey was important on a number of levels. The first was symbolic. The Manchester Quarterly Committee had drawn up the itinerary for Armitt's trip. Whether or not it was their intention from the outset is unclear, but Armitt traveled a route that connected each lodge to the next. As he finally closed the loop through Manchester, his travels connected the Order geographically. (See Map 4.2) The geographic unity was reinforced in the narrative form Armitt gave as a report in the *Odd Fellows' Magazine*. Significantly, immediately following the resolution of the crisis, the entity that had been created in this way was referred to as the "Manchester Unity" for the first time.[126] By 1826, all the Leeds lodges had been reunited with the Order. Attesting to this new solidarity, Leeds was chosen to host the 1830 AMC.

Second, his trip was decisive because it revealed the tools necessary to maintain a permanent basis for that national level cooperation. These tools were of two kinds, one kind institutionalized the person; the other personalized the institution. Subsequent AMC votes altered the three offices of the Order so that they could have the same effect as Armitt's journey but without the extraordinary effort of a personal tour of the

---

[123] Felicity Heal, *Hospitality in Early Modern England* (Oxford: Oxford University Press, 1990).

[124] The lodges in Leeds were the only exception. They felt they needed to give their deputies another hearing before deciding.

[125] The nineteenth-century Odd Fellows who wrote histories of the Order all agree on this shift. Spry, *The History of Odd-Fellowship*, 9–12; Wilkinson, *The Friendly Society Movement*, 15–16.

[126] *Minutes, and Other Documents ...*, (Dec. 12, 1825) 205.

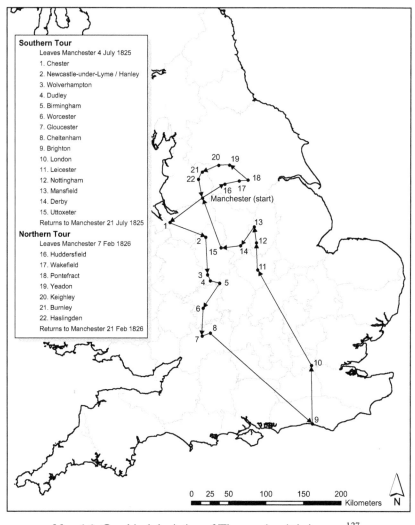

Southern Tour
Leaves Manchester 4 July 1825
1. Chester
2. Newcastle-under-Lyme / Hanley
3. Wolverhampton
4. Dudley
5. Birmingham
6. Worcester
7. Gloucester
8. Cheltenham
9. Brighton
10. London
11. Leicester
12. Nottingham
13. Mansfield
14. Derby
15. Uttoxeter
Returns to Manchester 21 July 1825
Northern Tour
Leaves Manchester 7 Feb 1826
16. Huddersfield
17. Wakefield
18. Pontefract
19. Yeadon
20. Keighley
21. Burnley
22. Haslingden
Returns to Manchester 21 Feb 1826

Map 4.2 Graphical depiction of Thomas Armitt's journey[127]

nation. At the Nottingham AMC (1827), for example, the representatives voted to change the duties of the Grand Master of the Order such that members would have the right to present their case to him personally

---

[127] Data compiled from Armitt's account in Armitt, "Biography," 57–65, 113–115. Map produced by Dr. Christine Bertoglio.

as the final step for settling any disputes.[128] At the Dudley AMC (1828), members voted to create a committee whose job it was to circumvent exactly the type of behavior that had made it possible for the Leeds' deputies to take over the AMC in their attempted coup. The amendment called for,

one of the oldest past officers from every district present at the AMC be appointed to act as moderators, who shall sit in a room apart from the Grand Committee room and who shall examine into the nature of all business coming before such committee, and if any thing appears to them frivolous or vexatious, or brought there with an intent to destroy unity, or sow the seeds of discord amongst brethren ... shall have a power to quash or make void such injurious props.[129]

While enlarging current or creating new offices institutionalized the role that Armitt had personally played in settling disputes, there were certain problems that would always require personal trust. In particular, the three offices of the Order would always involve faith in the person who held the office rather than in the legal restrictions on the office itself. Given this, it is not surprising that between 1814–1846, only thirty-five men were asked to fill the ninety-six possible openings.[130] Even more striking, in those same years only five men held the position of Corresponding Secretary, the only position that included remuneration. In 1837, members created an automatic vetting process wherein the Deputy Grand Master of the previous year would become the next Grand Master.

In 1835, the AMC voted to include a biography of the leading officers of the Order along with a fine metal etching portrait, which further personalized the institution. (See Figure 4.3.) As the unnamed author wrote in the first biography for the then sitting Grand Master, James Mansfield, "It being vitally important for the welfare of the Order, that the nicest discrimination should be used in the election of its chief officer, so it is equally gratifying, when one is chosen possessing the necessary qualifications to govern the community with dignity and honor ... "[131] He went on to advertise those qualifications. These biographies had many purposes but the level of detail about the specific services they performed without pay for the Order suggests that one of those purposes was to assure members of the trustworthiness of their officers. It was a version of what the savings banks patrons did when they

---

[128] *Minutes, and Other Documents* ..., (June 11, 1827) 246; (May 26–27, 1828) 262.
[129] *Minutes, and Other Documents* ..., (May 26–28, 1828) 262.
[130] Data drawn from the list of officers in Burn, *An Historical Sketch of the Independent Order of Oddfellows M.U.*, 123.
[131] "Biography. Mr. James Mansfield," *The Odd Fellows' Magazine* (1835–1837), 1.

Figure 4.3 Fine metal etching of Thomas Armitt
© Cambridge University Library, Cambridge, UK.[132]

advertised their own disinterestedness to demonstrate their honesty. The medals that the officers received from their lodges, districts, or the Order were listed as evidence of the esteem in which they had been and so should be held. Armitt's biography, the second one published in the magazine, included a depiction of his by-then famous journey.[133] On the one hand, the Order developed institutional mechanisms through which status and reputation could be broadcast across great distances. But, on the other, the personal characteristics of particular individuals played a significant role in facilitating, reinforcing, and perpetuating the institution itself.

The hospitality, which figured so prominently in Armitt's report, also became a permanent feature of the Order through the AMCs. The honor of hosting an AMC became something of a competition among districts to display the greatest loyalty, and of course assert their importance in the Order. Banners were made, halls rented and festooned, local histories were written, and sometimes historical sites along with the best routes to walk to see them were highlighted in pamphlets given to attending

---

[132] Armitt, "Biography," frontispiece.
[133] Although it was titled "Biography," Armitt actually wrote it himself. Armitt, "Biography."

deputies.[134] Offering each district a chance to host an AMC gave them an opportunity to show off their local community to Odd Fellows from other communities. But it also increased each local lodge's stake in the success of the Order at large. Through the years, choosing the sites for AMCs replicated and reinforced the geographical unity symbolized by Armitt's journey. As noted above, the choice of Leeds as the site for the AMC in 1830 demonstrated good faith and solidarity with the erstwhile defectors. Sometimes the location for the AMC was chosen to reward a particularly zealous Odd Fellow for services rendered. In 1832, for example, it was held in Monmouth to honor John Renie who was almost single-handedly responsible for spreading the Order throughout Wales and was a (some might say, the) major contributor to the early issues of the magazine. In the event, he died the day before the AMC. But his services did not go unrecognized: the deputies took a collection and started a subscription for his widow and children, which ultimately amounted to £80.

After years marked by constant fighting, attempted coups, and several near collapses of the entire Order, the Odd Fellows who attended the 1826 AMC finally agreed on a new system of reciprocity. Abandoning attempts to determine the exact costs who owed what to whom, they agreed instead that the extent to which one lodge relieved the travelers of another would become a measure of its benevolence. They applied the same rationale to a General Fund for the Order. Rather than requiring members or lodges "to bear an equal share of the incidental expenses of the Order" as they had tried to do in the early 1820s, the sub-committee for the general fund at the 1826 AMC proposed a fund designated "The Independent Order's Benevolent Fund." This new fund would defray the expenses of the Order, but it would also be used to relieve the distressed lodges and members of the Order and would be directed toward external charitable causes in the name of the Manchester Unity. The generosity of each lodge would thus become a measure of the benevolence of the Order. Making this official, spreading "the principles of benevolence and charity" replaced "Mirth and Harmony" as the goals of the Manchester Unity in 1826.[135]

By translating specific debts into benevolence and charity, the Odd Fellows were able to focus the attention of members on the power of their

---

[134] See, for example, *A Brief Sketch of Durham Compiled for the Use of the Officers, Board of Directors and Deputies of the Independent Order of Odd-Fellows, Manchester Unity Friendly Society, Attending the Annual Moveable Committee of the Order Held at Durham, May 1855* (Durham: Private circulation, 1855).

[135] *Minutes, and Other Documents* . . ., 214.

combined efforts rather than on the uneven cost of supporting travelers or lodges that experienced excessive instances of illness or death. Anthropologists note that reciprocity among equals is often achieved by "the refusal not to calculate credits and debits."[136] The Odd Fellows saw what they were doing in precisely these terms. The new principles of charity and benevolence would, one Odd Fellow reasoned, "make man what he ought to be to man – a BROTHER – to remove all the stumbling blocks of envy, malice and suspicion – to restore confidence."[137] But the transformation went beyond simply figuring out how to fund the Order without disaffection. The idea that together Odd Fellows were capable of giving charity far beyond the means or station of any individual member, and "rank it upon the basis of masonry, if not surpass it in philanthropy," as one Odd Fellow put it, proved incredibly compelling.[138] The pages of the *Odd Fellows' Magazine* and provincial papers began filling up with examples of their charity, and regularly featured proposals for new ways they might bestow further charity – schools, orphanages, and hospitals were just some of their ideas.

In the early 1830s, the Order took a page from its own history to solve a new problem. As noted above, when the magazine was first published in 1824, it did not enjoy a wide circulation. The editors tried to figure out how to extend it. They suggested that it be mandatory for each lodge to subscribe to a certain number, but to no avail. The AMC voted to put all the profits from the sale of the magazine toward an Order-wide Widows and Orphans fund. But even this was not enough on its own. Circulation only started to increase when the Odd Fellows began discussing the act of subscribing to the magazine, and thereby contributing to that fund, as a test of manliness. In the process, the wives of members, many of whom were financially capable of being members on their own account, were suddenly cast in utterly dependent terms. The pages of the magazine filled with panegyrics to feminine helplessness, "the bereft widow and the fatherless, weeping over the cold and lifeless remains of him that was their happiness, their support, their future prospect, and their all in this world..."[139] And, conversely, Odd Fellows could not be considered real men, if they did not respond to the call to care for their future widows. "Is he a man," asked one contributor to the magazine, "who can coolly contemplate the approach of age and want . . . and not wish to rescue the

---

[136] David Graeber, *Debt: The First 5,000 Years* (Brooklyn, NY: Melville House, 2011), 79.
[137] Wardle, "Preface to the New Series of the I. O. F's Magazine," 3.
[138] H. F. Green, "School for Children," *The Odd Fellows' Magazine* (1828–1831), 98.
[139] E. Huddart, "TO THE EDITOR AND COMMITTEE OF MANAGEMENT FOR THE ODD FELLOWS' MAGAZINE," *The Odd Fellows' Magazine* (1835–1837), 105.

aged (and then widowed) partner of all his joys?" The author concluded, "he ceases to be a man, and becomes a monster!"[140]

In response to this new campaign, subscriptions for the magazine increased significantly. In Briton's Pride Lodge, for example, a member noted that his lodge had only ever taken one copy of the magazine, but when he "explained the change, and the object to be attained by its increased circulation," forty-one members of his lodge signed up for their own copy. Similar increases happened in lodges all over the country, so that the number of subscribers increased from 2,000 in 1834 to 12,000 in 1837 and then 15,000 in 1840.[141] The Widows and Orphans fund became an important resource for the families of members, providing hundreds of thousands of pounds in relief over the course of the next seventy years. But the effect of this indirect method of funding the Order, where the Widows and Orphans fund held such prominence, was to gender the organization officially male for the first time.

Raising up the Widows and Orphans Fund as one of the chief aims of the organization in the 1830s also helped the Odd Fellows to deflect negative attention away from the alcohol-fueled conviviality at the heart of their brotherhood, further contributing to the official exclusion of women. As noted earlier in this chapter, given the middle class shift away from drinking in respectable clubs, alcohol and charity were no longer considered part and parcel. Overindulging in alcohol was seen as an affront to new notions of "independence." And "independence" was increasingly linked to masculinity and political reform.[142] In the early nineteenth century, radicals argued their case for political rights by gendering "dependence" as a female rather than class condition.[143] Men of all classes should have rights, the argument went, by virtue of the role they played taking care of their wives and children. In the early 1830s, the Odd Fellows used their Widows and Orphans fund to do similar work. Showing that they cared for their own dependents, a prominent Odd Fellow explained, would "increase our comfort and happiness at home and our respectability abroad." He and others suggested that they should at the same time omit the "narrations of our Bacchanalian revelries, I mean Anniversaries" from the pages of the

---

[140] "TO THE EDITOR AND COMMITTEE OF MANAGEMENT FOR THE MAGAZINE," *The Odd Fellows' Magazine* (1835–1837), 435.

[141] John Myers, "To the Editor and Committee of Management of the Magazine," *The Odd Fellows' Magazine* (1835–1837), 433; Spry, *The History of Odd-Fellowship*, 46.

[142] Clark, *The Struggle for the Breeches*, chapter 8.

[143] Matthew McCormack, *The Independent Man: Citizenship and Gender Politics in Georgian England* (New York: Manchester University Press, 2011), 123–126, 132, 171.

magazine and focus on more useful and respectable matters.[144] Note, he did not suggest that they stop drinking, but rather that they stop advertising it – and start advertising the good they did for their helpless wives and children at home.

Charity thus came to serve a number of purposes in the organization. While it was an end in itself, it acted as a unifying force as well as the measure of the Odd Fellows' respectability. In response to anyone who questioned their practice of meeting in pubs, the regular drinking together, the funeral orations they gave, or the secrets they kept, the Odd Fellows would simply list the amount they gave in charity as a defense. The effectiveness of their method of unity depended on the exploitation of contemporary gender norms to hide their less than respectable mode of cooperation and to showcase their benevolence.

Yet, in the same way this mode of creating solidarity depended on the exclusion of women, it also had other culturally specific limitations, as the split between the British and American Odd Fellows makes clear. The Odd Fellow lodges in America had been loosely federated with the British lodges since they began opening in the early 1820s. In spite of some early resistance to secret societies, the Order grew rapidly in Maryland, Pennsylvania, and New York in particular, and helped to facilitate the migration of many British Odd Fellows to the United States. But, as part of their attempts to legitimize a secret society in the early Republic and also to appeal to their respectable, middle class-membership, the American Odd Fellows had adopted a more religious tone in their rituals and lectures than the British Odd Fellows used. They also added a more elaborate hierarchy of degrees for members who became officers. At first, the British Odd Fellows followed suit. Indeed, the purpose of Thomas Armitt's journey in 1825 and again in 1826 was in part to explain the new Patriarchal degree, which extolled the virtues of the Old Testament patriarchs, to the other lodges.[145] The new degree, only open to Past Grands (officers who had previously served as a Grand Master), constituted a separate and superior lodge with respect to the regular lodges. The Board of Directors in Manchester initially thought that the Patriarchal lodge would help to safeguard the interests of the Order. But the hierarchy it created caused dissension among them at a time when they were desperately trying to forge bonds of unity. The deputies of the 1829 AMC in Sheffield argued that the degree was "calculated to create jealousies, and to separate chief friends" and so they voted to disestablish it.[146] The result was that by the 1830s, the Odd

---

[144] J. Peiser, "To the Editor," *The Odd Fellows' Magazine* (1834–1835), 384.
[145] Carnes, *Secret Ritual and Manhood in Victorian America*, 87.
[146] Armitt, "Biography," 116.

Fellows in America and those in Britain no longer spoke "the same language," as leading American Odd Fellow J. W. Ridgely put it. And consequently, "it was impossible for those in the States to distinguish between members belonging to the Manchester Unity and those belonging to other [Orders]," or, for that matter, between true Odd Fellows and frauds.[147] Ridgely was part of the Deputation sent to the Wigan AMC in 1842 with the goal of finding a common language. Instead, two years later, the two Orders formally split over the problem of mutual unintelligibility.[148]

This episode highlights the importance of the common language of Odd Fellowship as a source of unity and a guard against imposition within the British Order. It also makes clear how dependent that unity was on a shared culture. The culture of Odd Fellowship was a work in progress over the course of the century, but where the Odd Fellows drew lines of exclusion played as big a role in promoting accord as the affirmative reforms made to their rituals, literature, and social life.

★★★

Six convivial lodges in Manchester became the Independent Order of Odd Fellows, Manchester Unity through a combination of the unintended consequences resulting from efforts to solve particular problems under particular historical conditions and through the actions of some very committed members. These processes were marked by a variety of failed attempts, and yet, often, these failures led to unanticipated methods for solving hitherto intractable problems. Failure exposed particular sources of distrust, which could then be addressed. The Odd Fellows made

---

[147] "The AMC and the American Deputation," *The Odd Fellows' Quarterly Magazine* (1842–1843), 115.

[148] The American Odd Fellows officially became a white-only organization in the early 1840s when free blacks interested in joining the Order were turned away because of their race. The result of that exclusion was the origin story of the Grand United Order of Odd Fellows in America, one of the most important black fraternal organizations of the nineteenth century. Peter Ogden, a person of color born in the West Indies who was already an Odd Fellow in a British lodge himself, traveled to Liverpool and convinced the Grand United Order in England to grant dispensations to open black lodges in the US. Yet, unlike the British Odd Fellows who actively excluded women starting in the 1830s, both white and black Odd Fellow organizations in America admitted women in auxiliary branches. The class dimensions of this gender story are important, as Marc Carnes suggests, but further research comparing the three organizations would be illuminating. For more on the two Orders, see Theodore Ross, *History and Manual of Odd Fellowship* (New York: The M. W. Hazen Co., 1888; Charles H. Brooks, *The Official History and Manual of the Grand United Order of Odd Fellows in America* (Philadelphia: Grand United Order of Odd Fellows, 1902), and Carnes, *Secret Ritual and Manhood in Victorian America*.

extensive use of their own convivial origins when solving difficult problems of trust. In this piecemeal way, the Odd Fellows were able to transform strangers into brothers, brothers into a brotherhood, and a brotherhood into an international system of reciprocity. Because they all belonged to the same Order and because that Order had acquired social meaning, Odd Fellows could necessarily trust other Odd Fellows – whether or not the Odd Fellow in question was personally known. As a new lecture in 1834 stated, "The Brethren of our Order, who have been admitted to our company, have imbibed our sentiments and shared our esteem, may be assumed, whenever unhappily in misfortune, to be honourable and deserving objects of all the aid in our power to afford."[149]

It should be by now be clear that the institution that emerged from these processes was neither the most efficient, nor the most logical. Rather, it bore the marks and contours of a particular set of historical circumstances. The structure developed out of the solutions members came up with in response to new sources of distrust. These continuing problems required different strategies for ensuring cooperation both locally and nationally. Face-to-face interactions and sociability continued to be important even for facilitating trust at a distance, but so too did print media, uniform and transparent rituals and lectures, charitable giving, and collective performances. The particular combination depended on the issue being addressed. In the process of responding to contingent problems in particular historical contexts, creating the conditions of belonging to the Odd Fellows also entailed excluding those who could not belong. In this way, women and Americans became official outsiders as part of the same set of processes through which separate Odd Fellow lodges became the Independent Order of Odd Fellows, Manchester Unity.

Once the Order had become a national institution, it slowly gained public recognition as such, which of course created a new set of dynamics. The Odd Fellows' peculiar mode of solidarity, which combined benevolence and charity with an alcohol-fueled conviviality, became the subject of intense public scrutiny.[150] Much was at stake. When the

---

[149] *The Lectures Used by the Manchester Unity of the Independent Order of Odd Fellows* (Clerkenwell: John Griffin Hornblower, 1846), 14.

[150] For an example of this scrutiny in the national press, see "EYE-WITNESS," "The Odd Fellows at the Crystal Palace," *The Times*, Aug. 6, 1856. The Odd Fellows celebrated their anniversary at the Crystal Palace, drawing more than 20,000 members and their families to London for the occasion. The "eye-witness," who wrote to *The Times* describing the scene claimed that it was marked by drunkenness, dancing, and general debauchery. Two different Odd Fellows wrote response editorials to explain their practices. (Edward Mitchell, "Odd Fellows at the Crystal Palace," *The Times*, Aug. 16, 1856; James Curtis, "The Odd Fellows at the Crystal Palace," *The Times*, Aug. 11, 1856.)

Manchester Odd Fellows began to unite their local lodges, their benefits were collected ad hoc and paid out based on what was available. But by the late 1830s and certainly by the early 1840s, most lodges were offering stipulated sickness and burial benefits. The very success of their cooperation, uniting over 250,000 members all over Britain as well various colonies by the 1850s – and controlling among them hundreds of thousands of pounds – meant that the performative bonds that held them together might not be enough to secure those benefits. Various members throughout the Order began to call for more substantial, and, specifically, a more scientific basis for their institution. But it was only when the Corresponding Secretary for the Order absconded with over £4,000 that the need for such a change was taken seriously by the members at large. In an effort to deal with this contingent source of distrust, the Manchester Unity sought legal protection, which, in turn, required actuarial reform. To outsiders, mixing "notions of beer and insurance" seemed utterly incongruous.[151] Yet, as we will see in Chapter 5, the conviviality that made their institutional structure function would also be put to work securing the Odd Fellows against contingencies that even actuarial science could not predict.

---

[151] "Mr. Tidd Pratt's office can be no sinecure," *The Times*, Nov. 6, 1863.

5 Trusting Numbers
Sociability and Actuarial Science in the Manchester Unity

If we turn our eyes from the past to the future, we exchange our uncertain and doubtful light for absolute darkness and blindness ... we cannot know, we cannot tell, what an hour may bring forth ... from whence the blow shall come, upon whom or when it shall fall.[1]

Alfred Smith, Odd Fellow from Ripon, 1835

The insurer's activity is not just a matter of passively registering the existence of risks, and then offering guarantees against them. He "produces risks," he makes risks appear where each person had hitherto felt obliged to submit resignedly to the blows of fortune.[2]

Francois Ewald, 1991

From humble and, in the case of the Odd Fellows, convivial beginnings, by the middle of the nineteenth century friendly societies had become critical to the social welfare of millions of Britons. In addition to the great and growing body of law protecting and regulating them, "friendly society" had also become an important cultural category, standing as the symbol of both the high hopes and great fears legislators had about the social and economic security of the working classes. Legally registered societies numbered somewhere around 14,000 with over 2 million members. A further 14,000 were thought to exist as unregistered societies.[3] Unregistered until 1850, the Odd Fellows were the fastest growing and most successful of the Affiliated Orders, with a membership that

---

[1] Alfred Smith, "A Second Discourse," *The Odd Fellows' Magazine* (1834–1835), 205.

[2] Francois Ewald, "Insurance and Risk," In *The Foucault Effect: Studies in Governmentality: With Two Lectures by and an Interview with Michel Foucault,* Michel Foucault et al., eds., (Chicago: University of Chicago Press, 1991), 199–201.

[3] The Friendly Society Registrar, John Tidd Pratt, estimated that the number of unregistered societies was equal to those he registered. (*Report from the Select Committee on the Friendly Societies Bill,* P.P., 1849 (458), xiv, 219.) Twenty-five years later there were 32,000, comprising over 4 million members, with an estimated 4 million more when the members' families were included. (*Fourth Report of the Commissioners Appointed to Inquire into Friendly and Benefit Building Societies ,* P. P., 1874, xvi; see also appendix iv.)

increased from 250,000 at mid-century to 900,000 at the end.[4] Influen-tial people became members, including the famous political reformer Lord Chancellor Henry Brougham and the moral reformer Samuel Smiles.[5] No less than thirty-three Members of Parliament were Odd Fellows, as well as four bishops.[6] William Gladstone joined the ranks of the second largest Affiliated Order, the Ancient Order of Foresters, and said of friendly societies in general that they "had become so important that no history of this nation would deserve attention which excluded [them]."[7]

While their numbers and importance would only continue to grow in the second half of the century, the organizations that provided social welfare to so many working people and their families were also thought to be gravely unstable from a financial perspective. The prominent actuary Charles Ansell told the House of Commons Select Committee on the Friendly Societies Bill in 1849 that "the great majority are insolvent, without any doubt whatsoever."[8] Claims about friendly society insolvency had been a favorite critique of politicians and social reformers since the great mathematician Richard Price first noticed them in the late eighteenth century.[9] Even though actuarial tables for morbidity were severely flawed until the mid-nineteenth century, appraisals of the workingman's friendly society always involved the same two assertions. First, it was alleged that friendly societies charged an inadequate amount to members in order to actually insure against the sickness and death liabilities they carried. Second, these insecure financial matters were made worse by the universal custom of expending already deficient monies on practices of pub-based sociability, involving group drinking, rituals, processions, annual feasts and the like. However much they praised their self-helping spirit, over the course of the long nineteenth century, the consensus about friendly societies was that they were financially and socially unsound.

---

[4] For mid-century numbers, see F. G. P. Neison, "Contributions to Vital Statistics," *Journal of the Statistical Society of London* 9, no. 1 (1846): 138. For the membership numbers in 1904, see PGM Robert Moffrey, *The Rise and Progress of the Manchester Unity of the Independent Order of Oddfellows, 1810–1904*, Web. Nov. 25, 2017, www.isle-of-man.com/manxnotebook/history/socs/odf_mdly.htm.

[5] Wilkinson, *The Friendly Society Movement*, 13; Samuel Smiles and Thomas Mackay, *The Autobiography of Samuel Smiles* (London: Routledge/Thoemmes, 1997), 104.

[6] "The Work of the Order in 1892," *The Monthly Magazine of the Independent Order of Odd Fellows, Manchester Unity Friendly Society* (1892), 371.

[7] William Gladstone, *Industrial Review*, no. 870 (June 15, 1878).

[8] *Report from the Select Committee on the Friendly Societies Bill*, P. P., 1849, xiv, 219.

[9] Richard Price, *Observations on Reversionary Payments* (Dublin, 1772), 120–121.

Historians have defended friendly societies against the attacks of early nineteenth-century actuaries whose tables would have destroyed any friendly society using them, but once accurate tables were available around mid-century, they fault friendly societies for their resistance to reform. In particular, they note an incompatibility between sociability and solvency.[10] Perhaps, they could not help the fact that they "opened their doors with an intrinsic insolvency," but once actuarial science had developed the tables for sickness rates among laborers, the problem was, a leading friendly society historian makes clear, "a will to reform rather than the lack of knowledge."[11] According to this view, the "unconscionable time" it took for the "old practices" of ritualized sociability to die and the resistance to the implementation of appropriate actuarial reforms undercut long-term financial stability, ultimately leading to state intervention.[12]

Such a judgment leaves us with a puzzling historical problem. That is, how do we explain the fact that, in spite of widespread resistance to actuarial reform and the insistence on maintaining their convivial aspects, friendly societies did manage to provide some form of mutual aid to a significant proportion of the population throughout the nineteenth century? They did not do so perfectly and sometimes they had to close the boxes that held their funds permanently.[13] But taking a single year in the Odd Fellows' provision of mutual aid, 1872, for example, the Order paid out no less than £400,000 for sickness and funerals.[14] Rather than run from these allegedly insolvent societies, working Britons flocked

---

[10] Cordery, *British Friendly Societies, 1750–1914*, 176.

[11] Ibid., 130; Gosden, *The Friendly Societies in England*, 14, 23.

[12] Gosden, *The Friendly Societies in England*, 11, 220. As noted in the introduction, most historians rely on Bentley B. Gilbert's work for the idea that there was a necessary conflict between solvency and fraternalism in the late nineteenth-century context. See Bentley B. Gilbert, "The Decay of Nineteenth-Century Provident Institutions and the Coming of Old Age Pensions in Great Britain," *The Economic History Review*, xvii, no. 3 (1965), 557 and Bentley B. Gilbert, *The Evolution of National Insurance in Great Britain: The Origins of the Welfare State* (London: Michael Joseph, 1966), 70, 171. Recently, several historians have conducted empirical studies demonstrating that the extent of friendly society insolvency has been exaggerated. (Macnicol, *The Politics of Retirement In Britain, 1878–1948*, 116–134; Nicholas Broten, "From Sickness to Death: Revisiting the Financial Viability of the English Friendly Societies, 1875–1908," 107–120.)

[13] We only have anecdotal evidence for why friendly societies failed until 1874, when the National Registrar for Friendly Societies began collecting data on the causes of closures. And even those records are fragmentary as many members continued to suspect that the government wanted to collect their financial records for nefarious reasons and so did not fill out the forms.

[14] Moffrey, *The Rise and Progress of the Manchester Unity*, Web. Nov. 25, 2017.

to them in droves. Friendly society membership not only doubled between 1850 and the 1890s, it also shifted increasingly away from the isolated, local club toward the Affiliated Orders—that is to say, toward those friendly societies like the Odd Fellows who were best known for the importance they placed on practices of ritualized sociability.[15] What was it, one might wonder, that enabled friendly societies to thrive for well over a century in spite of the actuary's claim that "the ruin of any society, under such conditions, is inevitable?"[16]

The puzzle persists only if we continue to view it from the perspective of nineteenth-century actuaries. The real surprise is not why the old practices continued, but how friendly society members came to accept actuarial science at all. With enough data, an actuary claimed to be able to calculate and predict probable future patterns, not just in the natural world, but in the life of a human being, as well. The working-class members of friendly societies were not the only ones who found this difficult to believe. Even the actuaries to the most successful life insurance companies in the eighteenth and early nineteenth century did not trust their premium rates exclusively to actuarial science. As we will see, seeing like an actuary required nothing less than a cultural transformation even for actuaries. It should not surprise us, then, that the working-class members of friendly societies did not immediately trust in this emerging science either.

Considering the cultural transformation necessary to see like an actuary is only part of the explanation, however. It is also worth asking what friendly society members thought they were doing when they resisted actuarial reform. Attending to the explanations members gave for their actions and the debates that ensued within the context of the history of these organizations, it quickly becomes clear that the emphasis on sociability was neither backward looking nor necessarily in opposition to financial stability.[17] Instead, these practices became a cultural resource

---

[15] Taking the combined membership numbers of only the two largest of the Affiliated Orders, the Independent Order of Odd Fellows and the Ancient Order of Foresters, the Orders grew from 815,535 in 1872 to 1,600,223 in the 1890s. (P. H. J. H. Gosden, *Self-Help: Voluntary Associations in 19th-Century Britain* (New York: Harper & Row Publishers, Inc., 1974), 40; Macnicol, *The Politics of Retirement In Britain, 1878–1948*, 115.)

[16] F. G. P. Neison, *Contributions to Vital Statistics*, 3rd ed. (London: Simpkin, Marshall & Co., 1857), 417.

[17] The importance of understanding what contemporaries thought they were doing and the language they used to talk about their actions as a means of getting at the relationship between social structures and human agency is an insight I borrow from the work of several early modern historians. For a theoretical framework for these relationships, and especially good example, of this method, see Phil Withington, "Company and Sociability in Early Modern England," *Social History* 32, no. 3 (2007): 291–307.

that members adapted in order to deal with all the exigencies of life in an industrializing society, not just those related to the liabilities of sickness and death. The Odd Fellows, the first of the Affiliated Orders to begin implementing actuarial reform, only did so because of an historical accident. As noted in Chapter 4, in 1846, the Order's long time, well loved, and deeply trusted Corresponding Secretary, William Ratcliffe, stole over £4,000 from the treasury of the national offices.[18] Worse than the theft itself was the fact that the Order could do nothing about it. Ratcliffe escaped prosecution on the technical grounds that the Odd Fellows were not a legal friendly society and so had no standing in court.[19] "Confidence in the Order was rudely shaken" by this betrayal, which led the national leadership to seek legalization, a move that would require actuarial reform.[20] Yet, even as they began implementing financial reforms in the latter half of the century, it was the continued emphasis on various forms of sociability that enabled them to secure their members against contingencies that even actuarial science was incapable of predicting.

Whether providential or risk-based, mutual aid societies have existed in some form all over the world and throughout history. But the Affiliated Orders were unique to the Anglophone world in the nineteenth and twentieth centuries. The Odd Fellows were the first to go through a transition, however incomplete, from one way of seeing to the other.[21] An internal history of their organization, then, gives us unique access to the specific historical processes through which a significant number of nineteenth-century working people navigated one of the great paradigm shifts of modern life. By making sense of the actions of hundreds of thousands of working people over the course of more than a century, this story will also show us how they learned to trust the numbers that underpinned that shift.

★★★

Although we tend to think of the shift from providence to risk as a late seventeenth-century phenomenon, a function of the development of probability and statistics, friendly society members of the late eighteenth and early nineteenth centuries did not yet understand the world in terms of risk. They were not alone in this either. Even the actuaries of the most

[18] Moffrey, *The Rise and Progress of the Manchester Unity*, Web. Nov. 25, 2017.
[19] As noted earlier, because of their federated structure, they fell under the Corresponding Societies Act and thus were an illegal organization.
[20] Moffrey, *The Rise and Progress of the Manchester Unity*, Web. Nov. 25, 2017.
[21] Beveridge, *Voluntary Action: A Report on Methods of Social Advance*, 36.

successful life insurance companies of the eighteenth century had what Lorraine Daston calls an "anti-statistical" bias.[22] Actuarial tables were not treated as quantitative measures of the chance that something would happen based on observed statistical regularities. Instead, those tables measured the expectation that something *should* happen, given the divinely ordained organization of the universe. In the eighteenth century, for example, probabilists assumed that death rates were constant at any age between adolescence and middle age.[23] In these age ranges, if one person died before another, it had moral and spiritual, not medical or biological, meaning in it.[24]

There is nothing "natural" about a statistical or probabilistic way of seeing.[25] Statistics, for its part, requires a level of abstraction that can move far enough away from an individual thing so that it loses its particularity and can then be enumerated, made equivalent to another thing, categorized in a variety of ways (depending on the application), added up within these categories, and finally averaged. As Adolphe Quetelet, the Belgian statistician, explained in 1835 "the greater the number of individuals observed, the more do individual particularities, whether physical or moral become effaced, and allow the general facts to predominate ... "[26]

Yet even for Quetelet, who is now famous for his work on what he called "social physics" and for inventing the concept of the "average man," the shift from seeing individual people and all their idiosyncrasies to seeing populations comprised of equivalent individual units was difficult to make. In 1825, he attempted to use Pierre-Simon Laplace's sampling method, which applied a ratio of birth and death rates to a sample population as a means of determining the entire population of a country without taking a complete census. As he undertook the work to analyze the data from the Low Countries, however, the local particularities seemed to defy generalization. As he examined the results, it seemed

---

[22] Lorraine Daston, *Classical Probability in the Enlightenment* (Princeton: Princeton University Press, 1988), 120.

[23] Ibid., 299. For an examination of similar assumptions in the history of American insurance, see Viviana Zelizer, *Morals and Markets: The Development of Life Insurance in the United States* (London: Transaction Books, 1983); Jonathan Levy, *Freaks of Fortune: The Emerging World of Capitalism and Risk in America* (Cambridge, MA: Harvard University Press, 2014).

[24] The major life insurance companies of the eighteenth century only disaggregated membership by age in the 1760s. (Geoffrey Clark, *Betting on Lives: The Culture of Life Insurance in England, 1695–1775* (Manchester: Manchester University Press, 1999) 116.)

[25] Daston, *Classical Probability in the Enlightenment*, 173.

[26] Stephen M. Stigler, *The History of Statistics: The Measurement of Uncertainty Before 1900* (Cambridge, MA: Harvard University Press, 1986), 172.

that he would need as many "sampling units as there were people" if he hoped to represent accurately the widely divergent birth and death rates among people even in the same province.[27] Advances in sampling methods would ultimately make partial census taking more accurate. But it took the breakdown of the estate or caste-based social systems in Europe, which happened rather slowly and unevenly over the course of the seventeenth and eighteenth centuries, to make the idea of a homogenous population easier to imagine.[28] And even for the most statistically inclined, it was a difficult transition.

The history of probability and statistics is filled with similar examples that illustrate how an actuarial way of seeing required fairly significant cultural change.[29] Certain advances that were humanly conceivable and mathematically provable were not made because they were not socially acceptable.[30] We saw an example of this phenomenon in Chapter 1 with the fate of early fire insurance schemes in the seventeenth century. In the middle of the eighteenth century, when probability and statistics began to be used more regularly in certain kinds of insurance applications, there continued to be very strong cultural resistance for the risks associated with human life. In the first place, assigning a value to lives was thought potentially dangerous and definitely distasteful. In continental Europe, it was illegal and condemned "as an incitement to fraud and murder, and rejected on more philosophical grounds as an impious conflation of the sacred sphere of human life with the profane operations of the marketplace."[31]

[27] For more on this story, see ibid., 161–169.

[28] Alain Desrosières, *The Politics of Large Numbers: A History of Statistical Reasoning* (Cambridge, MA: Harvard University Press, 1998), 31–34; Theodore M. Porter, *The Rise of Statistical Thinking, 1820–1900* (Princeton, NJ: Princeton University Press, 1986), 25.

[29] For especially good accounts of the cultural histories of probability, see Daston, *Classical Probability in the Enlightenment*; Ian Hacking, *The Emergence of Probability: A Philosophical Study of Early Ideas About Probability, Induction and Statistical Inference* (Cambridge: Cambridge University Press, 2006). For similar approaches to the history of statistics see, Porter, *The Rise of Statistical Thinking, 1820–1900*; Desrosières, *The Politics of Large Numbers*; Joshua Cole, *The Power of Large Numbers: Population, Politics, and Gender in Nineteenth-Century France* (Ithaca: Cornell University Press, 2000).

[30] For two analyses of the politics of numbers, see Buck, "People Who Counted"; William Peter Deringer, "Calculated Values: The Politics and Epistemology of Economic Numbers in Britain, 1688–1738" (PhD diss., Princeton University, 2012). For the resistance to using numbers to determine causes of social phenomena, see Andrea Rusnock, *Vital Accounts: Quantifying Health and Population in Eighteenth-Century England and France* (New York: Cambridge University Press, 2002). For how "facts" came to acquire objective authority not subject to interpretation see Mary Poovey, *A History of the Modern Fact: Problems of Knowledge in the Sciences of Wealth and Society* (Chicago: University of Chicago Press, 1998).

[31] It was outlawed in Europe, with the exception of certain places in Italy where it was highly regulated. (Clark, *Betting on Lives*, 8.)

In addition to reducing the value of human life to a number and profiting from a divinely crafted product, buying life insurance was also closely associated with speculation. From the late seventeenth century, Britons had shown a strong and disastrous propensity to gamble on anything that contained an element of chance in it, and gambling through insurance had become quite common by the mid-eighteenth century. In fact, the first state regulation of insurance was called the Gambling Act (1774). It was an attempt to reduce the opportunities for speculation in insurance by requiring that the policyholder have a financial interest in what was being insured.[32] The association between gambling and insurance put the indemnification of life at odds with prudence, the great ideal of the age.[33]

But life insurance was also seen as speculative because although life tables had been around for a while, using them for the purpose of predicting and valuing life was not the norm for any of the insurance companies that proliferated in this period. The Society for Equitable Assurances on Lives and Survivorships, which ultimately became the most successful life-insurance company of all time, provides a helpful illustration of this. When the directors of the company applied for a Royal Charter in 1761 (after being rejected once before), the Privy Council made it clear that using actuarial tables was still considered speculative. "The success of this scheme must depend upon the truth of certain calculations taken upon tables of life and death, whereby the chance of mortality is attempted to be reduced to a certain standard: this is mere speculation, never yet tried in practice and consequently subject, like all other experiments, to various chances in the execution."[34] One of the keys to accurate predictions, as we will see later in this chapter, was testing the predicted rates, year after year, against what actually happened.

The subsequent history of the Equitable, as it came to be called, which is still in existence today, shows that actuarial science was held in such low regard, and for so long, that even the company's actuaries refused to rely solely on its predictions. Prior to the Equitable, "the first generation of insurance firms functioned like friendly societies, according to simple

---

[32] Clark, *Betting on Lives*, 22. For more on the Gambling Act in the nineteenth century, see Timothy Alborn, "A Licence to Bet: Life Insurance and the Gambling Act in the British Courts," In *The Appeal of Insurance*, Geoffrey Clark, ed., (Toronto: University of Toronto Press, 2010), 107–126.

[33] While this elicited censure in some circles, the speculative element actually made life insurance more attractive to its middle-class customers. For more on this, see Timothy L. Alborn, *Regulated Lives: Life Insurance and British Society, 1800–1914* (Toronto: University of Toronto Press, 2009).

[34] C. G. Lewin, *Pensions and Insurance Before 1800: A Social History* (East Linton (Scotland): Tuckwell, 2003), 381.

redistributive procedures."[35] Like the friendly societies of Daniel Defoe's day, what a person gambled on in these schemes were not the odds of beating the life tables, but the odds that the insurer and his other customers were trustworthy – that is to say, whether they would pay up when the time came. The Equitable was the first life insurance company to set premiums in accordance with actuarial tables, despite the government's rejection of their charter on this basis. Their subsequent success, however, was *not* due to their reliance on these tables.

As the next generation of actuaries would discover, William Morgan, the Equitable's actuary, exercised what they would describe as "an almost pathological prudence" both in setting premiums and making investments. Morgan learned this excessive caution from his uncle, Richard Price, whom we met in Chapter 2 as "Britain's foremost authority on actuarial mathematics" and author of the "celebrated Northampton Table" for mortality.[36] He was also an important moral philosopher. Price taught his nephew that tables were only a rough estimate of where to begin the assessment of a candidate. The rest of the assessment was moral, an evaluation of the candidate's character.[37] Consequently, when taking on new lives, Morgan interviewed each candidate individually and then interviewed character witnesses known to the candidate, not unlike the way new members of friendly societies were vetted. If a candidate presented significant moral risks (late in paying debts, heavy drinker, etc.), he might be refused. If the risks were of a less serious nature, an additional charge of between 11–22 percent was added to his premium. When the company's yearly surpluses showed a 60 percent excess of assets over liabilities as a result of this abundance of caution, Morgan refused to redistribute the money as dividends back to the members, warning that "extraordinary events or a season of uncommon mortality" might "catch the Equitable unawares."[38] Rather than actuarial tables, Morgan's prudence, both fiscal and moral, kept the Equitable solvent. The same was true of other successful life insurance companies. Use of actuarial tables did not come into widespread practice until the very end of the eighteenth century. Even then, "insurers stayed in business by the exercise of caution, by keeping a

[35] Clark, *Betting on Lives*, 7. On this point, also see Alborn, *Regulated Lives*, 22.
[36] Clark, *Betting on Lives*, 123; Charles Jellicoe, "General Meeting of the English and Foreign Representatives of Assurance Interests ... ," *The Assurance Magazine*, 1851, 368.
[37] As Clark points out, "'When taking new lives, the insurance company solicited testimony from 'gentle folk' in preference to 'medical men'." (Clark, *Betting on Lives*, 128.)
[38] Morgan quoted in Daston, *Classical Probability in the Enlightenment*, 180.

sharp lookout for fraud, and by following rules of thumb. Experience counted, counting didn't."[39]

Actuarial science, then, required a new way of seeing, both conceptually and culturally. Even those who could see – indeed even those whose business it was to see – in an actuarial way did not always feel comfortable or safe in doing so. They would always, as the French prospectus for the Equitable advertised, "modify the exact calculations of mathematics by those of prudence."[40] Prudence, that eminently eighteenth-century middle-class value, informed life insurance practices in the quality of lives selected, in the way premiums were set, and in the types of investments to which surpluses were put. "It took new beliefs and new values, not just the availability of new techniques, to make mathematically based life insurance attractive to buyers and sellers."[41] Scholars disagree on the nature of and process through which these new values and beliefs emerged. But the fact remains that they would not be in place for the middle-class customers of life insurance until the beginning of the nineteenth century, over a hundred years after reliable data on mortality rates existed. Just on the basis of the radical cultural shift involved in adopting an actuarial way of seeing, it makes sense that the largely uneducated members of the Odd Fellows were also reluctant to adopt it.

Besides good cultural reasons for being cautious about actuarial science, however, the science behind the laws of sickness, the key problem for friendly societies, was badly underdeveloped in the early part of the nineteenth century. P. H. J. H. Gosden pointed out long ago that "it was absurd to rail against the shortcomings of the societies when there was no scale by which to measure the deficiencies."[42] Great strides had been made in the statistical models predicting average life spans since John Graunt first published his path breaking interpretation of the London Bills of Mortality in 1662.[43] But very little had been done on rates of sickness. Richard Price created the first tables on sickness rates only in 1772, as we have seen.[44] Price's tables were based on the assumption that the

[39] Clark, *Betting on Lives*, 7.
[40] Quoted in Daston, *Classical Probability in the Enlightenment*, 181.   [41] Ibid., 173.
[42] Gosden, *The Friendly Societies in England, 1815–1875*, 99.
[43] John Graunt, *Natural and Political Observations Mentioned in a Following Index, and Made upon the Bills of Mortality* (London, 1662); William Petty, *An Essay Concerning the Multiplication of Mankind* (London, 1682). For comprehensive overviews, see Lewin, *Pensions and Insurance Before 1800*; Cornelius Walford, *The Insurance Cyclopaedia* (London: Charles and Edwin Layton, 1876).
[44] Richard Price, *Observations on Reversionary Payments*, xx, chapter 2.

probability of sickness increased uniformly throughout a person's life. There was no actual data in existence that could either confirm or disprove the validity of his tables. Friendly societies were the only organizations who had access to such information, and most did not keep any records, much less accurate rates of sickness, tabulated according to age, occupation, and so on. Price's tables were only tested when a few patronized friendly societies tried to use them. It turned out that for the early part of life they worked well enough. But, when it came to ages above 50, they were dangerously inaccurate, as the 1825 Select Committee on Friendly Societies was shocked to learn in the course of its investigations.[45]

A patronized friendly society in Scotland, the Highland Society, produced the first tables developed from actual observation in 1824. The Highland Tables, as they were called, showed that far from being uniform, sickness increased with age. Yet, while these tables were based on actual experience rather than mathematical probability, they used a particularly Scottish definition of sickness. Like most friendly societies, the Highland Tables defined sickness first as an illness that rendered one unable to work. But in order to receive sick pay, according to the Highland Tables, an individual had to have been a member for at least five years, unable to finance the period of unemployment with his own resources, and sick for (generally) more than five days. This much stricter definition was not noted until several English societies had adopted the Highland Tables and gone bankrupt under their guidance.

Subsequent attempts to develop sick tables did not fare much better. The first attempt to gather information on sickness experience according to English understandings of sickness (inability to work regardless of an individual's financial status) was collected by the Society for the Diffusion of Useful Knowledge and analyzed by Charles Ansell, actuary to the Atlas Assurance Company, in his *Treatise on Friendly Societies* (1835). The data had been collected between the years 1823–1827, but the friendly societies from which the data were compiled were too disorganized to provide reliable data and, in any case, there was too little information to achieve statistical regularity for the crucial age range above fifty. While the Highland Tables were later proved to be 36 percent too low, Ansell's tables were only slightly better at 19 percent below the actual rates required for solvency.[46] In any case, later actuaries agreed

---

[45] *Report from the Select Committee of the House of Commons on the Laws Respecting Friendly Societies*, P. P., 1825, iv, 4–5.

[46] Information taken from *Fourth Report of the Commissioners Appointed to Inquire into Friendly and Benefit Building Societies*, P. P., 1874, xxiii, pt 1, clxxxii; F. G. P. Neison, *Observations on Odd-Fellow and Friendly Societies*, 7th ed. (London: B. Steill, Paternoster Row, 1847), 7. Also see Gosden, *The Friendly Societies in England, 1815–1875*, 103.

that both would have devastated the friendly society movement if they had been adopted universally.

Francis Neison, actuary to the Medical, Invalid, and General Life Assurance Society and founding member of the Institute of Actuaries, had more room than most to "rail against the shortcomings of friendly societies" because he had developed the first "accurate scale with which to measure their deficiencies," in 1845. But even his tables were problematic. As part of his debate with Edwin Chadwick, the famous sanitation reformer, Neison set out to prove that population density and environmental causes did not have as big an impact on health as moral choices, like physical activity and avoidance of alcohol. And in his published study, he asserted, but did not yet have the data to prove, that occupation probably had a greater impact than location.[47] His tables were thus accurate in general but did not make it possible for a particular society to account for special occupational liabilities. Significant sickness data broken out by occupation would not exist until the Odd Fellows compiled the returns of their 250,000 members in 1850.

Whether or not the tables were in fact accurate mattered less, however, than the fact that what the general public saw of actuarial science as it developed was constant disagreements about these tables among its leading practitioners. Because of the relationship between actuarial science and controversial social problems, especially those related to the issue of poverty, disagreements among actuaries were often conducted in public papers and pamphlets. In response to Neison's tables, for example, John Finlaison, in his official capacity as actuary to the government, published competing tables based on the friendly society returns from 1846–1850. His tables diverged from Neison's significantly. See Figure 5.1.

Finlaison's tables were based on a bizarrely strict notion of sickness, both in terms of duration as well as what qualified as sickness. Excluding all chronic diseases, for example, his definition was completely inappropriate for friendly societies, where sickness was simply understood as anything that incapacitated a member from working. Yet instead of a private and professional discussion of one scientist to another, Neison criticized Finlaison's work publicly and in polemical terms,

Since the disastrous publication of the Highland Society's tables, in 1824, perhaps no other unfortunate event as the publication of what is termed the Government Tables [i.e. Finlaison's tables], has arisen in the history of benefit

---

[47] The French had a better sense by this point of how these mapped on to each other. See William Coleman, *Death Is a Social Disease: Public Health and Political Economy in Early Industrial France* (Madison: University of Madison, 1982).

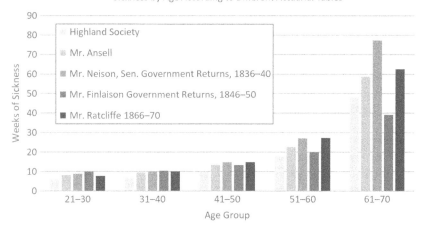

Figure 5.1 Comparative sickness by age according to different actuarial tables[48]

and friendly societies … a careful perusal of these observations must satisfy everyone having a practical knowledge of the management of friendly societies, of the imminent danger of circulating such documents under government sanction![49]

Neison did not stop there. He then went on to criticize the recommendations of John Tidd Pratt, the government appointed Registrar for Friendly Societies, in similar terms. Charles Hardwick, a self-trained actuary and Odd Fellow, would later say that it should not surprise us that the "partially educated working man may well hesitate … when he discovers that those in whom he is told to place implicit confidence, entertain no such profound veneration for the opinions or advice of each other."[50]

Somewhat ironically, given that it was his brother's fraud that forced the Odd Fellows to begin reform, Henry Ratcliffe, the new Corresponding Secretary for the Order was the one who ultimately "satisfactorily

---

[48] I have reproduced the numbers in the table included in the Royal Commission's report, illustrating how divergent the rates of sickness were in the late 1840s. See *Fourth Report of the Commissioners Appointed to Inquire into Friendly and Benefit Building Societies*, 1874, 183.

[49] Neison, "Contributions to Vital Statistics," xxii.

[50] Charles Hardwick, "A Few More Words about Management," *The Quarterly Magazine of the Independent Order of Odd Fellows, Manchester Unity* (1857–1858), 469.

settled" the laws of sickness in 1850. Although this did not end the public battles waged between actuaries, the sickness tables that finally became the standard were produced from an Order-wide valuation of the morbidity rates of actual members. The tables were subsequently refined in a series of quinquennial valuations throughout the century. Ratcliffe made separate allowances for age, location, and occupation. Not only did his study comprise over a million years of experience, it also drew data from every county in England, Wales, Scotland, and Ireland, and from twenty-six different occupations. In most cases, it confirmed the conclusions Neison had drawn from his less substantial study and the hypothesis he had ventured about the importance of occupation. But Ratcliffe's work was especially important for the amount of data it provided for sickness rates above the age of sixty. Thus, it was the Odd Fellows themselves who had the dubious honor of putting actuarial science in a position such that an actuary could declare the Manchester Unity insolvent.

If developing accurate tables was the first step in making friendly societies actuarially sound, it was by no means the last or even the most difficult. The complexities encountered when attempting to apply those tables to particular societies presented a far greater challenge. As Neison explained to the 1849 Friendly Society Commission, from an actuarial perspective "the subject of friendly societies is altogether a very complicated one. In fact, there is no branch of vital statistics so difficult to be understood."[51] Actuarial science was more complicated when it came to friendly societies because unlike life insurance companies, friendly societies promised benefits for a wide variety of risks, some of which were dependent on particular definitions that were not the same in each friendly society. In terms of the variety of benefits on offer, the Odd Fellows, for example, gave £10 for the death of a member, £5 for the death of his wife, between 7s and 10s per week sick pay (until death, which was generally reduced after six or twelve months chronic sickness), travel pay, and clearances. Each of these had local meaning. Sickness, as we saw, was not a medical concept. It was defined as the "incapacity from labor" and so had different criteria for every occupation.[52] As Neison and Ratcliffe both made clear, sickness rates also varied according to age, occupation, and, to a lesser extent, region. Most actuaries agreed that trying to calculate accurate sickness tables for ages over seventy was impossible and recommended annuities for this age range rather than

---

[51] *Report from the Select Committee on the Friendly Societies Bill*, P. P., 1849, xiv, 1.
[52] See Neison's answers to the committee *Report from the Select Committee on the Friendly Societies Bill*, P. P., 1849, xiv, 16.

sick pay.[53] Similarly, travel pay and clearances depended on the decision to travel, which, in turn, was dependent on a large number of variables, which then varied according to region.

Complicating matters further still, achieving actuarial soundness was an ongoing process that required the trained eye of an expert. It was not as though the Odd Fellows could have adopted the appropriate tables and then have been set for life. The various Select Committees and Commissions on Friendly Societies called throughout nineteenth century learned this seemingly anew each time they met.[54] But it was one of the few things on which all actuaries agreed. From the government's perspective, a set of model tables would have made both the goal and the method of making friendly societies sound much easier. Yet, as the actuaries took great pains in explaining, tables that might be accurate for the entirety of the Order – even tables based on the actual experience of the whole Order – were not necessarily appropriate for a particular lodge in, say, Monmouth.[55] Model tables drawn from a large enough aggregate to yield statistical regularities could only be safely applied to a society with a membership big enough to achieve the statistical average. The actuaries also agreed, however, that making societies big enough to overcome local particularities such that model tables might be appropriate would take away the powerful supervisory effect of small numbers and thereby make friendly societies more susceptible to fraud. In any case, they felt it would be unjust to ask healthy people to pay for the liabilities of the unhealthy people who would necessarily be included in such a large society. The only solution was to take the great masses of data required for regular patterns to emerge and adapt them individually to the local circumstances of individual clubs.

---

[53] This was because there were too few people who survived beyond age 70 for any statistical regularities to emerge.

[54] The five most important actuaries in the country – Francis Neison, Charles Ansell, John Finlaison, George Davies, and (John's son) Alexander Finlaison – were interviewed in 1847 by the Select Committee of the House of Lords and in 1850 by the Select Committee convened to examine the Bill that would legalize the Odd Fellows. They all agreed that model tables would be more than unwise; they would be unsafe. (*Report from the Select Committee of the House of Lords on the Provident Associations Fraud Prevention Bill, Together with the Minutes of Evidence and Appendix*, 1847–1848 (489) xvi, 65–66; *A Bill to Consolidate and Amend the Laws Relating to Friendly Societies*, 1850 (273) iii, 37; Theodore M. Porter, *Trust in Numbers: The Pursuit of Objectivity in Science and Public Life* (Princeton: Princeton University Press, 1996), 109.)

[55] As Charles Ansell put it to the House of Lords Committee in 1848, "I doubt exceedingly the Propriety of promulgating any Table whatever that should be considered proper to be adopted universally ... A table that would be very proper for one Locality, or one class of persons, would be highly improper, in fact ruinous, for Miners and such people." (*Report from the Select Committee of the House of Lords on the Provident Associations Fraud Prevention Bill*, 1847–1848, 69.)

In addition to the periodic valuations and revisions of life and sick tables, each lodge would also have to be careful about how it invested its funds in the meantime. Neison even argued that careful investments were more important for solvency than accurate tables.[56] Solvency was calculated assuming a certain rate of interest, usually between 3–4 percent. If those rates were not achieved, contributions might have to be raised. For the Odd Fellows, all of this tracking and revising meant that they would have to prepare over 4,000 sets of tables, revise them annually in response to interest rate fluctuations, and then completely revamp them every five years in order to adjust to actual variations in mortality and morbidity rates.

Friendly society finance was so complicated, it turned out, that only a few people in the country were qualified to manage it. The job required, as Neison stated to the 1849 Select Committee on Friendly Societies, a very "peculiar education … to be competent to judge of it; it requires a specific education."[57] Later in the interview, he went a step further. Not only was friendly society finance too variable for model tables and too difficult for the members to manage, Neison also claimed that it was too much work for most actuaries. The actuaries Neison consulted on the subject felt that "the special knowledge necessary to advise safely is very considerable, and they do not think it worth their while to undertake it."[58] Only a very specific kind of actuary, then, trained not only in the finer points of actuarial mathematics, but also experienced enough with a particular friendly society's history to be able to take account of all its variables, could make a valid judgment.[59] The fact that actuaries often disagreed as to the best tables or courses of action, while vexing to the members of friendly societies and of the government committees appointed to investigate friendly societies alike, only further underlined the necessity of having a professional actuary in charge.[60] Neison suggested that "members should

---

[56] Neison, "Contributions to Vital Statistics," 1846, 125.
[57] Report from the Select Committee on the Friendly Societies Bill, 1849, 11.
[58] Report from the Select Committee on the Friendly Societies Bill, 1849, 23.
[59] On the importance of "experience," rather than strict mathematical ability or precision, see Porter, Trust in Numbers, chapter 5.
[60] For evidence of the consternation this caused among Odd Fellows, see Report from the Select Committee on the Friendly Societies Bill, 1849, 133. The actuaries interviewed by the various Friendly Society Committees and Commissions argued two ways on this issue. First, they believed that eventually, there would be enough data to bring the judgment of actuaries into closer agreement. And second, since an actuary's reputation was materially affected by the relationship between the judgment he made for an insurance company or a friendly society and the reality of their experience, the impact of inaccuracies in his judgment would have significant consequences. Thus, this problem could be left safely in the hands of professional actuaries whose interests it served to be as accurate as possible.

calmly reflect, that the radical and scientific part of the question is neither a simple nor a very generally understood one, even among the most highly educated classes; and it can therefore be no reflection on the intelligence of any individual member to ask for advice elsewhere."[61]

Obviously, stressing the complexity of their science and the need for expertise in interpreting it was part of the monopolization and professionalization of the actuary's field.[62] But, for my purposes, the necessity of the actuary and his judgment in achieving actuarial soundness highlights a different point. From the perspective of friendly society members, the list of things they were being asked to trust in this process was rather long. Not only would accepting actuarial science mean trusting an outsider to tell them how to run their lodge and what rates to set for contributions and benefits, but also what kind of people to admit. And all this even before they got to the question of trusting the peculiar assortment of numbers purporting to predict the future.

★★★

Yet, the working-class members of friendly societies did not resist actuarial science simply because they were ignorant of how it worked. Rather, they operated their organizations on a very different set of assumptions, assumptions that happened to be fundamentally opposed to the claims of the actuary. Because members believed the future was clouded by "absolute darkness," they structured their organizations such that as a group they would be able to help each other through whatever blows they were dealt.[63] From their perspective, the only way to protect oneself was with the help of others. Thus, the relationship they focused on was that between the members themselves. This is why sociability continued to be so important. Even though the Odd Fellows did not begin as a friendly society, they too shared this perspective about the future.

The origin and organization of friendly societies in Britain reveals the meaning that working people ascribed to insecurity and the limits of what they thought they could do about it. "The uncertainty of worldly prosperity – the calamities – misfortunes – troubles human life is liable to" was the whole purpose behind creating mutual aid societies in the first place and was often stated explicitly in the preamble to the rules of the club.[64]

[61] Neison, *Observations on Odd-Fellow and Friendly Societies*, 35.
[62] For more on this point, see Poovey, *A History of the Modern Fact*; Porter, *Trust in Numbers*, chapter 5.
[63] Smith, "A Second Discourse," 205.
[64] "Rules and Regulations to Be Observed by the Society at Annan Called the Trades Society, as Approved of, and Confirmed by, the Quarter Sessions Held at Annan ... 1801," In *Friendly Societies; Seven Pamphlets, 1798–1839* (New York: Arno Press, 1972), 3.

Members committed to paying into the "common stock" of the society in order to aid members "whom the Lord shall afflict in the course of his Providence."[65] Yet, what might be called a "providential bias" did not mean that they "submitted resignedly to the blows of fortune." The great proliferation of friendly societies beginning in the 1760s itself registers the deliberate and thoughtful action working people took to guard against the key economic vulnerabilities to which their lives were subject.[66]

So, too, do the membership qualifications common to the vast majority of workingmen's clubs.[67] People already "afflicted" by Providence with known diseases, the sick, weak, or infirm, (especially illnesses that bespoke of moral laxity like the "foul disease") or those who worked in dangerous trades were universally barred from joining.[68] Older men (usually over the age of thirty-five) were excluded for the same reason.[69] Their fate was clear, and even relatively affluent artisans could not honestly obligate themselves to take care of someone who would likely prove a major drain on limited resources.

While membership was generally restricted to the young and apparently healthy, the financial structure of friendly societies was based on the assumption that the time, extent, and nature of any member's need were unknowable. Scholars have hitherto assumed that friendly societies tried to approximate actuarial calculations when setting rates, even if the relationship itself was based on custom rather than science in the early years before adequate tables had been developed.[70] This was not the case. Rather than a specific relationship between what an individual paid in and what he would potentially receive, these rates varied in a direct relationship to a club's ability to pay for cases of illness or death *as they emerged.* In the

[65] "Rules and Regulations to Be Observed by the Society at Annan," 7.

[66] For an analysis of the geographic spread of early friendly societies, see Gosden, *The Friendly Societies in England, 1815–1875*, 22–23; Gorsky, "The Growth and Distribution of English Friendly Societies in the Early Nineteenth Century."

[67] I use the term "workingmen's clubs" to distinguish friendly societies started and run by working men from clubs started by patrons. While workingmen's clubs often received donations from local patrons, they were not subsidized by them in a systematic way. Patronized clubs did not usually discriminate in these ways because their goals were different, and their resources were not as constrained.

[68] Kent & Sussex Friendly Brothers' Society, *Rules & Regulations of the Kent & Sussex Friendly Brothers' Society: Established at Hawkhurst, Kent, the Fifth Day of May, 1823.* (Cranbrook, UK, 1824), 20.

[69] The Trades Society at Annan excluded anyone over thirty-six and the Friendly Brothers' Society in Kent anyone over thirty. "Rules and Regulations to Be Observed by the Society at Annan," 7; Kent & Sussex Friendly Brothers' Society, *Rules & Regulations of the Kent & Sussex Friendly Brothers' Society*, 19.

[70] Gosden, *Self-Help: Voluntary Associations in 19th-Century Britain*, 54; Cordery, *British Friendly Societies, 1750–1914*, 49.

Friendly Brothers' Society in Kent, for example, the initiation fee went up or down "as the stock of the society may require."[71] While it was common to reduce the amount of sick pay after a certain period of prolonged illness, usually twelve–fifteen weeks, it was also common to reduce it in relation to the amount of money remaining in the box. The Annan Trades Society normally gave 6s., lowering it to 4s. after thirteen weeks of sickness. But if the stock "should at any time be reduced below one hundred pounds," sick pay was reduced to 5s. and 2s., respectively.[72]

In addition to varying contributions and benefits as the common stock was depleted, further shortfalls were often made up through levies. These kinds of collections were conducted ad hoc in response to contingencies as they arose. Some clubs explicitly stated the conditions under which a levy would be instituted. The Town Porters' Friendly Society in Edinburgh, for example, vowed never to deprive members of sickness relief. But, in order to make good on that commitment, they required that "every Member binds and obliges himself to pay sixpence in addition to the usual quarter-accounts" until the stock exceeds £120. If the collection did not put the funds above that amount, the members would vote to raise "or lower the Sick or Funeral-money as the Funds will admit."[73] In cases of death, the lump sum given to the family or friends of a deceased member, ranging between £2–£10, was almost always raised in whole or in part through a levy. For the Odd Fellows, funds were collected on a case-by-case basis and given "as far as circumstances would admit" for the first part of the nineteenth century.[74] Even the first

---

[71] Kent & Sussex Friendly Brothers' Society, *Rules & Regulations of the Kent & Sussex Friendly Brothers' Society*, 22. The Finch Friendly Society varied their entry fee as the stock went above or below iterations of £10. (*Articles Agreed upon by a Friendly Society: Meeting at Thomas Finch's at the Sign of the Tiger, in Lindfield, in the County of Sussex*. (London: Printed for the use of the Society, 1757), 3.)

[72] "Rules and Regulations to Be Observed by the Society at Annan," 7–8. See also article 3 of the Finch Friendly Society. Each member agreed to give "Three pence for his share of the Reckoning." (*Articles Agreed upon by a Friendly Society: Meeting at Thomas Finch's at the Sign of the Tiger*, 4.)

[73] "Articles and Regulations for Governing the Town Porters' Friendly Society, Instituted … 1688; and Revised and Amended … 1833," In *Friendly Societies; Seven Pamphlets, 1798–1839*, 20.

[74] As James Roe, a senior officer from the North London District, put it in his testimony to the Select Committee of the House of Lords in 1848, "up to 1824 there was no regular rate of payment in sickness, nor of contribution. About that time, when sickness occurred, the members used to contribute among themselves." (*Report from the Select Committee of the House of Lords on the Provident Associations Fraud Prevention Bill*, 1847–1848, 87.) This extempory mode of collection and distribution of funds continued beyond 1824 as well. Attempting to clarify how their organization worked to detractors in 1828, one Odd Fellow elaborated, "in sickness, a brother, *if requisite*, is supported, and supplied with regular medical advice. If in distress, his case is humanely inquired into, and the balm of charity bestowed, *according to circumstances*. If he is necessitated to travel, in search of

Friendly Society Act, passed in 1793, recognized the improvised nature of most friendly societies, defining them as "societies of good fellowship, for the purpose of raising from time to time by subscription of the several members … , or by voluntary contributions, a stock or fund for the mutual relief and maintenance of all…"[75]

If early nineteenth-century friendly societies were characterized by ad hoc collections and stock-dependent rates of contributions and benefits, they cannot meaningfully be described as insolvent. While they often acted preemptively, excluding cases of known disease or infirmity, they did not attempt to predict the future of any individual member nor did they seek to attain even an approximate sense of the liabilities their members represented. Instead, they responded to need when it arose, and they called on members to meet that need by contribution when the stock fell short.[76] And when it fell so low that they could no longer meet the calls upon it, they closed the box and divided the remainder between the members. What contemporary observers criticized as shortsighted and even selfish behavior was closer to Daniel Defoe's concept of a contractual and circumscribed neighborliness rather than an attempt to mimic insurance principles.

The effectiveness of this system depended a great deal on admitting only members willing and able to pay their share when the need arose. Exclusions on the basis of health, age, or dangerous occupation helped to ensure that members had the ability to contribute. The question of willingness was, of course, more difficult to determine since it depended on trust. This is where the larger context of the credit economy becomes so important. As we saw in Chapter 1, because the vast majority of economic exchanges from the seventeenth through the nineteenth centuries were conducted on the basis of personal credit, "people were constantly involved in tangled webs of economic and social dependency which linked their households to others within communities and beyond, through the numerous reciprocal bonds of trust in all of the millions of bargains they transacted."[77] Trust was the boundary condition for local credit networks: trustworthy people were admitted and untrustworthy people excluded. The same was true of friendly societies. The

---

employment … he is enabled to meet with 'friendship and protection,' in almost every town or village, from Berwick-upon Tweed to Penzance." (Emphasis mine. "To the Editor of the Manchester Gazette," *The Odd Fellows' Magazine*, (1828–1831), 73.)

[75] 33 Geo. III. c. 54.

[76] In fact, taking collections as needed was not different in practice from the way poor rates were raised under the old poor laws.

[77] Muldrew, *The Economy of Obligation*, 97.

requirement that two current members, and sometimes three, vouch for the "character" of a new candidate, for example, was standard in friendly society rules.[78] After a vote by the entire group, the new member swore an oath, obligating himself to fulfill his promise of mutual aid.[79]

But the problem of trust did not end at the point of admission. The question that most concerned members of both credit and friendly society networks was how to ensure that others would fulfill their obligations when the debt came due or the collection was taken in the future. Historians have shown that for credit networks, friendship and sociability were critical for communicating and maintaining trust.[80] In the most basic sense, friends could vouch for one another's trustworthiness. And, engaging in sociability – whether it took the form of hospitality, visiting, charity, the forgiveness of debts or gift giving – helped to forge and maintain bonds between serially linked creditors.[81] Such practices also signaled one's continued participation in the ongoing web of obligation. The same was true for friendly societies. Group drinking, feasting, and processions, on the one hand, and fines for fighting and other kinds of divisive or disreputable behavior, on the other, reinforced and policed the bonds between members.[82] Signaling the great importance of trust in particular, the penalty for any member caught defrauding or dealing dishonestly with his club was almost always expulsion.[83]

The Odd Fellows shared a "providential bias" with other friendly societies, but they had further objections to actuarial science based on the internal logic of their organization. Actuarial reform would require a set and definite relationship between contributions and benefits. In their strictly convivial days, contribution fees were simply the cost of belonging

---

[78] Some friendly societies held the recommenders accountable for the future actions of the candidate, assigning a fine should that member prove to be a bad character. Others held committees to examine the candidate in person. Most sent current members to visit the candidate's place of business or friends and held a vote at the following club night. See *Rules and Orders of the Friendly Society of Millthrop, Instituted the 12th Day of May, 1788*, 6; *Laws & Regulations to Be Observed by the Brethren of the Loyal Lodge of the Ancient and Honorable Order of Independent Odd-Fellows, Held at … York*, 3.

[79] See, for example, *Articles Agreed upon by a Friendly Society: Meeting at Thomas Finch's at the Sign of the Tiger*, 1–2.

[80] Muldrew, *The Economy of Obligation;* Heal, *Hospitality in Early Modern England*; Tadmor, *Family and Friends in Eighteenth-Century England*.

[81] For examples, see Tadmor, *Family and Friends in Eighteenth-Century England*, 109; Muldrew, *The Economy of Obligation*, 95–172.

[82] Sociability combined with fines was a characteristic means of promoting harmony in most eighteenth-century clubs and associations. For more on this aspect of associational life in this period, see Clark, *Betting on Lives*, 163–164, 230, 325.

[83] For a particularly strong statement about the punishment for dishonesty, see *Rules and Orders to Be Observed by a Friendly Society, Meeting at the House of Mr. George Westwood, at the Sun Inn at Hitchin in the County of Hertford* (London, 1752), 10.

to the group. Later as mutual aid became more central to the Odd Fellows, fees functioned as an ongoing commitment to fulfill the obligation to mutual aid, just like they did in regular friendly societies. At the level of the Order, however, the Odd Fellows had stopped trying to calculate exact debts between lodges in the 1820s, as we saw in Chapter 4, because they found that such calculations led to distrust. Reorienting their goals away from "mirth and harmony" and toward the more encompassing ethos of "benevolence and charity" had enabled them to build an international system of mutual aid.

While originally intended as a means of ensuring that migrating Odd Fellows would find relief when traveling in search of work, the shift toward benevolence ended up doing new kinds of work as the century wore on. The benevolent ethos also helped the Odd Fellows deal with a great variety of other financial challenges. By the 1840s, for example, the membership composition of lodges had shifted increasingly toward unskilled rather than skilled laborers, which tested but also proved the effectiveness of benevolence as a guiding principle.[84] The growth of the proportion of unskilled laborers increased the number of people requiring sick pay every time they were out of work due to illness or accident. It also increased the occasions where members were unable to pay their dues at all. There is no statistically relevant data on this point, but the minute books of local lodges record instances with rising frequency from the 1840s on. If membership had been based on a direct link between payments and contributions, members would have lost their benefits at the time they needed them most. Instead, what often happened was whenever a member could not pay his dues "due to no fault of his own," his lodge would take a subscription to pay them until he was back on his feet. In 1849, for example, the Farmer's Rest Lodge in Knowsley set Brother James Lea "good on the books" for over a year because his

---

[84] In an Odd Fellow Lodge in Derbyshire, for example, the number of initiates who described their occupation as "laborer" or "miner," as opposed to a skilled occupation, was 60 percent of the whole from 1838–1890. But with a closer look at the years 1838–1847, a sharp increase in the number of unskilled laborers as a proportion of the entire lodge membership is apparent, from 41 percent in 1838 to a high of 66 percent over the course of 1846–1847. Data drawn from *Membership Book, Winster Area, 1838–1890*: Derbyshire Record Office, D6198/1/1. John Russom, an Odd Fellow from Tarporley, estimated in 1840 that 90 percent of Odd Fellows were "labouring men." (J. Russom, *An Essay on Odd Fellowship: Being an Explanation and Vindication of Its Principles, Etc.* (London : Hamilton, Adams, and Co), 1840, 17.) For an examination of this shift in friendly society membership more broadly, see Neave, *Mutual Aid in the Victorian Countryside: Friendly Societies in the Rural East Riding, 1830–1914.*

was "a very distressing case."[85] Similar acts of friendship and benevolence can be found in the extant records of all the Odd Fellow lodges.[86]

The benevolence at the heart of the solidarity between lodges also made it possible to distribute financial burdens that threatened to overwhelm local lodges, and that would have forced any other isolated friendly society to close its box. At the Annual Moveable Committee meetings each year, the Benevolent Fund Sub Committee met to decide on cases of distress throughout the Order. One could practically trace every instance of a mine collapse, an outbreak of cholera, or a dip in the trade-cycle throughout the country simply by perusing the records of this committee. If there were not enough funds available for the requests deemed worthy of consideration, a circular was sent to all the lodges asking them to subscribe to the cause. An especially poignant case of benevolence by subscription took place in 1850. An Odd Fellow named Robert Wallace, who happened to be the MP for the Borough of Greenock, became "embarrassed in circumstances." Unskilled laborers may have experienced reversals more frequently, but Wallace's case demonstrated that even those in the highest stations were vulnerable. In the end, members all over the Order sent donations to a man most had never met totaling £133 11s. 9d.[87] They relieved the Parliamentarian's distress for the same reasons they relieved the less fortunate members of their own lodge: "That the man is a brother is his title – that he is in distress is his claim."[88]

Alleging that an early nineteenth-century friendly society was insolvent was akin to questioning the oath members took to relieve each other in time of need. A true test of solvency for an organization based on this

---

[85] They eventually agreed to extend this reprieve indefinitely until Lea found employment. See entries for Jan. 22; May 28; Oct. 1; Nov. 26, 1849 in the Resolution and Minute Book, Farmer's Rest Lodge, 1838–1864: Knowsley Record Office, KA 31/C/M1.

   In the Loyal Falmouth lodge, George Angel had an accident that incapacitated him from labor in the spring of 1867. His lodge gave him sick pay even though he had not been a member for the required six months. A member of the same lodge, J. J. Libby, was given 10s. because he was in "distressed circumstances." And as late as 1869, the Loyal Falmouth Lodge paid the outstanding contributions of Henry Mitchell, who was in arrears five months, because he was in "distressed circumstances." On the same night, they voted to pay for "H. Head's" contributions for the same reason. (Minute book, no. 3, Minute Books, 1866–1870, Loyal Falmouth Lodge, Dec. 21, 1869, May 28, 1867, Oct. 13, 1868: Cornwall Record Office, Truro, X1111/1/2.)

[86] Even in one of the first lodges to adopt actuarial reforms, the ethos of benevolence is nevertheless evident. During the Cotton Famine, the Pleasant Retreat Lodge made a whole group of members "good on the books" until they could find work. (*Preston District Minute Books, 1856–1876, Pleasant Retreat Lodge*, Nov. 24, 1862: LRO, DDX 433/2.)

[87] Spry, *The History of Odd-Fellowship*, 114.

[88] Alfred Smith, "The Benevolence of Odd Fellowship," *The Odd Fellows' Quarterly Magazine* (1842–1843), 38.

type of mutuality would have to include the extra money one member might be able to give or the refusal on the part of another to ever ask for relief. Lord Beaumont, who chaired the 1847–1848 Select Committee of the House of Lords on Provident Associations Fraud Prevention Bill, came to understand the critical role benevolence played in absorbing uncertainties within and between Odd Fellow lodges after interviewing several leading Odd Fellows. Summing up their testimony, he perceptively remarked, "therefore, it would be difficult to reduce all those Contingencies to the nice Calculation of the actuary."[89] In other words, in addition to rates of sickness and death, the actuary would have to try to assign value to the commitment made by a group of mutually obligated friends and brothers.

It should not be surprising, then, that when the actuary Francis Neison did publicize his calculations that predicted catastrophic insolvency for the Odd Fellows, most members were not just incredulous, they were also offended. From their point of view, the financial stability of the lodge and of the Order was measured in terms of the number of brothers one could call on in time of need and the strength of the bonds between them. This was, in fact, their precise definition of prosperity. The notion that prosperity was demonstrated by the strength of the brotherhood can be found in all the anniversary reports from the start of the *Odd Fellows' Magazine* in 1824 to well into the 1850s.[90] As Alfred Smith, an Odd Fellow from Ripon, put it, "since the year 1834, Odd Fellowship has increased in numbers from sixty thousand to one hundred and eighty thousand members! This is prosperity indeed!"[91] He went on,

Every one who knows anything of Odd Fellowship, knows that it is in a most prosperous state. I have made inquiries of people from all parts of the country, and I hear of nothing but increasing numbers and flourishing finances. ... [T]he wise regulations of our Order have always met, and meet now, all its requirements, and we have much to spare, why, in the name of common sense, are we to make ourselves wretched by inventing distant and imaginary evils?[92]

When the future was unknowable, counting brothers mattered; calculating liabilities did not.

---

[89] *Report from the Select Committee of the House of Lords on the Provident Associations Fraud Prevention Bill*, 1847–1848, 23.

[90] A typical account in the magazine read: "Bridgenorth. – This district is in a very prosperous condition. New members are almost every lodge night enrolled ... " ("Progress of Odd Fellowship," *The Odd-Fellows' Chronicle* (November 29, 1844), 29.)

[91] "Memoir of Alfred Smith, P. G.," *The Odd Fellows Quarterly Magazine* (1842–1843), 2.

[92] Alfred Smith, "The Independence of Odd Fellowship," *The Odd Fellows' Quarterly Magazine* (1844–1845), 42.

The benevolence of the brotherhood and the sociability used to promote it were developed in response to the contingencies the Odd Fellows faced over the first half of the nineteenth century, as we saw in Chapter 4. Over the years, they became part of the structural and conceptual relationships between members and the Order, as well as between lodges. The continual growth of the Order both convinced them that they were doing something right and assured them that their future, though unknown, was nevertheless secure. Actuarial science asked them to rid their organization of sociability because such practices wasted money and to give up acts of benevolence because they were not reducible to calculation. And it asked them to trust that a stranger and his numbers provided a better guide to the future than the brotherhood that had been increasing steadily for over forty years.

***

By mid-century, however, a number of pressures from different sources combined in such a way that suggested the benevolence of the brotherhood was no longer enough to secure the Odd Fellows' future. First, the culture of a benevolent brotherhood was clearly not enough to prevent major fraud, as William Ratcliffe's theft had recently proved. Second, certain people had begun calculating liabilities rather than just counting brothers, professionals like Neison, working to develop their burgeoning field, and also actuarially minded members within the Order itself, like Henry Ratcliffe and Charles Hardwick. Third, these actuaries may have "produced risks" where only obligations had hitherto existed, but regardless of what regular members understood about risk, most lodges were offering set benefits at this point.[93] Instead of limiting gifts to what "circumstances will admit," it had become standard to state explicitly the sickness and burial benefits members could expect, which meant that pre-determined out-payments were promised without being associated with a designated income. Finally, while it was true that the Order was growing, from an actuarial perspective more members meant more liabilities.[94] The mismatch between the benevolent history of the Order and the insurance benefits they were in fact offering was not immediately

---

[93] Charles Hardwick, *A Manual for Patrons and Members of Friendly Societies. The History, Present Position, and Social Importance of Friendly Societies: Including Oddfellowship, and Other Affiliated Provident Institutions of the Working Classes; Comprising the Gradual Development of the Science Termed "Vital Statistics"* (Manchester: John Heywood, 1859), 3. For the shift in the way sick gifts were paid for, see Minute Book, Duke of York Lodge, No. 17, October 1, 1835. Instead of paying 6d. per levy, the sick benefit was set at 10s. per week and members were asked to increase their weekly contribution from 7d. to 8d.

[94] Wilkinson, *The Friendly Society Movement*, 34.

obvious to most members. But in the process of grappling with it over the second half of the nineteenth century, the Odd Fellows created a new connection between sociability and actuarially sound practices, one that would secure the Order against contingencies that actuarial science could never predict.

The initial resistance to actuarial reform was at first quite intense; 15,840 members severed their ties with the Order rather than submitting to what they saw as "an insidious attempt to divert the Order from its original benevolent purposes and designs, and to assimilate it in principle to an assurance society."[95] Those who remained were divided over precisely this question: what kind of institution would the Odd Fellows be? Would they continue to be a benevolent institution, a "band of brothers...with common ties and common interests unit[ing] the members in a warmer and firmer bond than can be expected to exist where mere paying and receiving are concerned?"[96] Or, would they be a "Mutual Assurance Compan[y] of the People," "regulated by calculations and principles that take into account the future as well as the present?"[97] The opposing sides did not fall into the rural/urban or working class/middle class divides we might expect. Most of the defecting lodges, for example, were from urban Manchester and Salford, and these rebels included not just a working-class membership, but their largely middle-class leadership as well. In fact, while the divide was often sharp, those who fell on one side or the other shifted over time. James Roe, a senior officer of the Order, also testified in front of Lord Beaumont's committee in 1847. After hearing Roe's explanation of how the internal organization of the Order worked, Beaumont asked this clarifying and telling question: "This society is of a peculiar Character, being a Benevolent Society in addition to being a Provident Society?" "Yes," Roe confirmed.[98] More important than what kind of people identified with which side were the steady stream of contingencies that compelled

---

[95] "Annual Moveable Committee, Glasgow," *The Odd-Fellows' Chronicle* (June 1845), 132. They ultimately left the Order permanently, starting a competing Order of Odd Fellows rather than submit to the proposed actuarial regime. The new Order was called the National Independent Order of Odd Fellows and was also headquartered in Manchester. For more on the "national split" see Wilkinson, *The Friendly Society Movement*, 35–37; Burn, *An Historical Sketch of the Independent Order of Oddfellows M. U.*, 106–109.

[96] Alfred Smith, "An Essay on the Nature and Advantages of Odd Fellowship," *The Odd Fellows' Magazine*, (1838–1839), 8.

[97] Charles Hardwick, *The History and Present Position, and Social Importance of Friendly Societies, Including Odd Fellowship and Other Affiliated Provident Institutions of the Working Class* (Manchester: John Heywood, 1869), 1; Charles Hardwick, "Prospects and Condition of the Order," *The Odd Fellows' Quarterly Magazine*, (1844–1845), 400.

[98] *Report from the Select Committee of the House of Lords on the Provident Associations Fraud Prevention Bill*, 1847–1848, 93.

them to keep asking different versions of that same question: What kind of institution were they?

There is no better navigator to the productive power of this question and the role it played in the financial security of the Odd Fellows than Charles Hardwick, an Odd Fellow from Preston who eventually became the Grand Master of the entire Order. A printer-turned-writer, historian, painter, and member of several other local civic associations, Hardwick joined the Preston Retreat Lodge in 1841. He became quite active in his lodge when Order-wide actuarial reform was first seriously considered in 1845.[99] After teaching himself actuarial science and then conducting a valuation of his own lodge and district, Hardwick began traveling around the country giving lectures detailing his findings.[100] He made it his personal mission to convince reluctant Odd Fellows of the necessity of adopting actuarial reforms. His mission was ultimately a success. But along the way, the evolution of his own thoughts on the question of benevolence also gave him a unique perspective on the importance of sociability for achieving actuarial soundness.

Hardwick did not hide his impatience with the argument that because the Order was a benevolent society, they should not be judged by the same terms as insurance companies. "Call it charity or benevolence if you will;" he warned, "yet the natural laws which influence the average amount of sickness, and the rate of mortality experienced by the members still demand *unconditional* recognition in the framing of the financial laws." He gave no credence whatsoever to a loaves and fishes effect, exclaiming,

I freely confess that I am deplorably ignorant of any rule in mathematics that can convert three times three shillings into fifteen. Yet till some such sublime science be discovered, I fear the rates of payment and benefit in Friendly Societies, notwithstanding their philanthropic objects, as in other assurance companies, must submit to the vulgar rules in common arithmetic.[101]

[99] "Charles Hardwick, GM, Portrait Gallery," *The Quarterly Magazine of the Independent Order of Odd Fellows, Manchester Unity* (1857–1858), 322. He contributed a great many articles to *The Odd Fellows' Magazine*, too numerous to list. But the titles of several of them make it quite clear what his key concerns were: "A Few More Words about Management" (1858); "Vital Statistics: Our recent Experience" (1862); "Progress of Financial Improvement" (1864); "The New Financial Law" (1865).

[100] His lectures proved so popular, he was asked to publish something on the subject. At first, he did so in pamphlet form, selling "two large editions" and then he expanded it into a book that went through three editions. The book titled *The History, Present Position, and Social Importance of Friendly Societies* was first published in 1859; a revised second edition was printed in 1869 and another in 1893. For more on his publication history, see *"Obituary: Charles Hardwick, P. G. M.," The Monthly Magazine of the Independent Order of Odd Fellows, Manchester Unity Friendly Society*, (1889), 259.

[101] Hardwick, *The History and Present Position, and Social Importance of Friendly Societies*, 5.

But he was also annoyed with overzealous critics who were not Odd Fellows, actuaries like Neison and social reformers like Lord Albemarle, whose ignorance of the Order's inner workings led them to pronounce its financial condition worse than it actually was.[102] As Hardwick explained, "when the uneducated men discover that their case is made out to be worse than they know it really to be...they denounce the whole of the assertions of this party, as false and slanderous."[103]

After distrust of ill-informed outsiders, Hardwick thought that the other major obstacle to reform was the inability on the part of the general membership to recognize sickness and death as personal risks that they brought into their lodges. In order to attach the predictions of actuarial science to individual members, he dropped all "logarithms, decimal fractions, or algebraic processes" in his lectures and any terminology that might be confusing "to minds unaccustomed to arithmetical calculations."[104] He also discarded the standard actuarial tables, with their column after column of impenetrable figures. In the place of numbers, Hardwick used graph lines, each one representing a decade of life. (See Figure 5.2.) Each row contained a bold line going from left to right for sickness and right to left for mortality, very clearly indicating the death and sickness rates an Odd Fellow could expect to experience at a given age.[105] Illustrating the "utter injustice" of admitting members of different ages at the same rates, he personalized the numbers even further, telling a story about how much Thomas, age forty, was cheating John, age twenty, if both joined at the same time and paid the same rate.[106]

---

[102] For his defense against Lord Albemarle, who attacked the character of the Odd Fellows in The *Times*, see Charles Hardwick, "Another Clap of Thunder," *The Quarterly Magazine of the Independent Order of Odd Fellows, Manchester Unity*, (1859–1860), 74.) Neison denounced the Odd Fellows for their enormous expenditure on management, claiming that it was "150 percent of that paid away to sick members." But 90–95 percent of what he had understood to be funds used for running the Order was actually monies given away in charity, both internally and to local causes. (Ibid., 74; Neison, *Observations on Odd-Fellow and Friendly Societies*, 20.)

[103] Charles Hardwick, *Friendly Societies: Their History, Progress, Prospects, and Utility: A Lecture* (Preston: Simpkin, Marshall, and Co., 1851), 34.

[104] Hardwick, *The History and Present Position, and Social Importance of Friendly Societies*, 4.

[105] The diagram included measured two and a half feet by three feet with roughly a seventy-two-point font. Hardwick recommended that members hang it in the lodge room to keep the laws of sickness and mortality "always before them." Such stark reminders of one's mortality must surely have had some effect. See Charles Hardwick, *Insolvent Sick and Burial Clubs: The Causes and the Cure; or, How to Choose or Found a Reliable Friendly Society. With a Large Illustrative Diagram, Suitable for Suspension in Club-Rooms, Showing, at a Glance, the Average Annual Sickness and the Expectation of Life at Various Ages.* (Manchester: John Heywood, 1863).

[106] Ibid., 18–19; Hardwick, *The History and Present Position, and Social Importance of Friendly Societies*, 66.

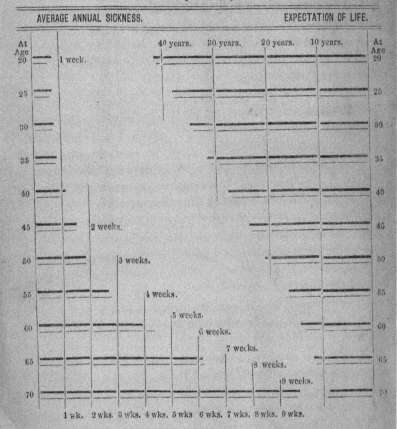

Figure 5.2 Charles Hardwick's mortality and morbidity diagram
© Boston Public Library, Boston, MA.[107]

---

[107] Hardwick, *Insolvent Sick and Burial Clubs*.

Indeed, equity was Hardwick's answer to the charge that actuarial reform would make the Odd Fellows a self-interested, pounds and pence, "act of parliament benefit society."[108] In the benevolent version of the Odd Fellows, vulnerability to the impenetrable whims of fortune was assumed to be equal, and so each member had given what he could when the need arose. When members had cited the golden rule in favor of this system, the emphasis was on doing what could be done in that moment. Hardwick and others protested that this was unjust because regardless of what was known or unknown about the future, by the 1840s the Odd Fellows had been advertising specific sickness and burial benefits as part of membership. Therefore, justice required that the money received in each lodge be earmarked to meet this obligation. The objection "we all pay alike, and should all receive alike ... may be generous, but it is neither just, equal, nor impartial," one actuarially inclined Odd Fellow pointed out.[109] He then encouraged every Odd Fellow to ask himself the question, "Am I acting justly in bestowing charity from funds which are not exclusively my own, or am I acting unjustly?" Hardwick went even further, citing a revised version of the golden rule on behalf of this new understanding of equity.[110] It was only fair that each Odd Fellow fulfill the contract he had agreed to by paying into the box proportionate to the benefits he expected to receive, nothing more and nothing less, just as he expected others to do.

Hardwick's actuarial lessons combined with this new understanding of equity did help to change the minds of a lot of members about what the rates of contribution should be and what benefits should be attached to those rates.[111] By 1875, the vast majority of lodges had implemented actuarial reforms, putting the Odd Fellows "foremost among the Orders through the successive steps which it has taken towards the attainment of financial security," according to the 1871–1874 Royal Commission on

---

[108] Robert Dawson Ferguson, "Stability of Lodge Funds," *The Odd Fellows' Magazine*, (1844–1845), 90.

[109] George Candelet, "The Force of Truth," *The Odd Fellows' Quarterly Magazine* (1846–1847), 41.

[110] Hardwick, *The History, Present Position, and Social Importance of Friendly Societies*, 209.

[111] His important role in effecting actuarial reform is made clear in his memoir and obituary, both published in *The Odd Fellows' Magazine*. He was also toasted regularly at anniversaries of lodges throughout the country. See, for example, the anniversary report for the North London District in 1863, when the district officer "proposed 'Friendly Societies,' coupled with the name of P. G. M. Hardwick..." ("Oddfellowship, Anniversaries, Presentations, Etc.: North London District," *The Quarterly Magazine of the Independent Order of Odd Fellows, Manchester Unity*, (1863–1864), 59.)

Friendly Societies.[112] Yet, while there was a decided shift toward a more scientific approach to mutual aid within the Order, there was little change to the importance placed on sociability within the lodges. Contemporary legislators and social reformers found this troubling as they were certain that there existed an "utter incongruity in combining notions of beer and insurance."[113] In their view, what little money that the eight million working Britons by this point associated with friendly societies had at their disposal should all be directed toward funding their future welfare.[114] The national Registrar for Friendly Societies, John Tidd Pratt, spearheaded a publicity campaign designed to eradicate friendly society sociability by refusing to certify rules that allowed any portion of a club's funds to be used for convivial purposes – even when those funds had been separated from insurance funds. He went so far as to publish an advertisement in every newspaper in the country threatening to sue any registered friendly society that applied collected funds toward "liquor at monthly meetings, band at anniversary dinners, dinners to persons carrying banners, donation to the Lancashire Relief Fund, &c.."[115]

At first, Hardwick agreed with the critique of the so-called "old practices" of sociability. He thought that the expenditure on mysterious symbols, quasi-masonic regalia, and the anniversary feasts was not just a waste of money, it was an embarrassing anachronism for an institution as important as the Odd Fellows. He described these practices as "ancient mummery," "gewgaws," and "trumpery."[116] But as he toured the country giving his lectures on actuarial science as it applied to friendly societies, he changed his mind. "A strong suspicion has lately crossed my mind," he explained, "that the originators of these societies were wiser in their generation, in this respect, than either I or the actuaries."[117] Whereas "learned actuaries" found that it cost £10,000 to rent and furnish offices splendid enough to give them the air of longevity so critical for attracting customers, the Odd Fellows simply marched through the streets for funerals or anniversaries in the regalia they had

---

[112] *Fourth Report of the Commissioners Appointed to Inquire into Friendly and Benefit Building Societies*, 1874, xxxvii.

[113] "Mr. Tidd Pratt's Office Can Be No Sinecure."

[114] In addition to the 4,000,000 Britons estimated to belong to friendly societies in the early 1870s, the Royal Commission on Friendly Societies added another 4,000,000 people, who, as recipients of the benefits, were "interested" parties. (*Fourth Report of the Commissioners Appointed to Inquire into Friendly and Benefit Building Societies*, 1874, xvi.)

[115] *Report of the Registrar of Friendly Societies in England*, 1863, (449) xxix, 58–59.

[116] Hardwick, *The History and Present Position, and Social Importance of Friendly Societies*, 10, 151–153.

[117] Ibid., 152.

owned for decades and signed up new members on the spot.[118] The regalia, "once purchased," Hardwick pointed out, "lasted for years, and was even convertible into cash."[119]

While he still believed in the absolute necessity of "submitting to the vulgar rules of mathematics" where insurance matters were concerned, Hardwick no longer saw benevolence and insurance as oppositional principles. He had found that the "profession of brotherhood" inscribed in every Odd Fellow ritual caused members to recognize obligations between each other that did not exist in strict insurance offices. "It causes them to meet together in social converse, and to devise plans for the amelioration of the condition of their unfortunate brethren, or widows and orphans. It causes them to voluntarily fulfill many of the duties necessary to the carrying out of the objects of their associations."[120] Lodge secretary was one of the key duties performed out of brotherly love rather than for payment in most lodges.[121] As a result of actuarial reforms, the work each secretary performed had increased significantly – detailing the vital statistics for each member, tracking rates of sickness and mortality according to age, maintaining the now multiple accounts of the lodge in addition to various investments, and finally compiling all this data into quarterly, yearly and quinquennial returns for the use of the Order. The "profession of brotherhood," in this case, actually made it possible for a working-class organization to *afford* to achieve and maintain actuarial solvency.[122]

The continued importance of the "profession of brotherhood" in the Order and the "social converse" that facilitated it were made especially apparent during the Cotton Famine of 1861–1865. This embargo on cotton exports during the American Civil War brought the Lancashire textile industry to its knees, destroying the livelihood of 60,000 Odd

---

[118] Critiques of these dubious practices appeared in literature throughout the nineteenth century. For an examination of this phenomenon, see James Taylor, *Creating Capitalism: Joint-Stock Enterprise in British Politics and Culture, 1800-1870* (Woodbridge: Boydell & Brewer Ltd, 2014), 79–80. For the necessity of grand buildings for the success of public companies, see Iain S. Black, "Spaces of Capital: Bank Office Building in the City of London, 1830–1870," *Journal of Historical Geography* 26, no. 3 (2000): 351–375.

[119] Hardwick, *The History and Present Position, and Social Importance of Friendly Societies*, 152.

[120] Ibid., 160.

[121] The annual cost of managing the Order itself, about £900, was not charged to members. It was recuperated through the sale of rules, lectures, and the like. (Wilkinson, *The Friendly Society Movement*, 66.)

[122] Hardwick even attributed the lower rate of sickness that actuaries consistently found among friendly society members to the brotherhood as well. "The very feeling of fraternity in the breast of a member of one of the affiliated bodies is, of itself, instrumental in keeping down the rate of average liability." (Hardwick, *The History and Present Position, and Social Importance of Friendly Societies*, 158.)

Fellows in the process.[123] Although many local friendly societies were
forced to close their boxes, the Odd Fellow lodges in Lancashire were
not.[124] At first, lodges used their own accumulated reserves to help their
members. But once it became clear that the embargo would go on for a
long time and those reserves would not be enough, the Board of Directors issued an Order-wide subscription appealing to the benevolence of
the brotherhood to relieve the continued distress.[125] Over the course of
five years, Odd Fellows throughout Britain and the Empire sent in more
than £10,000 in donations.[126]

Hardwick played an important role in encouraging people to give "with
the confidence." In one of several articles he published on the subject, he
declared that "Brotherly Love is no myth."[127] Even though he cautioned
that the donations should be given in the form of loans secured against the
distressed members' own funeral benefit rather than as outright charity, he
had come full circle in terms of the place he allotted to benevolence in the
meaning of Odd Fellowship. "Our great friendly society is not simply an
insurance company," he clarified, "it is likewise an affiliated body of
brethren, banded together for the purpose of carrying into practical effect
the great principles of philanthropy and of charity in its widest and most
legitimate sense."[128] Where the government's Registrar for Friendly Societies, Tidd Pratt, saw the by-products of sociability – and specifically
"donations to the Lancashire Relief Fund, &c." – as an affront against
the actuarial soundness of friendly societies, Hardwick had come to see
them as critical to their financial stability in a much broader sense. Unlike
strict insurance companies, the Odd Fellows had hundreds of thousands
of brothers to call on in their time of need. See Figure 5.3.

In the last quarter of the century, the Odd Fellows continued to
discuss the appropriate relationship between benevolence and actuarial
soundness, but by then, the dialectical relationship between them had
also taken on a structural and legal life. Even though the Order as a whole
had reduced its financial deficiency to between £6–700,000 by the

---

[123] John Watts, *The Facts of the Cotton Famine* (London: Cass, 1968); W. O. Henderson,
The Lancashire Cotton Famine, 1861–1865 (New York: A.M. Kelley, 1969). For more on
the Cotton Famine as it impacted Odd Fellows, see Charles Hardwick, "Friendly
Societies and the Cotton Famine," *The Quarterly Magazine of the Independent Order of
Odd Fellows, Manchester Unity* (1863–1864), 4.

[124] Watts, *The Facts of the Cotton Famine*, 140.

[125] For a copy of the subscription call, see Charles Hardwick, "The Distress in the Cotton
Manufacturing Districts," *The Quarterly Magazine of the Independent Order of Odd
Fellows, Manchester Unity* (1861–1862), 202–203.

[126] Wilkinson, *The Friendly Society Movement*, 62.

[127] Hardwick, "The Distress in the Cotton Manufacturing Districts," 203.

[128] Ibid., 202.

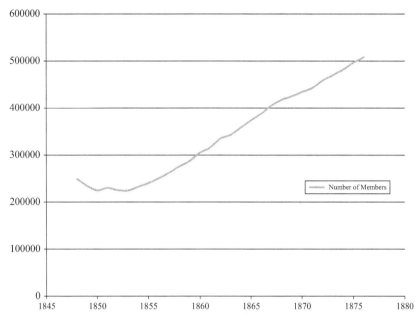

Figure 5.3 Graph showing the membership of the Manchester Unity, 1848–1876

mid-1880s, the continued struggle to achieve full solvency was marred by fluctuating returns on investments, the statistically irrelevant size of some lodges, and also the concentrated regional impact of spikes in sickness and mortality rates. There were also lodges that refused to reform. In order to help lodges who were distressed even after implementing reforms and as a means of compelling those who refused to reform at all, the Odd Fellow leadership set up a Relief Committee whose benevolent fund would be financed through an Order-wide levy. Funds would be dispersed on a case-by-case basis and only on the condition that specific steps were taken to ensure future financial stability. Some of the more affluent lodges thought this tax was unjust, and they refused to pay it. After all, they had put their house in order. Why should they have to bail out those who had not? The Odd Fellows' Board of Directors sued one of these defecting lodges in court. Working through the argument of the lodge in question, the presiding judge asked: "What is the argument adduced on behalf of the lodge? It is this, as it seems to me,"

because we now find that owing to our lengthened existence we have become a profiting society and a more rich lodge and society than other lodges, we will by our own motion split off from the parent society, and so carry away with us our money, disregard all the benefits we have received for fifty years past.[129]

He ruled that this lodge had to remain in the Order and had to continue to pay the levy or else return all the acts of benevolence it had ever received from the Order. Between 1891–1900, whether through voluntary or structural benevolence, the Odd Fellows gave £8,158 10s in donations to "necessitous lodges."[130]

The law, in this case, may have been on the side of benevolence, but it reveals a new problem that actuarial science introduced into Odd Fellowship. Hardwick's actuarial lessons not only helped members see the individual risks they brought to the lodge. It also taught them that they should be paying only for those risks. In other words, the logic of actuarial science introduced the rationality of pecuniary self-interest into the brotherhood. Calculating liabilities made counting brothers seem less important. The result was that it no longer seemed fair that richer lodges should have to care for poorer ones, or richer members for poorer members. Moreover, some members no longer felt the need to meet together at the lodge. They paid for their own liabilities, what more was required? "Lodge attendance" and how to increase it became an ever-present topic of discussion in the magazine throughout the 1880s and 1890s. The Board of Directors even sponsored an essay contest to see if someone could come up with a way to increase the diminishing number of attendees. The answers the members came up with were to increase the importance of brotherhood. Benevolence and mutuality were still critical for financial solvency, but they would require new justifications.

New justifications came in response to new problems. In the 1880s and 1890s, friendly societies began to experience a peculiar version of the "old age poverty" problem that generated so many debates in British society at large, leading ultimately to the Old Age Pensions Act (1908). Scholars have shown that poverty among the elderly increased in the late nineteenth century due to the fact that people were living longer and experiencing longer periods of sickness after the age of sixty-five.[131] Members of friendly societies also experienced these increases in morbidity rates among their older members. For Odd Fellows over sixty-five, for example, rates rose between 1848 and 1893 from 1.8 percent of the

[129] Moffrey, *The Rise and Progress of the Manchester Unity*, Web., Nov. 25, 2017.
[130] Landis, *Friendly Societies and Fraternal Orders*, 48.
[131] Macnicol, *The Politics of Retirement in Britain, 1878–1948*, 125–126; James C. Riley, *Sick, Not Dead: The Health of British Workingmen during the Mortality Decline* (Baltimore, MD: Johns Hopkins University Press, 1997).

"total weeks of sickness to 31.6 percent."[132] Some of those in receipt of sick relief were physically ill. But because friendly societies defined sickness as the inability to work, many were receiving sick pay because they were simply too old to work (or no work was available) and so were effectively receiving a pension.[133] These "quasi-pensions" were expensive; they had not been funded in advance and consequently formed a significant drain on friendly society funds.[134] Even though Joseph Chamberlain, Canon Blackley, and others exaggerated the impact old age poverty had on friendly society insolvency rates for political purposes, members of friendly societies – particularly of the Affiliated Orders – recognized the financial implications of the problem and took steps to address it.[135]

The approach the Odd Fellows took to this issue was in keeping with their ongoing efforts to achieve financial stability through a combination of actuarial science and benevolence. In terms of the former, the 1881 AMC ordered tables to be drawn up for a superannuation fund, the 1882 AMC approved them, and from then on superannuation funds were offered to all members. Additionally, the Order adjusted rates of contributions in light of their ongoing quinquennial valuation results, and paid to have Alfred Watson, the leading actuary on friendly society matters in the country at that point, conduct a new investigation into their sickness and mortality experience in 1893.[136] The superannuation schemes did not at first attract a significant number of members, but some lodges made it a condition of membership for new members, which dealt with future iterations of the problem.[137]

---

[132] Macnicol, *The Politics of Retirement in Britain, 1878–1948*, 126.

[133] Macnicol shows that employment opportunities were constricting for this age group, leading many friendly societies to treat the member as "unable to work" when he simply could not find work. (Ibid., 125–131.)

[134] Hardwick had first suggested such a scheme in the late 1850s in response to the volatile sickness rates above the age of sixty-five. (Charles Hardwick, "Recent Legislation Affecting Odd-Fellowship and Friendly Societies," *The Quarterly Magazine of the Independent Order of Odd-Fellows, Manchester Unity* (1859–1860), 24–25.)

[135] For an empirical analysis of Joseph Chamberlain's claims about friendly society insolvency, see "Old Age Pensions and the Friendly Societies," *Charity Organization Review* 10, no. 55 (1901): 26–30. For the steady attention to and success with actuarial reform from the 1870s, see Moffrey, *The Rise and Progress of the Manchester Unity*, Web. Nov. 25, 2017.

[136] The Ancient Order of Foresters also started a pension fund. (J. Lister Stead, "Friendly Societies and Old-Age Pensions, a Reply to Mr Chamberlain," *National and English Review* 25 (Mar. 1895): 69–70. Moffrey, *The Rise and Progress of the Manchester Unity*, Web. Nov. 25, 2017.)

[137] At the Derby AMC in 1892, a rule was added to the general laws that new members had to join a superannuation fund. ("The Work of the Order in 1892," 369–374.)

But that still left the problem of what to do about the elderly members who were in receipt of a pension for which they had not paid. Asking new members to belong to an Old Age Pension fund, some members argued, might be perfectly fair because they knew what they were in for and paying in early ensured a lower rate. But such a requirement would place an unbearable burden on the already old, who were not able to afford higher contribution rates at that point in their lives. As a Norwich Odd Fellow wrote, whatever the solution ultimately agreed upon, "the arrangement should not be made to bear too hardly on the older members."[138] An Odd Fellow from Staffordshire went further, reasoning that after a lifetime of paying into the lodge, "how cruel it would be to tell a poor old infirm brother that he had no claims" because he was not "afflicted with any specific disease."[139] He suggested paying the elderly as long as it was possible, which most lodges did. And yet, rather than bankrupt the Order as politicians like Joseph Chamberlain insisted it would, the Odd Fellows were fully solvent by 1904, capable of making good on their promised benefits to over a million members.[140] They even had a £33,346 surplus.[141]

★★★

Instead of leading to their demise, fraternal commitments provided a safety net in a world that was not always reducible to calculable risks. The "profession of brotherhood," as Hardwick discovered, played a critical role in sustaining the organization for many years, and kept a great many aging Odd Fellows out of poverty in the last decades of the nineteenth century. The dire predictions about the Odd Fellows' financial future did not come true for the same reason similar critiques of early nineteenth century friendly societies were off the mark – they were made from strictly actuarial perspectives. An actuarial way of seeing is anachronistic for the early period in the limited sense that accurate actuarial models did not yet exist. But it is also wrong in a broader and more important sense because it imposes a logic that ignores the way contemporary actors saw and understood their world. In other words, it actively disembeds

---

[138] John Chambers, "Letters to the Editor," *The Monthly Magazine of the Independent Order of Odd Fellows, Manchester Unity Friendly Society* (1893), 145.

[139] R. Farrow, "Letters to the Editor: Pensions or Sick Pay," *The Monthly Magazine of the Independent Order of Odd Fellows, Manchester Unity Friendly Society* (1893), 350.

[140] Chamberlain said, "If [friendly societies] continue to give old age pay in the form of sick pay, the result will be bankruptcy." (Quoted in Gilbert, *The Evolution of National Insurance in Great Britain*, 185.)

[141] For the results of the seventh valuation of the Order, see Moffrey, *The Rise and Progress of the Manchester Unity*, Web. Nov. 25, 2017.

friendly societies from their social and historical context – so radically so that the actions of hundreds of thousands of people over the course of nearly a hundred years are deemed inexplicable, even "unconscionable." For the second half of the nineteenth century, pronouncing upon friendly societies from an actuarial perspective blinds us to a much more complicated and interesting process. The internal history of the Odd Fellows shows that their financial stability rested on the dual principles of what one member described as "the good results from combining science with altruism."[142] When economic or scientific imperatives led to inequities, they kept asking a version of this question: would they be "actuarial friendly society men," whose "souls were in pawn to the devil of arithmetic, who blew our ideals sky-high," as one member posed it in 1915, or would they be "actual friendly society men?"[143] What kept them afloat for so many years was not relying exclusively on the one or the other, but the questioning itself: what does it mean to be "actual friendly society men?"

One of the biggest challenges for historians of the eighteenth and nineteenth centuries is making sense of the persistence of so-called traditional practices and structures even as British society was in the throes of "the great transformation." Modern knowledge forms like actuarial science have their own internal rationalities that, even as they were being developed, seemed to unfold in comprehensible ways and to have the capacity to reorder the world in their own image. This new story makes it clear, however, that taking the actuarial way of seeing as the only way to understand friendly society finance blinds us to at least three things. First, we miss that actuarial science had its own baggage. Not only did actuarial tables require a great deal of human intervention to make them work. When applied to friendly societies, the act of individuating members according to their various liabilities also undermined the mutuality that had held them together. Second, we miss the fact that actuarial science was incapable of predicting all of the casualties to which working Britons were subject. And it was benevolence that picked up where actuarial science fell short. Third, by adopting "modern" notions of science as both subject and narrator of that subject's history, significant parts of the story are rendered meaningless; they no longer belong in a story they actually helped to create. In this case, by treating friendly societies as if they were unsound insurance companies rather than financially precarious but socially powerful mutual aid associations, we lose an

---

[142] Landis, *Friendly Societies and Fraternal Orders*, 49.
[143] Quoted in D. Weinbren, "Mutual Aid and the State," Paper presented to the *Economic History Society Conference*, Cambridge University, 2011, 4.

entire set of rationalities for thinking and talking about how to make social obligations meaningful and effective in modern societies.

As we will see in the Epilogue, the late nineteenth-century parliamentarians and social reformers who looked to friendly societies, and to the Affiliated Orders in particular, for their model of mutual insurance were specifically interested in the way they produced welfare through solidarity. Over the course of the century, the Odd Fellows had figured out various means of getting erstwhile strangers to commit significant financial resources toward the mutual welfare of all the members of the Order. They also figured out how to protect this international system of reciprocity from fraud. Solving the problem of trust among strangers involved allowing for multiple rationalities to operate at once. Just as it had in the late eighteenth and early nineteenth centuries, however, the question that proved so difficult to answer was how to combine the moral power of the local friendly society with the financial strength of the whole nation without the power to exclude? If the system were compulsory, would the moral effects be attenuated? What scale of organization would be best for balancing the moral and financial effects? If everyone paid a share, on what principle would individual contributions be determined? Friendly societies, in other words, continued to be good to think with even as the British state reached the height of its power.

Epilogue
Alternative Endings

Under the [National Health Insurance] Act friendly societies would become something different altogether.[1]

Brother Marsh, Oddfellow from Southampton, 1911

[T]he degree to which the friendly societies triumph over their difficulties will depend on the life and spirit of service in them, on their being ready to meet new needs by new methods, in the old spirit of social advance by brotherly co-operation.[2]   William Beveridge, 1948

I began this book by trying to open up the way we think of friendly societies in the British past by bringing their ethical dimensions back into view. In each chapter, I examined the ways in which contemporaries adjusted the relationship between the ethical and institutional in order to deal with exigent questions of trust in the context of collective responsibility. The importance of this relationship lasted long after the state took over the role of providing social security in the twentieth century. If the origin of friendly societies should not be restricted to the particular working-class organizations that dominated the nineteenth century, the story of friendly societies cannot end with the decline of those particular institutions in the twentieth. The verdict that friendly societies went into terminal decline and "are now an anachronism," as one sympathetic historian put it, misses the ethical and institutional dynamic at the heart of these societies and of the concept of friendly society more broadly.[3] In these final pages, I want to show what happened to that dynamic as friendly societies began to join forces with the state in the provision of social welfare.

When the problems of poverty caused by old age, unemployment, and illness pushed beyond the existing systems of welfare in the last decade of

---

[1] "Oddfellows Conference at Salisbury," *Western Gazette*, May 19, 1911.
[2] Beveridge, *Voluntary Action: A Report on Methods of Social Advance*, 83–84.
[3] Bentley B. Gilbert, "The British National Insurance Act of 1911 and the Commercial Insurance Lobby," *Journal of British Studies* 4, no. 2 (1965): 148.

the nineteenth century, the state began considering a more comprehensive approach to these problems.[4] And it was the particular way that friendly societies had structured the relationship between mutuality and insurance that first attracted Lloyd George and his Treasury assistant William Braithwaite to seek the support of the friendly societies in their plans for national health insurance in the early twentieth century. Like their late eighteenth and early nineteenth-century predecessors who sought a means to provide for the needy without demoralizing them through that provision, both men saw the voluntary mutualism in friendly societies as the key to navigating these tricky waters.[5] Friendly societies covered some form of sickness and/or old age relief for more than 6 million Britons, but there were at least that many more who had no coverage at all.[6] George and Braithwaite wanted to extend the experience and values of friendly society mutuality to the entirety of the working population.[7] Under the initial plans for a new system, these workers would be enabled to join friendly societies with the help of the state. The role of the state would be kept to a minimum, merely providing the financial resources to subsidize members who could not afford the stipulated contributions, very much like John Acland proposed doing in the 1780s. Ideally, legislators hoped, friendly societies would get a boost in membership, but they were also hopeful that their practices of mutuality would remain unchanged.

However, unlike late eighteenth and early nineteenth-century proposals, which were implemented by founding and patronizing new

---

[4] The precise set of issues and political pressures that actually attracted the focused attention of the state in this period after decades and decades of piecemeal solutions is of course highly controversial. The literature on this question is legion. For a comprehensive survey, see Bernard Harris, *The Origins of the British Welfare State: Society, State, and Social Welfare in England and Wales, 1800-1945* (New York: Palgrave Macmillan, 2004).

[5] Jose Harris, "Victorian Values and the Founders of the Welfare State," *Proceedings of the British Academy* 78 (1992): 170–171; Nicholas Deakin, *Welfare and the State: Critical Concepts in Political Science* (London: Routledge, 2004), 45–48.

[6] These numbers include other types of organizations that had come under the protection of the Friendly Society Acts and could thus call themselves friendly societies in the late nineteenth century. "Holloway" and "deposit friendly societies" operated on the principle that Revd. John Becher (discussed in Chapter 3) proposed in the early nineteenth century, where mutual insurance for sickness and burial would be combined with a savings scheme in the form of a pension. While the type of insurance they provided had become increasingly popular in the late nineteenth century, they did not have meetings or any form of sociability. The biggest deposit society, the National Deposit Friendly Society, actually funded William Beveridge's study of friendly societies that resulted in his third report, *Voluntary Action*, but it was those friendly societies that had local branch meetings that were more important for modeling state social insurance.

[7] Gilbert, "The British National Insurance Act of 1911 and the Commercial Insurance Lobby," 128–129.

friendly societies and, so, had little impact on existing societies, the effect that the National Insurance Act (1911) had on existing societies was profound. First, due to various political pressures, instead of relying solely on traditional friendly societies as state providers, the benefits of the National Insurance Act (NIA) would be administered through trade unions, centralized friendly societies (which had no meetings), collecting societies (insurance companies that employed agents to collect dues at their customers' homes), and industrial, for-profit insurance companies. They would all be in competition for the same pool of previously uninsured workers. As new kinds of workers were added to this pool in subsequent Acts, the number of Britons covered expanded from approximately one-third of the adult male population in 1911 to more than one half by 1936.[8]

Second, in addition to an increasing number of new members, the administration of insurance benefits was incredibly complex. In particular, each approved society would administer twenty-one classes of insurance for twenty-two categories of member (including women), maintaining records on each person, their payments, sickness experience, and employment status.[9] New regulations concerning the administration of state insurance were issued at a dizzying pace, calling for changes in practices that were already poorly understood.[10] Handbooks attempting to explain the ever-increasing complexity of the regulations were published apace.[11] One such handbook, meant merely to introduce the useful literature that could help approved societies manage state

[8] Marvin Rintala, *Creating the National Health Service: Aneurin Bevan and the Medical Lords* (Portland, OR: Frank Cass, 2003), 22.

[9] Timothy Alborn, "Senses of Belonging: The Politics of Working-Class Insurance in Britain, 1880–1914," *The Journal of Modern History* 73, no. 3 (2001): 594. For details of the various classes and categories, see Percy Cohen, *The British System of Social Insurance; History and Description*, (New York: Columbia University Press, 1932), ch. 1.

[10] P. G. M. J. R. Barley made this clear in a speech given at the High Court of the Ancient Order of Foresters in 1919, "there has been too much experimenting by the authorities in connection with State insurance; too much irritation; too much of a tendency to sap the vitals of voluntary insurance by needlessly monopolizing the time and energy of our officials for State purposes." (Quoted in Frederick Ludwig Hoffman, *National Health Insurance and the Friendly Societies* (Newark, NJ: Prudential Press, 1921), 3.) The annual reports of the Loyal Order of Ancient Shepherds, one of the other major Affiliated Orders, from the years 1915–1920 discuss these issues in detail. See appendix J in ibid., 81–99. Amendments to the law were added in 1913, 1918, 1920, 1922, 1924, 1928, 1932, 1934 and 1936. (Rintala, *Creating the National Health Service*, 22.)

[11] The handbooks were issued from the Ministry of Health originally under the title: *National Health Insurance, 1911: handbook to the administration of sickness and maternity benefits by approved societies* (London: H. M. S. O. , 1913). A new one was issued with each amendment to the law.

insurance, was nearly 500-pages long.[12] The for-profit collecting societies and insurance companies had an advantage in this respect. They made their money precisely from the kind of administration the state required and could use their existing staff and company organization to accommodate new members. The new state scheme provided them with an enlarged, captive audience to whom they could sell their other insurance products. Friendly societies, of course, were not profit-making enterprises. Their staff, such as it was, were members who volunteered their services.[13] The increased financial and administrative burden of delivering state benefits, then, would require a significant restructuring of the way friendly societies operated.

Ironically, the changes that "approved" friendly societies instituted in order to meet the new administrative requirements of state insurance had the unintended consequence of isolating state members from the culture of mutuality that had made friendly societies so attractive in the first place. For example, the Affiliated Orders began consolidating smaller branch lodges into bigger ones in order to distribute the new administrative work in a manageable way. These consolidations happened among local unaffiliated clubs as well. The result was an increase in the size of individual lodges through the first half of the twentieth century.[14] Larger lodge sizes undermined one of the major reasons that Braithwaite suggested operating state insurance through friendly societies – the power of face-to-face sociability to eliminate malingering. Nineteenth century actuaries had expressly named the sick visitor, a staple of all friendly societies, as the key reason why sickness rates were lower in friendly societies than in the larger population.

Larger lodge size might diminish the impact of face-to-face interactions, but the way in which the internal structure of friendly societies was changed in order to administer benefits had an even bigger impact in this respect. Under the new law, all employees were required to join an approved society to receive their state benefits. Workers were free to choose which society they wanted to join. Unfortunately, from the state's perspective, they made choices of convenience, not from a desire to

---

[12] W. Addington Willis, *National Health Insurance Through Approved Societies: being a practical legal treatise incorporating the operative orders and regulations* (London: University of London Press, 1914).

[13] Staff in all approved societies were depleted by the start of World War I. (Geoffrey B. A. M. Finlayson, *Citizen, State, and Social Welfare in Britain 1830–1990* (Oxford: Oxford University Press, 1994), 205.)

[14] For a breakdown of membership numbers by branch from 1899–1946, see Beveridge, *Voluntary Action: A Report on Methods of Social Advance*, 329.

socialize with their insurers.[15] The Affiliated Orders further exacerbated this problem by treating members who joined only for the purpose of receiving their state benefits differently from regular members. In fact, they created a wall of separation between what became two classes of membership. The distinction between the "voluntary" members, those who joined for the friendly society, and "state" members, those who joined to receive their state benefits only, was significant.[16] Approved friendly societies treated the two classes as if they were in fact members of two distinct societies. One was a friendly society run on combined actuarial and fraternal principles and the other an insurance agency run strictly on state dictated actuarial principles. What this meant in practice was that those working men and women who joined only to receive their benefits never encountered the ethical culture of friendly societies to which Braithwaite and later Beveridge had been so keen to expose them. In the Manchester Unity, for example, this new class of members would not be initiated into the Order and would not be expected to participate in regular practices of sociability.[17] Previously uninsured working people entered as individual strangers and, as state members, remained isolated from both regular members and other state members. Their behavior with respect to their benefits and even more broadly with respect to their own health and welfare was not impacted by their membership in an approved society, whether it was a friendly society or not.

The separation was so complete, in fact, that some people on the state side did not even know that a friendly society was any different from an insurance company. In 1941, Lord Beveridge headed a committee to investigate how a new system of social welfare could be rebuilt after World War II ended. From these investigations, he ultimately produced his famous "Beveridge Report." As part of his examination, he commissioned Mass Observation, the social research organization founded in 1937, to get a sense of how people experienced social welfare and what they thought they needed. In the process, it became clear that the approved society system had actually denuded the term friendly society of any association with mutuality. Beveridge was shocked to find that of the people interviewed, "approximately two out of five had no knowledge of the term 'Friendly Society.'" After further explanation, the investigators found that some did in fact know what a friendly society was even

[15] A Mass Observation survey in 1948 found that less than 2 percent of the new members joined a friendly society for their social activities. (William H. Beveridge, *The Evidence for Voluntary Action, Being Memoranda by Organisations and Individuals, and Other Material Relevant to Voluntary Action*, (London: Allen and Unwin, 1949), see table 17, 74–75.)

[16] "Oddfellows," *Devon and Exeter Daily Gazette*, January 14, 1914.

[17] "Odd Fellowship and National Insurance Act," *The North Devon Journal*, May 23, 1912.

if they were not familiar with the term. But that still left one of three who were "unaware even of the existence of the Friendly Society."[18] Perhaps, most devastating from Beveridge's perspective, upon questioning 150 people who claimed to be members of friendly societies, it turned out that they were instead members of different kinds of approved societies, namely, collecting societies or insurance companies.[19] Instead of expanding friendly society fraternalism and mutuality to the whole of the working population, then, the approved societies system had reduced the concept of friendly society to an organization that administered state benefits. It was one among many and not particularly notable.

Not only had the concept of friendly society lost its ethical early modern connotations, but also, measured by their ability to administer state benefits, approved friendly societies did not fare well. Indeed, the approved society system as a whole was universally considered a failure. The results of the system were measured by the metrics of insurance, that is, in terms of coverage, administrative uniformity, and efficiency. Not surprisingly, given the radically different types of organizations that could qualify as an approved society, and the different levels of membership one could buy into, state benefits were unevenly distributed.[20] Taken as a whole, the approved societies were found to be inefficient, but friendly societies especially so.[21] Over the period in which the approved society system was in effect, friendly societies did not attract a significant proportion of the previously uninsured workers, and their share declined from 27.3 percent in 1912 to 16.6 percent in 1938.[22] Even Lord Beveridge, who argued that friendly societies should be the sole distributors of state insurance in the 1940s, was disheartened by their performance. But he attributed their declining membership to the forced competition they sustained with for-profit insurance companies and then, after 1948, to the even fiercer competition with the state.[23] Whether friendly societies could have done more to compete against the private commercial insurance sector or the state is an open question.[24] But there is no doubt that when the state offered free medical attention and comprehensive social

---

[18] Beveridge, *The Evidence for Voluntary Action, Being Memoranda by Organisations and Individuals, and Other Material Relevant to Voluntary Action*, 17.

[19] Ibid., 19.

[20] Finlayson, *Citizen, State, and Social Welfare in Britain 1830–1990*, 267–270.

[21] For more on this point, see HC Deb 23 May 1946, vol 423 cc565–619.

[22] For an analysis of these trends, see Alborn, "Senses of Belonging: The Politics of Working-Class Insurance in Britain, 1880–1914," 565–566.

[23] William H. Beveridge, *A Beveridge Reader*, Karel Williams and John Williams, eds., *Works of William H. Beveridge*; v. 7 (New York: Routledge, 2015), 149.

[24] For more on this point, see Alborn, "Senses of Belonging: The Politics of Working-Class Insurance in Britain, 1880–1914"; Bernard Harris, "'The Big Society' and the

security in 1948, the role that friendly societies had played in this capacity was no longer necessary. The day of the working-class friendly society so characteristic of the nineteenth century was done.

As noted above, it is not surprising that friendly societies saw a decline in membership as a result of the new system given how closely associated their benefits were. But fixating on this point misses two important developments. First, while the state declined to use the specific institution legally known as friendly societies to deliver benefits under the National Health Service Act of 1948, it nevertheless drew on the ethical richness of the concept. As Beveridge put it to Parliament in 1946, it was "the consciousness among simple ordinary people of the needs of others – a feeling for others in like position with themselves, and the banding together for mutual aid" that " ... has led to State action in social insurance such as we now have." The new state health care system would, he continued, "have been impossible but for the experimenting and the pioneering ... of friendly societies."[25] More than simply learning how to do social welfare from friendly societies, however, the state was itself attempting to become a friendly society. On July 5, 1948, the day the National Health Service Act came into effect, *The Times* reported that it had succeeded in this respect, "Today, the British people join together in a single national friendly society for mutual support during the common misfortunes of life."[26] This national friendly society provided a minimum social security below which no Briton was supposed to fall, and worked to eradicate the problem of poverty just as friendly societies had done for their own members throughout the nineteenth century.

Second, while the working-class friendly societies that dominated the nineteenth century saw a decline in membership after 1948, they never disappeared from the social landscape of Britain. They continue to do important social work in the British present. In fact, they seem to have fulfilled Beveridge's hope that they "meet new needs by new methods, in the old spirit of social advance by brotherly co-operation."[27] Just as the members of friendly societies had adapted the dynamic between the ethical and institutional aspects of their organization to forge bonds of trust beyond local bounds in the first part of the century and then

Development of the Welfare State" (Annual Conference of the Social Science History Association, Unpublished, 2011); Stephen Yeo, "Working-Class Association, Private Capital, Welfare and the State in the Late-Nineteenth and Twentieth Centuries" In *Social Work, Welfare, and the State*, Noel Parry, Michael Rustin, and Carole Satyamurti, eds., (Beverly Hills, CA: Sage Publications, 1980).

[25] HL Deb June 22, 1949, Vol 163 cc75–136.
[26] "Social Security," *The Times*, July 5, 1948.
[27] Beveridge, *Voluntary Action: A Report on Methods of Social Advance*, 83–84.

adjusted that relationship again to meet the actuarial challenges of the mid-nineteenth century, they tweaked them yet again in the twentieth and twenty-first centuries. Today, friendly societies continue to serve local communities, and particularly the elderly. Indeed, the Affiliated Orders that still operate branch lodges have expanded the social services they offer. The Independent Order of Odd Fellows, in particular, remains a vibrant organization with member lodges in every county and major town in the UK and in several other countries, including Bermuda, South Africa, and New Zealand. Calling themselves a "friendship group," they host "musical nights, day trips, dances, and meals out" for their more than 280,000 members. And they "encourage members to build upon their friendship networks with others across the UK, and overseas, by socialising and showing mutual support."[28] They also provide a growing number of financial services. Members can buy into an array of mutual schemes that help reduce the cost of medical services not covered, or not fully covered, by national health care. Perhaps, most interesting, they provide advice to members on state services, covering a staggering 15,000 topics. By helping people access services they might not know about and enabling members to get the most out of those services, the Odd Fellows work to reduce the complexity of national health care and other social services.

The history of friendly societies obviously includes the working-class, voluntary mutual aid organization that dominated the nineteenth century. But it is not restricted to them. Like the ebb and flow between the local and the national, the voluntary and the state, "free-market" and public planning, the relationship between the ethical and institutional have long been adjusted to meet new problems as they emerged.[29] Specific problems of trust often determined the ratio between the ethical and institutional aspects of friendly societies. As we work to find new answers to questions about who owes what to whom and why in our contemporary world, we can open the concept of friendly society back up to possibilities Daniel Defoe imagined for it in the seventeenth century. One that "has such a Latitude in it," as Defoe put it, that "all the Disasters in the World might be prevented by it, and Mankind be secur'd from all the Miseries, Indigences and Distresses that happen in the world."[30] It is possible to imagine that new kinds of friendly societies

---

[28] www.oddfellows.co.uk/About-us, accessed Apr. 5, 2016.

[29] For a thoughtful exploration of these ebbs and flows in welfare provision, see Finlayson, *Citizen, State, and Social Welfare in Britain 1830–1990*; Geoffrey Finlayson, "A Moving Frontier: Voluntarism and the State in British Social Welfare 1911–1949," *Twentieth Century British History* 1, no. 2 (1990): 183–206.

[30] Defoe, *An Essay upon Projects*, 122.

can be formed around specific problems. The bonds between members could be based on any number of ethical imperatives; the institutional framework could help to incentivize any number of outcomes; and the funding could be sourced and structured in various ways to reinforce those goals. If this book manages to revive the larger concept of friendly society – in all of its ethical and institutional nimbleness – as a cultural resource we might mine today in the face of new problems of trust in the context of social responsibility, it will have succeeded.

Index

Note: Page numbers in *italics* identify references to be found in the footnotes of these pages.